PRAISE FOR *THE HAIKU HANDBOOK*

"For many years, *The Haiku Handbook* has been without rival and the fullest, clearest, and most engaging guide to its profound and fascinating subject. For readers of haiku, whether veterans or novices, for poets and teachers, William J. Higginson remains the best friend they can find. In its attractive new edition, this classic book is a must for every poetry shelf."
—**X. J. Kennedy, coauthor of** *An Introduction to Poetry* **and author of** *In a Prominent Bar in Secaucus* **(original poetry)**

"The most thorough treatment haiku has received in English."
—**John Espy,** *Los Angeles Times*

"Chronicles the haiku movement and presents its best work."
—**Cor van den Heuvel,** *New York Times Book Review*

"Sure to become the standard text on the subject."   —*Booklist*

"Verve, erudition, and catholic selection of examples . . . "
—*Virginia Quarterly Review*

"Informative and engaging."   —*Newsweek*

"Indispensable."   —**Alexis Rotella,** *East West Journal*

"Higginson consolidates, adapts and updates the work of his predecessors. . . . In tracing the development of haiku in the West, and especially in the U.S., Higginson is at once informative and extremely fair. He discusses the different approaches to English haiku lucidly, giving reasons for his own preferences without being dismissive of other people's."   —*Japan Times*

THE
HAIKU HANDBOOK

THE HAIKU HANDBOOK

How to Write, Teach, and Appreciate Haiku

25th Anniversary Edition

William J. Higginson and Penny Harter

FOREWORD BY Jane Reichhold

KODANSHA INTERNATIONAL
Tokyo · New York · London

Distributed in the United States by Kodansha America,
LLC, and in the United Kingdom and continental Europe
by Kodansha Europe Ltd.

Published by Kodansha International Ltd., 17–14 Otowa
1-chome, Bunkyo-ku, Tokyo 112–8652.

ISBN 978–4–7700–3113–6

First KI edition, 1989
Tradepaper edition, 2009
18 17 16 15 14 13 12 11 10 09   10 9 8 7 6 5 4 3 2 1

LIBRARY OF CONGRESS CATALOGUE-IN-PUBLICATION DATA
Higginson, William J.
The haiku handbook : how to write, teach, and appreciate
    haiku / William J. Higginson and Penny Harter ; fore-
    word by Jane Reichhold. -- 25th anniversary ed.
        p. cm.
Originally published: New York : McGraw-Hill, c1985.
Includes index.
ISBN 978-4-7700-3113-6
1. Haiku--History and criticism. 2. Haiku--Technique. I.
    Harter, Penny. II. Title.
PL729.H48 2010
808.1--dc22
                    2009036628

www.kodansha-intl.com

Contents

Foreword

The art of poetry is beyond words. Even more challenging to grasp is the way poetry transmits the thoughts of writer to reader. All writ ers look for a way to shape a group of words into an experience larger than its parts with images that will resonate long after they are read.

Picture this. A woman is standing at an open window, just staring into space. Her eyes are a bit unfocused. She is lost in a world of thoughts and ideas. Suddenly, a small brown bird alights on the windowsill. She is jolted from her daydreams and returned to the present. Her mind whirrs as she attempts to understand why a bird would land just here.

The bird cocks its head, perhaps seeking a new view of the stranger. Fascinated, the woman bends forward for a better look. Stillness surrounds the two as unspoken messages pass between them.

The bird takes a tiny hop toward the woman, who cautiously stretches out a hand as if in greeting or offering something unseen. The bird is alert but not frightened. Its tiny toes press against the painted wood. The woman's hand inches closer. The bird takes another step forward. Then with a calculated leap, it lands in her outstretched palm.

The woman is stunned. Although she extended her hand, she never expected the wild creature to come to her willingly. But it has. Its feathery breast now rests in the cup of her hand. Perhaps, she thinks, her warm palm awakens the memory of the bird's days sitting on a nest.

The woman feels the bird's rapidly beating heart, and it is as if her own untamed heart has come home to her. She feels the delicate frame of this marvelous little being. It seems weightless—made of air and will. The tiny sharp claws on those sticklike legs slip between the woman's fingers, and she knows the need to fly free. The waxy beak nudges between two fingers, and she knows the struggle to get what she wants.

She has to set the bird free, but as she does she begins to build a nest of words to cradle her memory of the bird. In this nest she can keep her experiences alive, as they were for her just a few minutes ago.

Some word-nests come easily. Others take hours. But each time she makes one, she passes it along, hoping the eyes of someone else will find it. For when her words enter the reader's mind, they bring—in a flash—a related, but entirely new set of images. The poem conjures up the c   upped hand—and then, miraculously, it *becomes* the cupped hand that held the bird. Now the miracle of her experience comes alive; it feels as if the bird is in the reader's hand. That is what haiku is all about. It teaches us to build a nest of words to protect our inspiration until a reader can experience it in his or her own way as poetry.

Haiku are the perfect size for holding our encounters with the natural world. Haiku are not big or plodding, or dark and riddled with the old conventions of abstract constructions. Haiku are brief, yet incredibly open and at the same time very exact. They offer an established, yet endlessly flexible, way to express oneself.

For twenty-five years, William J. Higginson and his wife—poet and teacher Penny Harter—have shown us how to write haiku. From their understanding of Japanese poetry, they have taught us how to shape haiku, how to word them, and how to share them. And, of course, how to understand and appreciate them. The couple have inspired thousands. They have led readers and writers forward step by shy step, knowing, as we all do, that poetry comes from the heart, but writing comes from practiced skills. With the gentle guidance in this book, any willing reader can become a writer able to capture a moment of inspiration—whether it involves a blade of grass, a mountain, or city street. So go for it! Explore and be blessed!

Jane Reichhold

A Note on the Translations and Some Words of Thanks

The primary purpose of reading and writing haiku is sharing moments of our lives that have moved us, pieces of experience and perception that we offer or receive as gifts. At the deepest level, this is the one great purpose of all art, and especially of literature. The writer invites the reader to share in the experience written about, and in the experience of the shared language itself.

In this handbook you will find haiku in ten different languages, from all inhabited continents of Earth. While I have made all the final versions of the translations unless stated otherwise in the text, a number of people have given of their time and expertise, that we might all share, as nearly as possible, the experiences and the languages of these poems. I am especially grateful to the following.

In Japanese, Emiko Sakurai was particularly helpful in identifying and translating poems that reflect the diversity and craft of Issa. Professor Kazuo Sato, head of the International Division of the Museum of Haiku Literature, Tokyo, lent valuable assistance in reviewing the haiku by modern Japanese poets, and spent many hours pursuing the owners of copyrights. Tadashi

Kondo has lent his insight and poetic sensitivity to a number of collaborative translations which we have done over the years, several of which appear here. Shortly before the manuscript went to press he reviewed all the translations from Japanese, offering many clarifications and suggestions.

In Spanish, Gary Brower and Mark Cramer first brought the variety and depth of continental and Hispanic haiku to my attention. Elizabeth Searle Lamb and Bruce Lamb critiqued some of my Spanish translations, and Maria Luisa Muñoz assisted me in my efforts on her own work. Merlin Marie dePauw provided help on some technical points, and assisted in obtaining permission from Spanish-language poets.

Denise Gordon and Penny Harter assisted with French, in some cases providing trots and in others helping to develop shades of meaning missing from my early versions. André Duhaime and Dorothy Howard gave me an advance opportunity to read the manuscript of their *Haiku: anthologie canadienne/ Canadian Anthology*.

In German, Petra Engelbert made near-final translations for many of the poems of Imma von Bodmershof, and Volker Schubert assisted me in reviewing poems and criticism by German authors and in making translations. Sabine Sommerkamp helped keep me abreast of the current scene in Germany and also produced some preliminary translations.

Wanda Reumer provided information on haiku in Dutch, and reviewed my translations. Katarina von Bothmer checked my work on Hammarskjöld's Swedish. Nina Zivancevic reviewed my translations from Serbo-Croatian.

All the translations from the Greek of George Seferis were made especially for this book by Manya Bean.

In addition to help on translations, my work on *The Haiku Handbook* has been assisted by many over the years. Two of the earliest to offer encouragement leading to this book were Eric W. Amann, the first editor to publish my translations and criticism, and May D. Harding, a spirited teacher who insisted that I devote the same concentration to writing essays that I did to writing poems and translations.

Harold G. Henderson offered a kindly ear to the brash young man I was when we met. He said that he hoped his students would surpass his work, and we had many a friendly argument as I tried to do that. I only hope that this handbook may be fit to stand on the foundation that he, R. H. Blyth, and Kenneth Yasuda, each in their different ways, built for my early studies in haiku.

Soon after I began actively publishing my translations I discovered Cid Corman's work on early and contemporary Japanese poetry, which helped me to formulate my own concerns as a translator. Cid's letters provided additional encouragement and direction; he was also responsible for putting Tadashi Kondo in touch with me, a service for which I remain very grateful.

In the last decade my increasing interest in twentieth century haiku in Japan has been fed by the excellent works of Makoto Ueda. Hiroaki Sato, that most prolific translator of modern Japanese poetry, has provided much new material for haiku enthusiasts to enjoy, and given me reason to re-examine some of my assumptions about form in Japanese poetry. He has also given me a good deal of personal help on one point or another.

Among my poet-colleagues in America, Anita Virgil, Cor van den Heuvel, and Michael McClintock have each stimulated my research and writing, and acted as sounding boards for ideas as I developed them. Cor also read through the entire first draft of this handbook and recommended improvements.

Thomas Rimer gave the near-final manuscript a thorough reading, and offered helpful suggestions, many of which were adopted.

Poets Bill Zavatsky and Ron Padgett, of Teachers & Writers Collaborative, Inc., encouraged and offered valuable criticism of my early writing on teaching haiku. Ron has also written on his own experience teaching haiku. Portions of a piece which he revised for this book at my request appear in Chapter 11.

For helping me find bits and pieces of information, and encouragement along the way, I am particularly indebted to L. A. Davidson, until recently the recording secretary of the Haiku Society of America; Elizabeth Searle Lamb, editor of *Frogpond*; Robert Spiess, editor of *Modern Haiku*; Hal Roth, editor of *Wind Chimes*; Étiemble, authority on haiku influence in modern European poetry; and Sonō Uchida, former Ambassador of Japan to Morocco.

C. H. Farr has been a patron of the arts through continued donations to this effort.

Bonnie Crown, agent extraordinaire, found me out and asked me to write a new book on haiku before she knew that I had already completed an outline. She then found me a publisher, and schooled me in patience—a quality which she exemplifies.

Tim McGinnis, my first editor at McGraw-Hill, had the patience and courage to demand my best, and wait for it; his suggestions substantially improved this handbook. Elisabeth Jakab, who became my editor during the last phase of manuscript preparation, pushed the work—and me—through to its conclusion. And Joan Eckerman, editorial assistant, provided steady encouragement throughout.

Penny Harter, whom I first knew as a poet and colleague in teaching students to write, has helped me see this project through in every way imaginable. She has been a sounding board, co-translator, typist of some early draft chapters, and critic. She has contributed an important chapter on teaching. She has also made our home as peaceful as possible in these three years, despite the many pressures on us as writers, workers, parents, and members of our community.

I am deeply grateful for all these assistances; remaining errors are mine alone.

                                                              W.J.H.

A Note on Japanese Pronunciations and Names

When space allows I include the originals of works quoted from languages other than English. Japanese originals are given in *romaji* ("Roman letter") transliteration. Most readers probably have at least a slight acquaintance with the pronunciations of other Western languages. For some, this may be the first introduction to Japanese. Since a transliteration of one language into the phonetic symbols of another is never more than an approximation, I include here a rough guide to pronouncing Japanese words and names.

In romaji most consonants sound quite like their values in English. *G* is always as in "*give*" or as *ng* in "si*ng*"; *n* at the end of a syllable is held longer than in English, and shifts toward *m* before *b*, *m*, and *p*. A double consonant (except *n*) indicates a vowel sound now lost, and yields a glottal stop.

The vowels of Japanese are all pronounced, with a few exceptions that do not concern traditional poetry. Each vowel represents a unit of duration, all roughly equal in length, unless a macron or doubling indicates twice the length. Vowels in romaji have approximately the same pronunciations as in Italian. The following table gives some American-English equivalents for Japanese vowels.

SHORT VOWELS*

LONG VOWELS*

a = *a* in f*a*, h*a*	*ā* = *aa* in *aa*h
i = *ee* in k*ee*p	*ii* = *ee* in kn*ee*
u = *o* in wh*o*	*ū* = *oo* in ball*oo*n
e = *e* in b*e*t	*ē* = *ey* in f*ey* (no diphthong)
o = *o* in *o*kay	*ō* = *ow* in bl*ow*

*"Short" vowels are clipped, about half as long in duration as "long" vowels.

Eastern and Western ways of handling names differ. Some writers try to avoid confusion by dealing with all the names in their texts in the same way. The variety of names encountered in this book argued for another approach, summarized below.

FULL NAME	SHORT FORM	AS INDEXED
R. H. Blyth	Blyth	Blyth, R. H.
Li Po	Li Po	Li Po*
Matsuo Bashō	Bashō	Bashō**
Tanizaki Junichirō	Tanizaki	Tanizaki Junichirō
Makoto Ueda	Ueda	Ueda, Makoto

*With a cross-reference: Rihaku, see Li Po.
**With a cross-reference: Matsuo Bashō, see Bashō.

In the West given names usually precede family names, but family names are given first in indexes, followed by a comma. In Asia, however, family names usually appear first. Thus, in the first four examples Blyth, Li, Matsuo, and Tanizaki are family names. In the West we usually use an author's family name for repeated reference, while in Japan those who write in traditional genres, such as most of those discussed in this book, are known almost exclusively by their personal names, which usually are pen names. Chinese names, such as Li Po, are so short that they are not generally abbreviated. To further confuse things, Japanese usually refer to classical Chinese poets by the Japanese pronunciations for the characters in their names, making one word out of family and personal names. Thus, Li Po becomes Rihaku.

The fourth and fifth examples represent modern developments. The novelist Tanizaki has become so well known here that his name often appears Western style, given name first. And writers of modern literature (i.e., in other than traditional genres) are usually called by their family names in both Western and Japanese texts. I retain the traditional Japanese order for these names. But I give the names of Japanese living in the West or writing in Western languages in the order they appear in on their own works, given names first, as in Makoto Ueda.

Japanese poets writing in traditional genres appear in the index under their pen names; a cross-reference will be found at their family names. In all other cases, the first name shown in the index is the family name, with a comma indicating a Western, or Westernized, full name.

Part One

HAIKU
OLD AND NEW

1

Why Haiku?

HAIKU HAPPEN

We often see or sense something that gives us a bit of a lift, or a moment's pure sadness. Perhaps it is the funnies flapping in the breeze before a newsstand on a sunny spring day. Or some scent on the wind catches us as we step from the bus, or bend to lift the groceries from the car. Something tickles our ankle and, looking down to see what it is, we see more:

> a baby crab
> climbs up my leg—
> such clear water

Or we are lying awake, alone with our thoughts, and as we turn to look at the clock

> at midnight
> a distant door
> pulled shut

and we find ourselves more alone, because of the being on the other side of that door, than when we had no thoughts for others anywhere in the world.

The first of these two short poems was written about three hundred years ago by the Japanese poet Matsuo Bashō. The second is by a twentieth century Japanese poet, Ozaki Hōsai. Both poems are haiku.

Moments that can give rise to haiku are not foreign to the Americas. Mark Cramer has translated the following poem, originally written in Spanish by the Mexican poet José Juan Tablada a few years before Hōsai wrote "at midnight":

> Tender willow
> almost gold, almost amber,
> almost light . . .

And just recently New Jerseyan Penny Harter found

> the old doll
> her mama box broken
> to half a cry

Haiku happen all the time, wherever there are people who are "in touch" with the world of their senses, and with their own feeling response to it.

WHAT HAIKU ARE FOR

The other day as my wife and I were going over the checkbook in the dining room one of our daughters, in the west-facing living room, called us to come look at the sky. She saw how the clouds' ragged edges took light from the sun, intensifying both the dark gray of the main body of the clouds and the pale blue of the late autumn sky. She was touched by the lovely picture it all made. She felt that we should see the sky for ourselves, should share directly the experience that triggered her feelings. So she called us.

As we looked at the sky, we saw what she saw. And at the

same time we thought back to other skies we had known. I felt the mixed feelings of time passing, the loss of the heat of summer and the beginning of the rush toward the winter holidays and the New Year. My wife spoke of the deeper colors that would come later, with the reddening of the sunset. As the three of us looked at the sky, almost wordlessly, we felt a sharing that goes far deeper than the words I have just used to describe the event can ever penetrate.

This is the main lesson of haiku. When we compose a haiku we are saying, "It is hard to tell you how I am feeling. Perhaps if I share with you the event that made me aware of these feelings, you will have similar feelings of your own." Is this not one of the best ways to share feelings? When we want to "reach" another person with our feelings, do we just say "I feel sad"? Or "I'm happy"? Unless we tell them *what* it is that makes us feel sad or happy, how can they share our feelings? In fact, we automatically ask this very question when friends say they feel happiness or sadness, pain or joy: "What is it? What's the matter?" Or "What put that smile on your face?"

Haiku is the answer to this "what?"

We know that we cannot share our feelings with others unless we share the causes of those feelings with them. Also, we know that sharing the causes for joy and sadness builds a sense of community among our families, friends, co-workers, and organizations. Stating the feelings alone builds walls; stating the causes of the feelings builds paths.

Most haiku present dramatic moments the authors found in common, everyday occurrences—small dramas that play in our minds. If we but see, but taste, as in these two haiku by Virginia Brady Young and Robert Spiess, respectively:

> On the first day of spring,
> snow falling
> from one bough to another

> Snowing . . .
> the dentist
> polishes my teeth

Haiku work, as we read them, by giving us a moment to look at some thing, some event, and see it more clearly than we have perhaps seen it before. The author had to stop to take note of this object, this event, and to write it down. If we take the time to read the poem, perhaps we will find ourselves

> pausing
> halfway up the stair—
> white chrysanthemums

with Elizabeth Searle Lamb, or

> not seeing
> the room is white
> until that red apple

with Anita Virgil. Of course, we cannot see the same chrysanthemums that stopped Lamb on the stairs, or know just what sort of apple turned Virgil's room white. But the next time we encounter chrysanthemums perhaps we will look at them more closely, become a sort of Georgia O'Keeffe of chrysanthemums. And Virgil's white room almost makes us instinctively look up at the walls of the room we are in now, reading this.

Haiku not only give us moments from the writer's experience, but go on to give us moments of our own. The central act of haiku is letting an object or event touch us, and then sharing it with another. If we are the writer, we share it with the reader. If we read a haiku, we share that moment, or one like it, with the writer.

Being small, haiku lend themselves especially to sharing small, intimate things. By recognizing the intimate things that touch us we come to know and appreciate ourselves and our world more. By sharing these things with others we let them into our lives in a very special, personal way.

2

The Four Great Masters of Japanese Haiku

MATSUO BASHŌ

Haiku begins in the great age of *renga*, a type of poetry enjoyed by many kinds of people in seventeenth century Japan. Matsuo Bashō (1644–1694) was a master of the renga, and made his living traveling around the country, teaching people everywhere he went the art and craft of writing renga, or linked poems. (See Chapter 13, Before Haiku, for a description of renga.)

In Bashō's day renga belonged to everyone, and particularly to the middle class, the people who lived in the hustle and bustle of one or another town of varying size. Bashō was deeply influenced by the Chinese poets of the T'ang Dynasty (seventh to ninth centuries A.D.), particularly Tu Fu, Li Po, and Po Chü-i, who are called To Ho, Rihaku, and Hakurakuten, respectively, in Japanese and many Anglo-Japanese texts. Among Japanese influences, Bashō particularly admired the *tanka* (see Chapter 13) of a

Buddhist priest named Saigyō (1118–1190) and the renga of Iio
Sōgi (1421–1502). All of these poets wrote from an aesthetic of austerity. They
often wrote about loneliness, or at least about being alone, usu-
ally with a touch of humor. For example:

Mid-Mountain Dialogue

you ask my purpose
    roosting in jade peaks
smiling yet without reply
    heart at self ease
peach blossoms running water
    sundown blazes away
having another sky & earth
    not among humans

Li Po

tō hito mo	even visitors
omoitaetaru	have stopped thinking of
yamazato no	mountain village
sabishisa nakuba	loneliness without which
sumiukaramashi	living would be unpleasant

Saigyō

Saigyō's poem is ironic; he is a monk, striving to live "without
attachments"—even to old, distant friends. It is easier for him to
forget the world, to be "happy", without the pleasure of having
visits from friends. At the same time, his poem jokes with the
Chinese tradition, particularly prominent in the poetry of Li Po
and his contemporaries, of writing poems as letters to far-away
friends. Similarly, in the Chinese example Li Po seems to be mak-
ing a serious statement about why he is living in the mountains.
But he pokes fun at himself, first by describing himself as "roost-

ing" like a bird, then by answering quite directly the very question he said he would not reply to.

This mixture of joking banter and seriousness pervades much of Chinese and Japanese poetry. The poems which Zen monks chose as their favorites, or composed themselves, are filled with images that strike deep into our feelings about the world. At the same time, these poems are likely to contain humorous puns, allusions to other poems or stories—sometimes serious, sometimes not—or frankly humorous scenes.

However, the renga of Bashō's youth had descended to mere commonness. When Bashō wrote his poem

kare-eda ni	on a barren branch
karasu no tomarikeri	a raven has perched—
aki no kure	autumn dusk

he was reacting against the petty superficiality of the language and feeling in the poems of his day. This poem, first published in 1680 and later revised to its present form, became the basis for Bashō's school of linked-poem composition.

As Bashō matured in his art he lightened his touch. In 1686 he published what has become the best known poem in the Japanese language, and decreed it the model for his mature style:

furuike ya	old pond . . .
kawazu tobikomu	a frog leaps in
mizu no oto	water's sound

The frog has been a traditional subject of Japanese poetry since the first recorded songs; by Bashō's day there were thousands, if not millions of poems involving frogs. But virtually every frog that appeared in a poem up to that time was celebrated for its singing. Even today, Japanese learn the songs of different species of frogs from records, much as we learn the calls of "song birds". But Bashō's frog leaps, making a small sound with his action, rather than his voice.

Bashō felt himself part of a rich poetic tradition. He was also concerned that poems should be created out of a deep unity of the poet and experience. This unity shows itself in the perceptual and expressive stages of poetic inspiration, as Makoto Ueda has called them. Of the first, or perceptual state, Bashō says "Learn of the pine from the pine; learn of the bamboo from the bamboo." One of Bashō's disciples explains that to be genuine a poem must contain the spontaneous feeling that *comes from the object itself.* In effect, the poet's first job is to share in the essential nature of the thing written about.

Bashō's disciple goes on to say that just as a mere "look at" an object is not enough to produce the deep seeing that begins inspiration, so the writing of a mere description cannot capture the essence of an object the writer's mind has penetrated. Bashō says, "In writing do not let a hair's breadth separate your self from the subject. Speak your mind directly; go to it without wandering thoughts."

Having shared in the life of an object, the writer must share this life with others through the medium of words. But these words must connect directly to the writer's mind, that is in turn directly connected to the object. This, the expressive stage, logically comes after the perceptual stage. But, as Bashō clearly says, the two stages ideally occur as one.

In the final poem, both the language of the poem and the mind of the poet should be transparent to the reader, who, on reading the poem, should see directly into the inner life of the object as the poet did. This is the ideal of Bashō-School haiku, an ideal almost all haiku poets since have striven to attain.*

*A vocabulary of several special terms grew up to express various nuances of this central ideal. Many of the distinctions made by Bashō and his disciples have become obscure over the years, but the ideal remains the same. Such terms as *sabi, wabi, hosomi,* etc., and all Japanese terms which are italicized on first appearance, are defined in the Glossary at the back of this book.

Another of Bashō's most famous poems sums it up. He had spent some hours getting to a temple on top of a steep, rocky hill. When he arrived, Bashō composed this hokku:

shizukasa ya	the stillness—
iwa ni shimiiru	soaking into stones
semi no koe	cicada's cry

We should not think of Bashō entirely as austere. In addition to many verses that seem like scenes for contemplation he wrote some that call for joy or abandon. Here is one:

iza yukamu	well! let's go
yukimi ni korobu	snow-viewing till
tokoro made	we tumble!

He can also see the humor in our insatiable desire for sensation:

kumo ori-ori	clouds occasionally
hito o yasumuru	make a fellow relax
tsukimi kana	moon-viewing!

Bashō was not known for haiku in his own day. He was a master of a kind of renga called *haikai-no-renga*, or "humorous linked poem". What we know as haiku Bashō called *hokku*, or "starting verse". For the haiku originated as the starting verse of a renga.

Bashō also became known in his day for another kind of writing, called *haibun*, which we can roughly translate as "haiku prose". Bashō's haibun vary from short, impressionistic sketches and diary entries to a series of travel journals. The most famous of these, *Oku no hosomichi* (literally, *Narrow Roads of the Interior*), is a world classic, as important in its way as *The Tale of Genji*.

The word *haikai* is often used to apply to all of the haiku-related literature: haiku or hokku, haikai-no-renga, and haibun. Bashō is probably the greatest master of all haikai literature, and so is considered The First Great Master of Haiku, or simply The Master. We will meet many more examples of his work throughout this book.

YOSA BUSON

Yosa Buson (1716–1784) was a prominent leader in bringing the influence of Southern Chinese painting into Japanese art. He also wrote poems, particularly in the haikai genre, and today is considered the second of the Four Great Masters of Haiku.

By Buson's day the haikai-no-renga of Bashō's followers had lost some of its steam, and Buson went back to Bashō for much of his personal inspiration. More than once Buson copied out entire manuscripts of Bashō's travel journals, adding his own enchanting sketches or paintings.

Buson's most characteristic verses have a sensual and objective quality that we readily accept from a painter. Here are two examples:

yūkaze ya	evening breeze . . .
mizu aosagi no	water laps the legs
hagi o utsu	of the blue heron
yanagi chiri	willow leaves fallen
shimizu kare ishi	clear waters dried up stones
tokoro-dokoro	one place and another

The second poem has all the characteristics of the sort of Chinese landscape painting Buson most admired. The thin branches of the leafless willows hang delicately down over the rocks now free of the brook's waters in the dryness of autumn. However, we should not be too hasty in accepting this as merely a picture. This poem illustrates the layers of allusion that can build up in what seems to be one simple little haiku.

In the preface to the poem Buson tells us that he was "practicing austerities" in the area called Shimotsuke in mid-autumn, and that the poem is a report of "the scenery right in front of my eyes, in the shade of an old tree said perhaps to be 'the pilgrimage willow'." Evidently, he refers to the *Narrow Roads of the Interior*, where Bashō writes the following passage in the same region:

> Now, the clear-water-flowing willow is still there at the village of Ashino on a path of the fields. The deputy of the area, a certain Kobu, offered now and again to show us this willow; wondered just where, today attending on the very shade of this willow.

ta ichimai	planting a patch
uete tachisaru	of field and leaving—
yanagi kana	ah, willow!

And Bashō, in his turn, assumes that we will know the "clear-water-flowing willow" as that tree of which Saigyō wrote this tanka:

michinobe ni	at the roadside
shimizu nagaruru	clear water flowing
yanagi kage	willow shade
shibashi tote koso	thinking to rest a while
tachitomaretsure	have come to a halt

This poem of Saigyō's is very well known, for it is the source of inspiration for the nō play *Yugyō Yanagi, The Priest and the Willow*. In the play a wandering priest is guided by "the Spirit of the Withered Willow". The spirit tells of a pilgrim who was looking for the source of the clear water at a temple, and found there a "golden light shining. A decayed willow tree suddenly revealed itself as Kannon of the purple willow. . . . it's become a holy place for walking pilgrimage." (Kannon is the Buddhist goddess of mercy.)

I have deliberately written the discussion of allusions in Buson's haiku

> willow leaves fallen
> clear waters dried up stones
> one place and another

in the present tense because to a reasonably literate Japanese these layers all exist simultaneously. Saigyō lived from 1118 to 1190; *The Priest and the Willow* was written by Nobumitsu, who lived from 1435 to 1516; Bashō's *Narrow Roads of the Interior* was first drafted in 1689. Buson, writing in the mid and late eighteenth century, certainly knew all this literature, and no doubt other stories and nō plays that relate to it as well.

Further, he felt that the haiku of Bashō had died out—one might say "withered" or "dried up"—by the time he came along, and Buson wrote several haiku alluding to the loss of Bashō's teachings. This is one of them. Literary allusions may turn up often in haiku, but in the hands of Buson they never appear without the clarity and power of a strong sensory image.

Even when his painterly love of the visual seems to give way to depicting human drama, small and large, Buson never gives up on his senses, as in these two examples:

hashi nakute	no bridge and
hi kuren to suru	the sun ready to set
haru no mizu	waters of spring

nusubito no	a thief
yane ni kieyuku	vanishes over the rooftops
yosamu kana	night chill!

In the first we feel the dread of someone—the author?—stopped at the edge of what is normally a little trickling stream, turned into a rushing torrent by the spring rains. Like the end of the first chapter in a mystery, the sky is about to go dark as we confront the problem. In the second we have a picture worthy of Goya. Shadows surround the puzzled expressions of the people, awakened by the sound of a thief. They just now begin to feel the chill night air as they stand around asking one another questions in their night dress.

Like Bashō, Buson was a very versatile writer. In addition to his painting—his major activity and source of income—he wrote not only haiku and occasional renga, but also verse in Chinese. Writing verse in Chinese had been fashionable centuries earlier, then waned in popularity until Buson's day. Buson wrote very engagingly in the classical Chinese five-word verse form. He also experimented in a sort of irregular Japanese verse that modern scholars have credited with being the first real use of free verse in Japanese, long before the influx of Western influence in the mid-nineteenth century.

In two outstanding works Buson very successfully mixed formal Chinese verse with informal Japanese free verse. The best known of these, *Shunpū Batei Kyoku*, literally "Spring Breeze Horse Levee Tune" (usually translated as something like "On the Banks of the Kema in the Spring Breeze"), also incorporates haiku by Buson and others. It has been translated into English several times.

Another example, one that demonstrates how well Buson worked the different pacings of formal Chinese verse and his own Japanese free verse together, is called *Denga Ka*, "A Lyric of Sluggish River". In the "Lyric" Buson takes on the persona of a woman in a very romantic setting, writing to her lover. She refers to the pleasure boat they share, and her inability to cut loose and go live with him in the city. The sensuality of the subject and the images is a strong foil for her fears.

A Lyric of Sluggish River

Spring waters	float plum blossoms
south flowing	Vine meets Sluggish
brocade hawser	do not loosen it
rapid stream	the boat like lightning

Vine Water   meets Sluggish Water
flowing together   like one body
in the boat   wishing to sleep with you
and be forever   people of Naniwa

You are like a plum tree on the water
      the blossoms on the water floating
            leaving   swift
I am like a willow on the riverbank
      the shadow in the water sinking
            following   impossible

Today these wonderful verses by Buson are not very well known to the Japanese. Buson is remembered mainly for his haiku and his paintings. But it is important to remember that Buson tried his hand at just about every kind of writing done in his day, and went well beyond others in his development of form. To all his work he brought a painter's love of shape, color, and movement. He also had a humorous eye for the human condition, and a great love of the literature and art of the past. In Chapter 14, Haiku Prose, we will find more of Buson's haiku in a setting that further illustrates the range of his artistry, humanity, and knowledge of earlier literature.

KOBAYASHI ISSA

The third Great Master of Haiku, Kobayashi Issa (1762–1826), was a country bumpkin compared to ascetic, priestly Bashō and worldly, sophisticated Buson. The majority of Japanese who like traditional haiku probably know and like Issa better than any other poet. Since he grew up in the country with a cruel stepmother and was banished from his home to city poverty in his mid-teens, Issa had a rather pessimistic view of human nature.

He came to prefer the company of small, seemingly insignificant creatures, and wrote many haiku on such topics as grasshoppers, flies and bugs, sparrows, and other less-than-glamorous beings.

One of Issa's best known verses shows his empathy with those who are often not appreciated:

yare utsu na	oh, don't swat!
hae ga te o suru	the fly rubs hands
ashi o suru	rubs feet

The fly prays twice as much as most humans.

However, Issa was a much more complex person than the standard fare of English language haiku books would lead us to believe. And his relative calm in accepting his difficult life is often obscured by excessively melodramatic and wordy translations of his poems. Professor Emiko Sakurai, of the University of Hawaii, has helped me select and translate the rest of the examples of Issa's haiku in this chapter. We have selected them with an eye toward correcting the imbalance in the popular view of Issa, and have translated them in ways that parallel the originals' lean, un-self-pitying language as nearly as possible.

Issa, though a child of the rural village, began his career as a poet in the city. Here are a few of Issa's views of life in the poorer quarters of Edo (modern Tokyo):

aki no yo ya	autumn night . . .
tabi no otoko no	a traveling man's
harishigoto	needlework

In the lamplight we see a figure bent over, a needle every now and then gleaming. We realize it is a man, alone, womanless. He has no mother, wife, or girl friend to darn his socks, sew up the split seam of a worn robe. Remember, we are dealing with a time almost two hundred years ago, and a culture where men did not do these things. A womanless man was undoubtedly poor. Certainly Issa was poor.

shigururu ya	drizzling . . .
oyawan tataku	tapping a large rice bowl
oshikojiki	deaf-mute beggar

But some were worse off than he.

kogarashi ya	a withering wind—
jibita ni kururu	seated in the falling dusk
tsuji utai	a street minstrel

The bitter wind drives off those who might otherwise stand and listen to the minstrel, as he laughs and sings, bringing joy to himself and the crowd. *Kogarashi* means literally "tree-witherer"; here not only a tree has been withered.

Like Bashō, Issa feels how one time penetrates another in the mixture of memory and present moment:

kagerō ya	heat shimmer . . .
me ni tsuki-matou	lingering in the eye
warai-gao	a laughing face

The rippling view through the rising heat brings to mind someone's rippling laughter, some other time. For Issa the laughing face is that of one of his children who died in infancy.

While we do not think of Issa as a sensualist, like Buson he can be very Romantic:

onna kara	the woman
saki e kasumu zo	leads into the mist—
shiohigata	low tide beach

This is not a bathing beauty, but a fully clothed woman who, barefoot, leads the way to see what treasures the tide has left. The appearance of shells, both empty and full of life, on the beach after the tide goes out has its opposite in the woman, who disappears into the mist. The sea reveals at least a small part of itself as the mist envelops one of those who come to see that revelation.

Issa had to fight for everything throughout his life: Mother love was denied him by his stepmother, who later tried to take away the property that was his birthright. He worked many years in the desolation of city poverty to make a name for himself as a poet. All of his children born during his lifetime died in infancy; the young wives who bore those children died before he did. (One child did survive to inherit his property; she was born to Issa's last wife after he died.) Through it all Issa seemed to draw strength from those small creatures whose lives are so fleeting, who seem so overwhelmed by the elements that we feel they need our encouragement:

> *suzukaze ya*   cool breeze . . .
> *chikara ippai*   with all his might
> *kirigirisu*   the katydid

It is easy to sentimentalize, and thereby trivialize, the life and poetry of Issa. Japanese, as well as Western translators, have often been guilty of doing so. But Issa's verses are usually clear of such sentimentality, the few popularly remembered exceptions notwithstanding. We must not mistake the sympathy, the empathy Issa feels for those who seem to be "underdogs" as pity. People who have not experienced such hardship feel pity for those who have. Issa himself lived through many hardships; when he encourages even grasshoppers and frogs in the face of their adversities, he encourages himself.

Issa is also capable of lovely serenity and aesthetic sensibility, and of seeing the humor that constantly plays about human concerns:

> *suzushisa ya*   the coolness . . .
> *hangetsu ugoku*   the half-moon shifts
> *tamari mizu*   puddles

> *asatsuyu no*   morning-dewed
> *asagao uruya*   morning glories he sells,
> *araotoko*   rough fellow

We should remember Issa as a complex person, capable of mixing humor and pathos, and sensitive to the beauty and mystery of life and our perceptions of it. A reading of his masterful autobiographical haibun, *Ora ga haru*, literally *My Spring*, gives a good idea of his range, and of his appreciation for poems by many poets in both the haiku and tanka modes. (See Resources at the end of this handbook.)

MASAOKA SHIKI

By the time the last of the Four Great Masters of Haiku, Masaoka Shiki (1867–1902), rose to dominate the world of traditional Japanese poetry, the renga had all but died out as a serious art form. Bashō was the last truly great master of renga, and though haiku was still thought of as hokku, the starting verse of a renga, none of the masters who followed Bashō devoted as much of their efforts to perfecting the renga as Bashō had. Buson struggled to establish a new style of painting during his lifetime. Hokku and renga were a diversion for him, although a very important one. Poetry parties over which he presided tended to become contests in composing hokku, rather than collaborative efforts at making a renga. And by the time of Issa poets made their reputations almost entirely on the basis of their individual poems rather than their ability to orchestrate a renga.

Just as Bashō became the pivot between the renga and the more independent hokku later developed by two centuries of disciples and new masters, so Shiki is at the same time the last of the Great Masters of Haiku and the first poet of modern haiku. He was the first to use the word "haiku", a term originally meaning a verse of haikai-no-renga (and previously seldom used), for the independent hokku. Some scholars and critics feel that Shiki destroyed the hokku/haiku by decreeing the end of renga. Actually, the independence of the hokku had been well established by Shiki's time, and it remained for a major critic to acknowledge the fact. Shiki was that critic, and his adoption of the word "haiku" for the short verses previously called "hokku" simply completed a process that had begun a century or more earlier.

However, Shiki was not concerned with only the haiku. He was also an innovator in the tanka, the other main type of traditional poem in Japanese. Before his death at the age of thirty-five he had established new schools of writing in both genres, an unusual feat. Japanese poets tend to concentrate on one or another of the main poetic genres, though they may occasionally dabble in another mode.

Shiki was seriously ill with spinal tuberculosis almost all of his adult life. While his strongly worded essays ranged forth across most of the Japanese literature of past and present, much of his poetry concerns the minutiae of sick-room life. The following tanka gives an impression of his clean, direct style, most unusual for his own day:

kame ni sasu	stuck in a vase
fuji no hanabusa	clusters of wisteria
hana tarete	blossoms hanging,
yamai no toko ni	in the sick-bed
haru kuren to su	spring begins to darken

There is a harmony between the purple of the wisteria flowers hanging down from the vase and the darkening spring. By using "spring begins to darken" Shiki brings an autumnal feeling into his tanka. This effect deepens as a Japanese reader notes that *tarete*, which means "drooping" or "hanging", also means "leaving behind", as in "He died, leaving behind just a bed and a table."

Perhaps only as we read the last line of Shiki's tanka do we begin to realize that this is a poem, a crafted piece of literature, and not just a picture in words. The haiku, even more than the tanka, often comes close to being merely a word-picture. Many failed haiku are just that. But if we are sensitive to the symbolic value which things and events have for us, then even simple word-pictures can mean a great deal to us, both as writers and as readers.

We share by means of words. But words that are too concerned with how *I* respond prevent *you* from responding freely to the object or event that caused my response. For this reason, Shiki demanded that the language of haiku be objective. He fought against the decadent haiku poets of his time who patterned their haiku after some of the more subjective verses of Bashō. Shiki believed that Buson was more objective than, and as great a poet as, Bashō, and he shocked the haiku world by saying so.

Shiki also insisted that verses on the actual objects and events of our lives are better than those made up in the imagination, though he did not prohibit the latter. The following poems point up this contrast between the subjectivity of Bashō and the objectivity of Shiki.

Bashō, in a famous passage of *Narrow Roads of the Interior*, lingers over the field where a long-past, historic battle was fought. He writes this haiku, one of his best known:

> *natsugusa ya*   summer grass . . .
> *tsuwamonodomo ga*   those mighty warriors'
> *yume no ato*   dream-tracks

Shiki, during a brief time in China as a war correspondent, also writes a battlefield haiku:

> *nashi saku ya*   the pear blossoming . . .
> *ikusa no ato no*   after the battle this
> *kuzure ie*   ruined house

In both poems there is a pun on the word *ato*, which may be written any of three ways: as a character meaning "track"; as a character meaning "after"; or in phonetic script which leaves the choice up to the reader according to the context. Bashō chooses "track" and Shiki writes the word in ambiguous phonetics. Though Shiki's *ato* is part of a phrase where it will be taken to mean "after" rather than "track", there are enough echoes of Bashō to suggest that his choice of ambiguity is not accidental. The entire middle line of Shiki's haiku is written in phonetic script. This would not be unusual, except that Shiki tends to write most of the words in his haiku in the less ambiguous characters, and since he was a war correspondent it is highly unlikely that he did not know the character for *ikusa*, "battle". More likely, he intends the reader to recall Bashō's poem, which begins with the *kusa*, "grass", of *natsugusa*, and ends with *ato*.

Thus Shiki writes a poem that gives us a vision of human nature and the rest of nature intertwined in contemporary battle ruins and pear blossoms, and at the same time he pokes a kind of fun at the naive veneration of ancient warriors expressed in Bashō's haiku. He contrasts the broad landscape of a battlefield, suggested in Bashō's poem, with the remains of a house, probably the home of some family now refugees, or worse. The bravery of legendary heroes, with the commonness of everyday living, both destroyed by war. By including a ruined *house*, rather than a ruined castle or fort, and writing at the scene of a recent battle, rather than of some long-ago event, Shiki has modernized the haiku, brought it into the present tense, and made the cruelty of war, rather than its grandeur, a fit subject for haiku.

There is a haiku by Itō Shōu, a well known haiku master of Shiki's day, which has the preface "Sekigahara Remembrance":

kono shita ni	under this,
eiyū no hone ya	heroes' bones . . .
nokoru yuki	left-over snow

This modern image, coupling the scraps of melting snow with the whiteness (in the mind) of the bones beneath it, is indeed striking. However, this poem is clearly closer to the poem of Bashō in feeling. Compare this patriotism that stands on the location of an old battle (fought in 1600) and alludes to Bashō's model poem for such an occasion, and the mixed feelings of one who stands in the smoking ruins of a battle just over, wondering why poets eulogize such insanity. Both are excellent poems, but they expose quite different sorts of consciousness.

Yet Shiki is not so different from Bashō, Buson, Issa, or the rest of us. Consider this poem of his in comparison with the woman Issa saw leading the way into the mist at the low-tide beach:

koginukete	rowing through
kasumi no soto no	out of the mist
umi hiroshi	the wide sea

Shiki, who stayed pretty well within the confines of traditional formal restrictions, was willing to stray to catch the lumbering awkwardness of a horse:

natsugawa ya	summer river . . .
hashi wa aredomo uma	there's a bridge, but the horse
mizu o yuku	goes through water

This haiku is practically a story, while the next is a mystery, one which we contemplate with mild curiosity:

aki harete	autumn clear—
mono no kemuri no	the smoke of something
sora ni iru	goes into the sky

In the next chapter we will look at some of the major figures who came into prominence after 1900, with just a few poems by each so we can get a feel for their styles and concerns—and how they continue the basic tradition of sharing that is the real core of haiku.

3

Modern Japanese Haiku

KAWAHIGASHI HEKIGOTŌ

Shiki left a number of disciples and confederates when he died in 1902. Kawahigashi Hekigotō (1873–1937) was most prominent among the younger generation who wished to continue renovating haiku. All of his earlier work is in traditional form, but much of it shows his freshness in taste, both as to subject and treatment. For example:

tō hanabi	far fireworks
oto shite nani mo	sounding, otherwise
nakarikeri	not a thing
tonbo tsuru	the dragonfly catching
sao yoru nami ni	pole, to the calling waves
sutete yukinu	abandoned and left

Fireworks, of course, are not particularly modern in Japan. Most fireworks haiku deal with the visual effects; the word *hanabi* literally means "flower-fire". But Hekigotō's fireworks are heard only, not seen. In effect, he has duplicated Bashō's movement from frogs' songs to frogs' actions in *furuike ya*. The sense of allure and entrapment in the second poem above builds an atmosphere similar to the Sirens of Odysseus. Each new part of the poem unfolds a shift in meaning. We move from "dragonfly catching"—an act—to the pole which performs that act. The pole has been left free, but seems trapped by "the calling waves". It is hard to imagine a way to pack more drama into such a short poem.

These two poems demonstrate the range of emotion and coloring that Hekigotō could build into the brief haiku, the contrast between an extremely ascetic, spare image by itself in the first and a heavily layered, compound image in the second. Hekigotō's virtuosity attracted many followers, including Ogiwara Seisensui, who had begun to abandon the traditional form of haiku. Hekigotō agreed with this. He wanted the poem to come as close to reality as possible, without the interference of man-made rules. With these principles he started the New Trend Haiku Movement. For the rest of his career Hekigotō experimented with disregarding the seventeen-sound pattern, often writing longer, rather "bumpy" haiku like these:

konogoro tsuma naki	recently wife died
yaoya	grocer's
na o tsumu	stacking greens
negi o tsumu	stacking onions
aruji musume	husband and daughter
tōku takaki ki	a distant, tall tree
natsu chikaki tateri	summer near, standing
tatamu yane ni	over folded roofs

In the first of these we see how the grocer and his daughter go on with their work, but always in the knowledge of the recent death. The relationship between husband and daughter, and between them and the work, has changed. This change affects the way they look, the rhythms and angles of their bodies—not to mention the way we look at them.

The second poem collapses space; the far-off tree looms over the jutting folds of the many roofs. Time also collapses; this is more apparent in the original, where *takaki*, "tall", and *chikaki*, "near", make the tree and summer one thing, both far and near. We feel the closeness of summer, and of the houses to one another, in the repeated sounding of *k* and *t* in the first seven words of the poem, and the opening of the soft sounds at the end brings in the distance.

TAKAHAMA KYOSHI

While editing *Hototogisu* ("cuckoo"), the magazine founded under Shiki's guidance, Takahama Kyoshi (1874–1959) had devoted most of its pages to the new fiction of modernist writers such as his good friend Natsume Sōseki and Sōseki's protégé, Akutagawa Ryūnosuke. Kyoshi himself wrote novels and travel diaries. After Shiki's death *Hototogisu* became almost exclusively a fiction magazine for a number of years.

But Kyoshi had been Shiki's other star pupil, equal to Hekigotō in importance. Though Kyoshi himself had said that Hekigotō was the most promising haiku poet among Shiki's students at the time of their master's death, he became increasingly upset by the liberties Hekigotō's group was taking. In 1912 he issued a statement to the effect that true haiku were written in the traditional way, with seventeen sounds and seasonal reference. He began putting haiku in *Hototogisu* again, and quickly attracted many fine poets who had not been pleased with developments in the New Trend Haiku Movement. Kyoshi became mentor to dozens of new poets in two succeeding generations, many of whom went on to establish schools of haiku composition and magazines of their own. Kyoshi also outlived virtually all of the other impor-

tant poets of his generation, and *Hototogisu,* under the editorship
of his son Toshio, continues to be one of the leading haiku mag-
azines. To this day his name and ideas dominate conversations
about modern haiku.

Kyoshi's strong opinions, bolstered by quoting Shiki's most
conservative statements, were widely disseminated by his stu-
dents and *Hototogisu,* the most important magazine in the haiku
world throughout the 1920s. Yet, for all his power, the haiku of
Kyoshi are very mild in tone, and tend to speak of specifically
Japanese subjects in a very traditional way. Most would be hard
for us to distinguish from verses written a century earlier:

ame harete	rain cleared—
shibaraku bara no	for a while the wild rose's
nioi kana	fragrance
tabisen to	this spring too
omoishi haru mo	when I had thought to travel
kure ni keri	has ended

Staying within the confines of the experimentalism of a cen-
tury earlier, Kyoshi still did write some powerful haiku in the tra-
ditional mode; here is one:

hakizome no	the first sweeping's
hōki ya tsuchi ni	broom . . . begins to get
narehajimu	used to the soil

Kyoshi breaks the flow of this poem in the middle, countering
the traditional rhythm. This break in the rhythm accords well
with the perception, which perhaps stopped Kyoshi in the act of
sweeping with the new broom. I wonder if Kyoshi saw the soil
on the just-used broom as the dot of black at the center of the
white area in the yin-yang symbol—and if he saw the breakdown
of the five-seven-five form forecast in the haiku of Buson, who
also often used a mid-poem break in his own haiku

OGIWARA SEISENSUI

While Kyoshi's long career as the main haiku master of all Japan was getting under way, Hekigotō's group was breaking up. Oriwara Seisensui (1884–1976), who had helped convince Hekigotō to drop traditional form, dropped Hekigotō and took the magazine he had established at Hekigotō's bidding in a new direction. In the pages of *Sōun* ("stratus clouds") Seisensui argued for a haiku that would illustrate the subjective feelings of the writer, rather than the objective world that caused the writer's feelings. Thus his poems reveal more of the writer than do Hekigotō's, with which they may be compared:

yume mo mizu ni	not seeing a dream
nete ita yo	slept the night
suzume no koe	sparrows' voices
ama no gawa mo	the Milky Way too
koku natta koto	has become intense
yūte wakareru	we said and parted

In the first, the noise of the sparrows points up the silence of the dreamless sleep. In the second, the intensity of the starry band becomes an image for the intensity of feeling with which the persons parted. This latter, almost a love poem, has a metaphoric or symbolic level similar to that found in the tanka of the old court poets. The tension in the poem arises from the interactions of the persons, not the depth of sensation one person experiences.

Seisensui's *Sōun* became the most widely read of the Free-Meter Haiku Movement magazines, and Seisensui kept up a heavy correspondence with many of the poets he published. This sometimes led to dialogues in verse, such as the following poem by Santōka and Seisensui's reply:

ushiro sugata no	shape of a back-side
shigurete yuku ka	going off in a drizzle?
hito o yobu ka to	calling someone?
tori no yobu koe	the bird's calling voice

A question suggests subjectivity in haiku; in the following poem Seisensui uses *ka* (a sort of verbal question mark) to further increase the sense of mystery and space in the metaphor of a thousand tatami mats:

umi wa michishio ka	sea at high tide?
tsuki wa senjō	on a thousand mats the moon
hikari o shiku	spreads light

TANEDA SANTŌKA

Taneda Santōka (1882–1940) married as a young man, took up modern business, and "dropped out" to become a beggar poet. Though on the fringes of society, he had studied haiku as a youth, and corresponded with and had haiku published by Seisensui in *Sōun*.

Santōka left the cities and lived in one or another small hut in the countryside, often walking miles each day jotting notes and haiku and occasionally accepting a little food from people he met along the way. His poems are full of the natural landscape most Japanese were leaving to enter the hectic modern life of the cities:

wakeitte mo	further in yet
wakeitte mo	further in yet
aoi yama	green hills

Santōka, like most of the wandering mendicants of old Japan, lived as he pleased. He also wrote that way:

> *nonbiri ibari suru*   taking a leisurely pee
> *kusa no me darake*   in lush sprouting grass

While the Japanese do not consider "four-letter words" taboo in the way that Westerners do, there are some images that one does not generally include in the more courtly poetry—but both Bashō and Buson, and a host of other haiku poets, have written poems with urine and other excreta in them.

> *ishi ni tonbo*   on a rock the dragonfly
> *mahiru no yume miru*   looks at midday dreams

Perhaps Santōka's dragonfly relates to Chuang-tzu's butterfly. In the old Chinese Taoist scripture, Chuang-tzu said that when he wakened from a dream he was puzzled: Was he a man who had dreamed of being a butterfly, or a butterfly now dreaming himself to be a man? Here it seems the dragonfly dreams Santōka.

At his best, Santōka recites the simple facts of his life, without considering style, form, or content. This simplicity produces his most moving poems, such as the following:

> *ko no ha chiru*   tree leaves fall
> *arukitsumeru*   walking on and on

OZAKI HŌSAI

Ozaki Hōsai (1885–1926) was also a beggar; he spent years begging and doing odd jobs around Kyoto temples before settling in a cottage on a small island of Japan's inland sea. While Santōka's poems are full of the loneliness of wandering out in the country away from people, Hōsai's city life seems to have been lonelier still:

> *seki o shite mo*   coughing, even:
> *hitori*   alone

Hōsai began writing while in middle school and was admitted to Seisensui's haiku circle by the time he was twenty. He was an excellent student, and seemed bound for a brilliant career in the life insurance business after graduating from law school at Tokyo Imperial University. But something went awry, and Hōsai gave up his home, family, and business to try first one and then another of the new, militant religions of Japan. The only thing he took with him into his new life was his haiku.

Hōsai abandoned traditional verse form, and, like Santōka, stayed within the simple confines of his life for his subject matter. He made his way doing menial work around the temples, which is sometimes reflected in his poems:

> *uchisokoneta kugi ga*   the misstruck nail
> *kubi o mageta*   bent its neck

We may imagine that Hōsai was irritated by this, but he seems to suggest that the nail is sad because it was hit incorrectly.

If Hōsai's life and religious seeking seem confused, his poetic vision was not. He was capable of sketching the people as well as the objects around him:

> *yuki wa haretaru*   snow stopped
> *kodomora no koe ni*   in the voices of children
> *hi ga ataru*   the sun shines

And himself:

> *nagisa furikaeru*   looking back at the beach
> *waga ashiato mo naku*   even my footprints are gone

Personal pronouns do not appear frequently in Japanese haiku; here Hōsai has used "even my" in anything but a casual way. At first suggesting self-pity, these words then call up the reflection "even *my* footprints, just now made, are gone—what of the hundreds, the many generations, that have gone before me?" Thus while seeming to mourn his own passing Hōsai actually joins in the universal lament for all the generations of mankind.

NAKATSUKA IPPEKIRŌ

Another poet of the generation of Santōka and Hōsai, Nakatsuka Ippekirō (1887–1946) was more modern in subject matter and treatment, as well as rhythmically unfettered. He gained a wide reputation because he vehemently refused to pay attention to traditional haiku form or seasonal references—the two characteristics which most Japanese still feel define haiku. To him these were superficial, and he frankly did not care whether traditionalists accepted his poems as haiku or not. At one time or another he worked closely with Hekigotō and Seisensui, and edited two different magazines of modernist haiku.

Ippekirō wrote many poems far longer than traditional haiku. In this example the opening words might have served another poet as a title or preface, but Ippekirō moves the reader straight into the poem without pause:

natsu-asa hinmin no ko ga	summer morn a child of the poor
hiki-kakaetaru	tugging and hugging
hitotsu no kyabetsu	a head of cabbage

Like most haiku, the original of this poem is one column of Japanese writing, but the verse-lines indicated seem natural to it.

The opening rhythm of the following haiku suggests that it is in an alternative rhythm occasionally used in the days of renga, but there is no convenient place to break the rest:

kuraku natsu no yo   darkening summer night
tsuchi o ki no ne no hashiru   through the ground tree roots run

Ippekirō found a variety of striking images, and put them into short verses in varying forms. I believe that the Japanese reader of such haiku naturally finds the irregular rhythms suggested by the grammar and syntax. The following two poems, selected for inclusion side-by-side in an anthology edited by Ippekirō himself and Seisensui in 1940, demonstrate some of the variety of Ippekirō's approach. I have left the rhythms of the translations for the reader to discover, as must be done with almost all haiku in Japanese.

yama-nobe no tori wa ori-ori ni sakebi fuyu no kumo
the mountain-side bird occasionally screams winter clouds

kusa ao-ao ushi wa sari
grass green-green the cows pass

Perhaps when a Japanese reader is forced to read a poem more than once to understand the grammar and rhythm the reader of a translation should have to also. But overemphasizing the formal aspects of any poem destroys its value for the human beings involved in it; we must read Ippekirō's poems for the brilliance of his images, the humanity of his observations, and the depth of his feelings for the objects and events he records, as we read—or should read—all haiku.

MIZUHARA SHŪŌSHI

While Seisensui was dominating the world of free-meter haiku from the helm of *Sōun*, and another influential member of Heki-gotō's group, Ōsuga Otsuji, broke ranks to move in a more conservative direction, Kyoshi kept on attracting new disciples. One of the more prominent of these was Mizuhara Shūōshi (1892–1981), who brought many other students into Kyoshi's camp. After a decade and more, Shūōshi broke with Kyoshi's *Hototogisu* group, however, taking a number of important followers with him. Shūōshi writes within the confines of traditional form and season feeling, but his haiku combine drama and color in ways not consistently achieved by other poets. Two contrasting haiku give an idea of his range:

tsubo ni shite	stuck in a vase
miyama no hō no	deep mountain magnolia
hana hiraku	blossoms open
ōki inu	the huge dog
tachimukaetaru	risen in greeting
satsuki yami	June darkness

And here are two more, from a group published in the mid-1970s under the title "Passionate Spring":

numa mo ta mo	swamp or paddy . . . ?
wakanedo aze ni	on the nursery ridge
tanishikago	a snail basket
moya nokoru	on the side where
kata ni hirakishi	mist remains the opening
botan ari	peonies are

Of the first of these, Professor Kazuo Sato suggests that it is dusk or hazy, so we cannot tell whether the landscape is wild or cultivated; but we do see a basket of edible snails on the ridge.

Shūōshi's dynamic haiku remain consistent throughout his long career. A number of his students and associates, however, went off in their own directions.

HASHIMOTO TAKAKO

Hashimoto Takako (1899–1963) began the study of haiku under another woman, Sugita Hisajo, who had been active in the *Hototogisu* group under Kyoshi and broke away to promote women's haiku. Takako's generation contains a number of well-known women haiku poets. But instead of shutting herself off in the slightly separate world of "women's haiku", Takako was a leading figure among those who had studied with Kyoshi and Shūōshi and broken away from both. She joined with Yamaguchi Seishi to found *Tenrō ("Sirius")* in 1948—a magazine that continues today.

Takako can write poems of great beauty and striking drama on very traditional subject matter, as in these two examples:

kiri no naka	amid fog
higurashi naku o	to the clear-cicada cries
ake to suru	dawn comes
hi o keseba	as the light's put out
jimushi no yami o	the ground beetles' darkness
isshoku ni	to one color

Many of Takako's haiku involve herself directly; she becomes an active participant, in both her sensations and her thoughts:

araigami	fresh-washed hair
yuku tokoro mina	everywhere I go
shizuku shite	making trickles
ryūtō ni	entrusting words
kotoba takushite	to a floating lantern
tsuki hanatsu	I push it adrift

The first of these, published in 1962, forms an interesting counterpoint to Larry Wiggin's sensual

> wind:
> the long hairs
> on my neck

which was first published in 1974 in the United States in *The Haiku Anthology*, edited by Cor van den Heuvel. Takako knows, as the second poem shows, that even her words are not immortal.

NAKAMURA KUSATAO

Three of Shūōshi's students who departed from the pleasant sensuality of their master were known as the "Human Exploration School". One of the group, Ishida Hakyō, became seriously ill during the war and never fully recovered. Nakamura Kusatao and Katō Shūson each led vigorous lives as haiku masters and magazine editors well into the 1970s, however. They have gone in somewhat different directions in their haiku, but both poets were deeply affected by the war.

Nakamura Kusatao (1901–1983) seems to have become strongly attached to the delicate meanings in the simplest small acts and observations.

naki tomo kata ni	like a dead friend putting
te o nosuru goto	a hand on the shoulder
aki hi nukushi	the autumn sun warms
mikazuki noseta	the crescent-moon-carried
mizuwa kochira e	water rings want to come
kitagaru yo	over here!

Kusatao wants to find the human, the comforting, in the
world around him, and in himself, as these two poems attest:

yake ato ni	the concrete left
nokoru tataki ya	in the fire's wake . . .
temari tsuku	a ball bounces
tsuma dakana	to hold my wife
shunchū no jari	treading spring noon's
fumite kaeru	gravel going home

Whether watching a child bounce a ball in the ruins of a
burnt-out house, or turning homeward to embrace his wife, Kusa-
tao shows us the tenderness and strength of one who has lived
through much death, and therefore all the more treasures life.

KATŌ SHŪSON

Katō Shūson (b. 1905) already had a vision of death and the
macabre before the war, as the dramatic pieces from his first col-
lection, *Kanrai*, "Midwinter Thunder", demonstrate; for example:

kanrai ya	midwinter thunder . . .
ima wa naki me o	under the burden of just-now-
oite iku	dead eyes, alive

It is not easy to watch the life go out of someone's eyes. We
carry such an image with us for a long time. Thunder always sug-
gests danger, but the winter thunder storm carries a special chill.
Through these things we do go on living, if we can.

Living under the air raids of the war deepened Shūson's sen-
sibility. Here is a haiku from a verse-diary of January 1945:

tōrō no	the praying mantis
ono o agetsutsu	still raising his axes
yakaretari	all burnt up

Indeed, the front pincers of the praying mantis do look a bit like axes. But Shūson's use of this metaphor is no casual selection of a mere physical look-alike for descriptive purposes. Here the metaphor not only etches a vivid picture on the retina of the mind's eye, it also takes us away from the sentimental idea of the insect imploring some power from heaven to rescue it, and gives us instead an image of anger amid the raging fire. (The Japanese *tōrō* has about the same associations as its English counterpart, "praying" mantis.)

And this is perhaps Shūson's most famous haiku:

> *hi no oku ni*   in the fire-depths
> *botan kuzururu*   saw the way
> *sama o mitsu*   a peony crumbles

It resulted from an air raid in which his house was destroyed and he and his wife became separated from their children. While we may read it to mean that he saw a peony crumble in the depths of the fire, I suspect that "the way/ a peony crumbles" is a metaphor for the way a frame building's walls buckle and then fall in a roaring fire, much the way the petals of a peony wither and then fall from the blossom. Our lives and the buildings we live them in may have some of the lush beauty of a peony; they have also its delicate vulnerability.

Though these themes are often present in his poetry, we should not think of Shūson exclusively as a poet of fire and death. In 1952 he took a trip to a hot-spring spa, and the peace of that place produced the following pair of verses. The Tsugaru Plain spreads out below the slopes of the spa, west of Aomori in northern Japan.

> *ganka tsugaru*   looking over Tsugaru
> *kata hanareyuku*   taking leave of my shoulder
> *natsu no chō*   the summer butterfly

> *uma arau*   washing the horse
> *shidai ni shōjo*   gradually the maiden's
> *hoho atsushi*   cheek warms

Like Kusatao, Shūson is concerned with people. These final
two examples of his work are from a group of haiku written in
1956, called "Steel Making People":

> *kajikamitsutsu*   in the numbing cold
> *kikai fuku te no* the hand wiping the machine
> *toki ni nigiri*   occasionally tenses

> *hiete takumashi*   cool and stout
> *abura hikari no*   the oily glistening
> *hiji gashira*   elbow tip

Shūson's haiku often have the quality of a "freeze-frame" or
"stop-action" shot that pulls a momentary flash of elbow out of
the total impression of a factory or foundry.

KANEKO TŌTA

The occasional use of metaphor in the poems of Shūson expands
widely in the work of Kaneko Tōta (b. 1919), a poet influenced
by Shūson who has now come to be one of the major figures of
Japanese haiku. Tōta seems to have incorporated into his work
many of the "new" techniques of the previous fifty years or more.
When he employs them, however, they seem all of a piece with
his work, rather than somehow stitched onto the haiku tradition
like patches. For example, is the following poem surreal, or sim-
ply a metaphor?

> *kawa no ha yuku*   the river's teeth go
> *asa kara ban made* from morning to evening
> *kawa no ha yuku*   the river's teeth go

During a trip to northern Japan Tōta stayed in a town where he encountered what he calls a "green bear" *(aoi kuma)*. We can take "green" in this instance to mean "tenderfoot" or young. Here are two of his poems on the green bear:

aoi kuma	green bear
chyaperu no asa wa	the chapel's morning
randa randa	pounding pounding
aoi kuma	green bear
karakuta akichi ni	in the junky vacant lot
kin no fu	cast iron stomach

The chapel bells pound the air as if to drive one to distraction. But the junk-filled empty lot becomes a picnic. The Japanese phrase which I have translated as "cast iron stomach" *(kin no fu)* has also the connotation that the bear is coming to understand metal.

Another group of haiku from the north concerns the salmon which swim up from the sea to spawn. In this group Tōta mixes his penchant for metaphor with pure, clean haiku classic in their simplicity. Three samples:

hone no sake	the bony salmon
ainu no boshi ni	to the Ainu mother and child
shigeri no ki	a luxuriant tree
hone no sake	the bony salmon
yoake no ame ni	in the rain at daybreak
umi no niku	flesh of the lake
hone no sake	the bony salmon
umi no ma-otome	a pure virgin of the lake
hiza daite	hugging her knees

In these three poems we see Tōta's ability to penetrate the minds of others, in this case the minds of a mother and child. The Ainu are the aborigines of Japan, who have been treated much the same way Euro-Americans treated the natives of North America. Just as there is something deeply satisfying in the appearance of a tree in full leaf, so the salmon—these *fish* in front of us— move the Ainu more than the mere fact of a full food supply. And what are the fish but the "flesh of the lake", as the birds are the flesh of the sky. Finally, we have the tender, innocent girl, "hugging her knees" as she watches the salmon, a picture with more mystery and depth in its simplicity than most artists can manage on however large a canvas.

CONTEMPORARY JAPANESE HAIKU

As we have seen, the Japanese haiku in the twentieth century continues to grow and change, expanding its ability to record and make available for sharing much of the diverse content of modern life. It is no longer restricted to a simple observation of natural phenomena—indeed, it never was so restricted. But as modern life has enlarged our experience and our sensibility haiku has enlarged to include the kinds of events and perceptions that modern people often find striking or touching, and may wish to record for their own future contemplation or sharing with others.

The writing and sharing of haiku engage hundreds of thousands of Japanese today, not just a few haiku masters. There are a number of large, national-circulation magazines in Japan with titles like *Haiku, Haiku Study,* and *Haiku and Essays.* There are hundreds of haiku-club magazines, also issued monthly. The smallest of these magazines contains hundreds of haiku per issue, and haiku from the smaller magazines often get reprinted in the larger nationals or in annual anthologies distributed locally or nation-wide.

Each of the twentieth century Japanese haiku poets we have looked at so far is or was a nationally known poet and the editor of one or more highly influential magazines. But the essence of haiku activity in Japan is in the small haiku clubs, where people from diverse backgrounds meet to compose, discuss, and publish their own and one another's haiku.

Itadori is one of several haiku monthlies published in the city of Matsuyama, the home town of Masaoka Shiki, Kawahigashi Hekigotō, Takahama Kyoshi, and Nakamura Kusatao. The magazine features a group of ten poems, each by a different poet, at the front of each issue. The following group from *Itadori*, called "Autumn Loneliness Selections", may serve as an example of the diversity and vigor of the mainstream of Japanese haiku in recent years. I have offered a few comments to explain the unfamiliar or show something of what I received from each poem. Readers need not limit themselves to my interpretations:

> *hirakikitta*   all rolled out
> *tairin no kiku*   this large chrysanthemum—
> *hinyari suru*   a chill
>
> > Ueda Isemi

Picture one large white chrysanthemum, right at its peak.

> *akiaji no*   autumn salmon
> *batabata haneru* the flipping leaping
> *no o tsukamu*   one I catch
>
> > *Takahashi Kazuo*

The apparent abandon of this poem cannot quite hide the grip of nature's cycle.

> *shiozuke no*   the flavor
> *daikon no aji*   of the salt-pickled *daikon*—
> *tsuki to futari*   the moon and I
>
> > *Fujimoto Kanseki*

The root of the *daikon*, a large white radish, is pickled in brine. The author eats alone, and makes the moon a companion.

> *fuyu no hoshi*   winter stars—
> *kokyō seseragi*   home town brook murmuring
> *taema nashi*   incessantly
>
> > *Matsuura Takuya*

What some smell, sound, or sight will do to the memory.

suteu naku	castoff cormorants cry—
sokobie no yo no	the deep cold of the dark at
ushōburaku	the birdkeeper's cottages

Sakai Yamahiko

Fishing with trained cormorants (large, black birds) takes place in the summer and early fall around Gifu, northwest of Nagoya. The boats move over the river at night, when the moon is not out, carrying bright flares, Fish are attracted by the light. The birds catch the fish; a loop around the neck prevents them from swallowing the larger fish, which they deposit in the boats. But now the season for fishing is over.

taifū semaru	a typhoon bears down
hama ni ryōma no	on the beach stands Ryōma,
futokorode	arms folded

Kinoshita Michiteru

When a typhoon is coming people scurry about, tying down this, closing that, barring doors and windows. Michiteru sees, or envisions, one man who stands calmly, watching the approaching storm. This man seems like Sakamoto Ryōma, a hero of Shikoku (the island on which Matsuyama is situated) who helped lead a movement to reform the government toward the end of the feudal era in Japan. The poem may be taken as an allegory for Ryōma's calm in the face of increasing Western interest (the "typhoon") in "opening" Japan. Still, there is a haiku moment here in the literal meanings: a man stands on the beach, calm in the face of the increasingly wild waves and sky.

akimatsuri	autumn festival
chigo osoroi ni	the children all alike
mayu kakare	eyebrow-decked

Oka Sueno

Gaily dressed and made-up children make a charming sight at the local harvest festival. But the contrast between the young and the meaning of the harvest can deepen the emotion with a touch of the lament, familiar to people of all cultures, "the grasses of the field, that withereth."

sue no inu	porcelain dog—
hinemosu shūshi	all day long autumn loneliness
ware o mamoru	watches over me

Takeda Chie

Some companions make us feel more alone.

tosaji kite	here in Tosa
shii no mi kaishi	buying pasania nuts
onnazure	man with a woman

Ebisuya Kiyoko

Pasania trees used to be quite common in southern Japan. The fruit is conical, something like an acorn, and is eaten raw or roasted. Most of the trees have disappeared. But in the old province of Tosa in southern Shikoku, noted for keeping its traditions alive, pasania trees still flourish. The man buying pasania nuts at the roadside stand is probably a tourist from some other part of Japan, enjoying the rustic setting.

chi ni hibiki	the ground echoes
hasa mata hitotsu	yet another rice rack
ame ni taoru	collapsing in rain

Izumi Sumie

The sheaves of rice, set out to dry on the *hasa*, soak up the untimely rain; the racks collapse under the added weight, with a thud.

From the classical aesthetics of appreciating a flower and the comforting rituals of the season and observing tourists, through the depths of loneliness mirrored in our surroundings, fantasies of a sporting or historical nature, even to the despair implicit in the way nature undermines our most serious and carefully thought-out plans for physical and economic well-being, these ten poems give a fair impression of the range of emotions, moods, and perceptions that find their home in modern Japanese haiku.

HAIKU ENDURING

In Japan there are many kinds of poetry, as there are in most vital cultures. There are still a number of poets who concentrate on writing the traditional tanka, the "short poem" (it is a little shorter than two haiku) that has been the main variety of Japanese lyric poem since the seventh century or earlier. There are poetic genres which have much the same place in Japan that the limerick does in the Anglo-American tradition. There are traditional folk songs in both relatively free and set forms. And, for the last hundred years or more there has been a vigorous growth of modern, free-verse poetry which, as in the West, is now understood to be the dominant force in serious literature. Not to mention the rise of an entertainment industry patterned on Western mass-media culture, with its popular-song writers.

But the haiku endures. Despite its limitations, both as to length and subject matter, and despite the competition with other poetic genres, writers of haiku go on recording their impressions of life in these short poems, and sharing them with others in ways as casual as a chance conversation over a cup of tea or coffee and as formal as a guest reading or lecture by a major poet or critic. A haiku written out on a special card by a master becomes a treasured art object. Almost every newspaper has its haiku column, and being chosen to select the poems for a haiku club's magazine is a great honor.

Why does the haiku endure in Japan? I think the reasons are few and easy to understand. We all admire one who has a gift with words, who can tell a vivid story or put an idea across so that we understand it. The haiku, due to its brevity, is at once demanding and not quite overwhelming in its challenges. We all can think of ourselves as occasionally having the kind of sudden awareness that makes for a haiku moment, and can also think of ourselves as being able to make a few words fit together so that others might share in that moment.

Sharing is one of the things we want most in life, to give something of ourselves to others, so that they might accept us and our experiences and perceptions as important. The haiku, while short, is long enough to give others an impression of who we are, some piece of the story of our lives. Yet it does not go on forever, like a self-indulgent autobiography, without getting to the point. And it leaves room for a response, so the sharing can become mutual.

Haiku poets, like any other poets, quickly try to find their own poems when they appear in print. But most haiku poets also read poems by other poets writing on the same subjects they have written about, for the fun of finding out how others responded to such-and-such an event, to the season, to the sights along some route. Since Bashō's *Narrow Roads to the Interior* thousands of poets have visited one or more of the places he visited and wrote of, to try the landscape or seascape out on their own eyes, and to try their hands at capturing some new essence of the place that Bashō may have missed—or, often enough, simply to say to the spirit of a poet who lived three hundred years ago, "Yes, I have been here too, and found it as you said."

4

Early Haiku in the West

HAIKAI AND HOKKU

Haiku in the West begins at the beginning of the twentieth century, with attempts to write haiku in French during a visit to Japan by Julien Vocance, Paul-Louis Couchoud, and others. They published a book of their efforts in 1905. Then a decent anthology of Japanese literature in French translation by Michel Revon was published at Paris in 1910. Revon called the hokku of Bashō "haikai", which became the term most often used in French and Spanish for the first half of the century. But not until World War I did haiku really begin to become an indigenous Western phenomenon.

In the trenches of 1915 Julien Vocance wrote a series of haikai called «Cent Visions de Guerre» ("One Hundred Visions of War"). While many of his "Visions" are rather grandiose and sentimental, some are sharply focused and come close to hitting the haiku nail on the head:

Sur son chariot mal graisée,	On its badly greased wagon
L'obus très haut, pas pressé,	The shell very high, unhurried,
Au-dessus de nous a passé.	Above us has passed.
Dans sa flanelle	Into his flannels
Ses ongles vont, picorant	His fingernails go, picking
Les petites bêtes.	The little beasts.

The first is weakened by an unimpressive metaphor in its opening line, but the second accurately portrays a trench-mate's search for the little creatures that would feed on him.

In 1920 haikai by a dozen poets appeared in the *Nouvelle revue française,* one of France's leading literary magazines, and the 1920's saw many haikai in French books and magazines. Here are some samples:

Un trou d'obus	A shell hole
Dans son eau	In its water
A gardé tout le ciel.	Held the whole sky.

Maurice Betz

Démontés après la fête	Dismounted after the festivities
Les petits chevaux de bois	The little wooden horses
Se serrent l'un contre l'autre.	Crowd against one another.

René Maublanc

Le ciel noir,	Black sky,
Les nez rouges,	Red noses,
Et la neige.	And snow.

René Maublanc

Le train arrivait;	The train was coming;
j'avais un baiser tout prêt:	I had a kiss all ready:
le train est parti . . .	the train left . . .

Jean Baucomont

Meanwhile, Basil Hall Chamberlain's second edition of *Japanese Poetry*, including his new essay "Bashō and the Japanese Poetical Epigram", was published in London and Japan at the end of 1910. (An earlier edition, without mention of haiku, had come out in 1880.) And Lafcadio Hearn's translations of hokku and tanka scattered through his many books on Japan were collected and published as *Japanese Lyrics* (Boston, 1915). Considering the distance between almost all of Western poetry and these traditional Japanese modes, Revon, Chamberlain, and Hearn acquitted themselves well. These, and a few other books, less well executed, provided French, Spanish, and English-language poets with a first look at Japanese haiku, which most of the British and North American poets called hokku, after Chamberlain.

Six months after *Poetry* magazine began, in the issue of April 1913, Ezra Pound's now famous "In a Station of the Metro" appeared. This may be the first published hokku in English. The poem underwent at least two later revisions, which are discussed in Chapter 9, The Craft of Haiku.* And Pound had four or five other hokku published in his book *Lustra* of 1916, along with the Metro poem.

Other poets followed Pound's lead. In dated order, we have:

from Thirteen Ways of Looking at a Blackbird

Among twenty snowy mountains,
The only moving thing
Was the eye of the blackbird.

Wallace Stevens (publ. 1917)

---

*Pound was apparently ready for hokku. In the San Trovaso Notebook, a copybook in which he recorded poems written in 1908 in Venice, he had written the following, probably before he had heard of hokku: "I have felt the lithe wind/ blowing/ under one's fingers/ sinuous."

Lines

Leaves are grey-green,
The glass broken bright green.

William Carlos Williams (1919)

Autumn Haze

Is it a dragonfly or a maple leaf
That settles softly down upon the water?

Amy Lowell (1919)

The twigs tinge the winter sky
brown.

Charles Reznikoff (1920)

All of the sections of Wallace Steven's "Thirteen Ways of Looking at a Blackbird" are short, imagistic. After this, Stevens would work at clothing his thoughts in images, rather than at developing his thoughts from images. William Carlos Williams's poem "Lines" is almost worthy of Shiki, and certainly looks forward to longer work Williams would do in the early 1920s and thereafter; one thinks immediately of his poem "Between Walls".

Amy Lowell wrote a few hokku that show the direct influence of specific Japanese models. For example, her poem "Peace", that runs "Perched upon the muzzle of a cannon/ A yellow butterfly is slowly opening and shutting its wings." is obviously an allusive variation on Buson's "Perched upon the temple-bell, the butterfly sleeps!" (Lafcadio Hearn's translation). However, Lowell's "Autumn Haze" resembles none of the extant translations; and the title asks us to believe that it was based on actual experience. I would vote "Autumn Haze" one of the best hokku by a self-styled Imagist, though Lowell would try more later, less successfully.

Though Charles Reznikoff was known at that time only to a few poets and not to the reading public, he has become increasingly important. And he continued to apply the haiku principle of getting down exactly the thing seen to many different kinds of material throughout his life, only occasionally adding his own pointed comments, as in this perfect *senryu* (see Chapter 15, Beyond Haiku), published in 1969:

> Horsefly,
> on the window of the automobile agency:
> you're out of business now.

Other poets who were to grow in importance in Europe and Latin America published what they called haikai. These are from a group of eleven, titled «*Pour Vivre Ici*» ("To Live Here", 1920), by Paul Eluard:

À *moitié petite,*	Half-little,
La petite	The little girl
Montée sur un banc.	Set on a bench.

Une plume donne au chapeau	A feather gives to the hat
Un air de légèreté	An air of frivolity
La cheminée fume.	The chimney smokes.

These, and the other sections of "To Live Here", demonstrate the combination of image and humor that pervaded the haikai before Bashō, though today they seem more like senryu. It is the vividness of such images, and the ideal turn of phrase in which to catch them, that appealed to European and American minds in the period between the world wars.

One such mind was that of José Juan Tablada, a Mexican poet and diplomat who visited Japan in 1900 and was much impressed with its art and poetry, but seems to have discovered the haikai in Paris during 1911 and 1912. In 1919 his book *Un Dia . . . poemas sintéticos* came out, consisting entirely of haikai except for a short verse prologue. Many of the poems in *Un Dia* are more expressions than presentations; Tablada uses vivid metaphors to capture some essential characteristic of an animal or object in general, rather than to present us with a particular example of that animal or object in the here and now. But even some of Tablada's frankly metaphorical pieces approach the ecstasy of experience that joins an especially Spanish quality to the emotionalism of some Japanese haiku. For example, probably Tablada's most famous poem from *Un Dia*, with a translation by Mark Cramer:

El Saúz	The Willow
Tierno saúz	Tender willow
casi oro, casi ámbar,	almost gold, almost amber,
casi luz . . .	almost light . . .

Tablada was a major figure in *modernismo,* the shift to the new that went on in all the arts with the growing twentieth century. For the rest of his life, Tablada wrote haikai and concrete, or visual, poems, as well as longer free-verse poems. One concrete poem by Tablada, written in French, has a special haiku touch. The page shows four pairs of footprints, as if made by a small bird hopping about, and the text reads:

Oiseau	Bird
Voici ses petites pattes	See its little feet
le chant c'est envolé. . . .	the song has flown. . . .

This appears to be the beginning of an interaction between haiku and concrete poetry that continues today in the West.

Tablada wrote haikai throughout his life, and influenced a number of other Spanish and Hispanic poets to do likewise. Here is one of his later haikai:

Looping the Loop	Looping the Loop
Vesperal perspectiva;	Evening perspective:
en torno de la luna	around the moon
hace un "looping the loop"	making a loop-the-loop,
la golondrina.	the swallow.

Many poets writing in Spanish have written haikai. Much of the work, however, wanders from the path of haiku into cute metaphors that have their basis in linguistic agility, rather than genuine experience. These two are among the best of the Spanish-language haiku I have seen in surveying materials through the 1940s; both are from the 1920's or earlier:

Canta, canta, canta,	Sings, sings, sings,
junto a su tomate,	next to his tomato,
el grillo en su jaula.	the cricket in its cage.

Antonio Machado

Pájaro muerto:	Dead bird:
¡qué agonía de plumas	such an agony of feathers
en el silencio!	in the silence!

Juan José Domenchina

Machado, in particular, made the haikai his own, and incorporated it into several sequences written in the twenties. We will encounter more of his work in Chapter 15, Beyond Haiku.

In the meantime, the great German poet Rainer Maria Rilke made his first attempt at a thing he called haikai, in French in September 1920; it failed as haikai and as poetry. His second go at it, in December of the same year, was in German, and came closer to the mark, although very wordy:

Kleine Motten taumeln schauernd quer aus dem Buchs;
sie sterben heute Abend und werden nie wissen,
daß es nicht Frühling war.

Little moths reel, shuddering, out of the boxwood;
they'll die this evening and never be the wiser,
that it is not spring.

This might qualify as an extended haiku, but the phrase "never be the wiser" seems superfluous. Finally, in French, the year he died (1926) Rilke managed a decent haikai that has a good deal of the spirit of senryu in it:

Entre ses vingt fards	Among her twenty rouges
elle cherche un pot plein:	she searches for a full pot:
devenue pierre.	turned to stone.

By 1929 the Greek poet George Seferis had found haikai, as his posthumously published diaries reveal. Here are a few of the sixteen haikai in his *Collected Poems*, in translations prepared for this book by Manya Bean:

Στάξε στὴ λίμνη
μόνο μιὰ στάλα κρασὶ
καὶ σβήνει ὁ ἥλιος.

Drip in the lake
only one drop of wine
and the sun goes out.

Στὸν κῆπο τοῦ Μουσείου

"Αδειες καρέκλες
τ' ἀγάλματα γυρίσαν
στ' ἄλλο μουσεῖο.

In the Museum Garden

Empty chairs
the statues returned
to the other museum.

Νύχτα, ὁ ἀγέρας
ὁ χωρισμὸς ἁπλώνει
καὶ κυματίζει.

Night, the wind
separation spreads
and billows.

Γράφεις·
τὸ μελάνι λιγόστεψε
ἡ θάλασσα πληθαίνει.

You write;
the ink lessened
the sea increases.

The first of these is a bit surreal to qualify as a haiku, but would probably arouse interest among some Japanese haiku poets. The second seems at first glance good, but prosaic. Then the ambiguity sets in. Did the statues return under their own steam? Where is the "other" museum? A museum garden is as good a place to "people-watch" as any. Both of the last two poems seem metaphorical in intent; the sea of the last in particular, to me, suggests the "sea of words"—the growing mass of written words that characterizes civilization.

Among other noteworthy developments before World War II cut off commerce with Japan, Georges Bonneau published a series of books with his decent translations into French from Japanese poetry, including *Le Haiku*, in the mid-1930s. Harold G. Henderson's English translations of Japanese haiku came out in a book called *The Bamboo Broom* in 1934. The Ecuadorian poet Jorge Carrera Andrade appended a group of twenty Japanese haiku in his Spanish translations to a collection of his short epigrams called *Microgrammas*, published in Tokyo in 1940. And then the war obliterated cultural exchanges.

HAIKU AND ZEN

When the distress of World War II began at last to clear, two important interpreters of haiku to the West found themselves in Tokyo. Harold G. Henderson was on the staff of the American occupation forces. And R. H. Blyth, a Britisher recently released from a Japanese internment camp where he had spent part of the war, was invited to tutor the Crown Prince. Each was responsible for a major jump in the movement of haiku to the Western hemisphere.

Blyth had studied with a Zen master for some time. He came to believe that Zen Buddhism was the dominant influence on the traditional Japanese arts, particularly haiku. During the 1940s he began publishing a succession of books on Zen, haiku, and related topics. His *Haiku: Volume I*, was the first of four volumes published between 1949 and 1952 under the title *Haiku*. In each of these books several hundred poems were given, with Blyth's sometimes brilliant, sometimes misleading translations, plus his very Zen-full comments on them. These books were sold at foreign language bookstores throughout East Asia and in the United States. Copies reached Europe. And a new interest in Japanese haiku began to grow among poets of the immediate post–World War II generation.

The so-called "San Francisco poets" and the "Beat poets" from the New York area, in particular, remembered the experimental hokku of the Imagists. Gary Snyder, already a student of Taoist and Zen philosophy, began writing haiku and short hokku-like pieces in his diary for 1952, published in *Earth House Hold*. Two samples:

> This morning:
>> floating face down in the water bucket
> a drowned mouse.

> leaning in the doorway whistling
> a chipmunk popped out
> listening

Allen Ginsberg, a main figure in the New York group, spent a good deal of time in California. An entry in his journal for the mid-1950s reads "Haiku composed in the backyard cottage at . . . Berkeley 1955, while reading R. H. Blyth's 4 volumes *Haiku*"; here are three samples:

> Looking over my shoulder
> my behind was covered
> with cherry blossoms.

Winter Haiku

I didn't know the names
of the flowers—now
my garden is gone.

Lying on my side
in the void:
The breath in my nose.

While the last one surely has what Zen masters laughingly call "the stink of Zen", the others have the humor and sense of the physical that pervades haiku. Ginsberg's diary entry also has some advice to himself on writing haiku, including:

Haiku = objective images written down outside mind the result is inevitable mind sensation of relations. Never try to write of relations themselves, just the images which are all that can be written down on the subject ...

Soon Jack Kerouac would also write "haikus",* like these:

Birds singing
in the dark
—Rainy dawn.

Useless, useless,
the heavy rain
Driving into the sea.

*While the "Beat poets" and others have anglicized the plural of *haiku* to haikus, most purists, myself included, retain the Japanese style, which makes no distinction between singular and plural, as in the English words *sheep, deer,* etc.

The first of these seems a perfect evocation—one awakens, wondering why the birds are singing while it is still dark outside. Then the underlying sound of the rain comes through, with the just perceptible greyness of dawn on the horizon. The second, with perhaps also a slight stink of Zen, still reminds me of one of Bashō's famous pieces that has a similar mood:

samidare o	June rains
atsumete hayashi	gathering, speeding
mogami-gawa	Mogami River

Meanwhile, Mexican poet Octavio Paz was writing his own very short poems, having visited India and Japan in 1952. I feel these to be haiku, though I do not know whether Paz takes them that way:

El dia abre la mano	The day opens its hand
Tres nubes	Three clouds
Y estas pocas palabras.	And these few words.

Niño y trompo

Boy and Top

Cada vez que lo lanza	Each time he flings it
cae, justo,	it falls, just,
en el centro del mundo.	in the center of the world.

Ante la puerta

Before the Door

Gentes, palabras, gentes.	People, words, people.
Dudé un instante:	I hesitated a moment:
la luna arriba, sola.	the moon above, alone.

The first of these, published in 1952, echoes Homer's "rosy-fingered dawn", but has surreal overtones, almost like a painting by Magritte. The second, except for one word, seems simply a portrayal of the concentration a child gives a plaything. The youngster stares fixedly at the spinning top, which becomes the center of all existence for him. But that "just" (the pun works in

Spanish, too) and the extra comma give the poem a little extra force, making it a touch didactic. Perhaps there, where nothing operates but the laws of physics, is true balance, true justice. The last of the three poems echoes a famous haiku by Bonchō (various surnames; d. 1714):

> *fuku kaze no*   the blowing wind's
> *aite ya sora ni*   buddy . . . in the sky
> *tsuki hitotsu*   a single moon

Paz would go on to publish in 1957 a complete Spanish translation of Bashō's *Narrow Roads of the Interior,* in collaboration with Eikichi Hayashiya. 1957 also saw the publication of Kenneth Yasuda's *The Japanese Haiku: Its Essential Nature, History, and Possibilities in English.* Yasuda's book, unlike Blyth's volumes on the subject, quotes a good deal of Japanese scholarship on the haiku, and hardly mentions Zen—the word appears four times in some two hundred thirty pages. The Paz translation and Yasuda's technical manual were but the harbingers, rising with a wave still building toward its crest.

5

The Haiku Movement in English

BEGINNINGS

In 1958 three books appeared that would capitalize on growing American interest in haiku, and expand it further. In Japan the Nippon Gakujutsu Shinkōkai published *Haikai and Haiku*, presenting translations from the works of Bashō, Buson, Issa, *and* Shiki, plus a sample haikai-no-renga, part of Bashō's *Narrow Roads of the Interior*, and one of Buson's longer pieces in mixed haiku, free verse, and Chinese. The book is generally what one would expect from a committee of scholars: useful appendices on the terminology of Japanese literary criticism and season words, and translations that are relatively accurate to the sense of the poems, but uninspired.

At about the same time Jack Kerouac's most widely read novel, *The Dharma Bums*, and Harold G. Henderson's updated version of his book from the 1930s, now called *An Introduction to Haiku*, arrived in American bookstores. Kerouac's book became the bible to a whole generation of American youth. In the opening fifty pages it introduces the reader to "Japhy Ryder", a character based on Gary Snyder. Japhy writes haiku—and suddenly so do a lot of other people. He also reads, among other things, "the complete works of D. T. Suzuki and a fine quadruple-volume edition of Japanese haikus." No doubt the books of R. H. Blyth. Several of the poets I know first discovered the haiku in Kerouac's novel.

Meanwhile, many other people, particularly teachers, were finding Henderson's *Introduction* an entrée to haiku. Although Henderson's translations have titles and end-rime, features normally absent from Japanese haiku, his versions are reasonably accurate and the riming much more skillfully done than some of the atrocities committed on haiku in the early decades of the century. He also provided readers with word-for-word trots of the originals. Unfortunately, he left out the modern haiku which he had included in his earlier book. And he made little or no mention of renga, haibun, senryu, or haiku sequences. Despite these limitations, Henderson's book became quite popular.

The combined effects of Kerouac's and Henderson's books started hundreds of Americans writing haiku. Already existing writers' clubs took up haiku, in much the same way as the Imagists had in London more than forty years earlier. Poets around the world who could read English, or who read *The Dharma Bums* in translation, took up haiku as a result of one or the other of these books.

One of the more interesting examples of this phenomenon is a section toward the end of Dag Hammarskjöld's journal, *Vägmärken*, published in 1963. Well over a hundred seventeen-syllable poems occupy the entries for August 1959 through December 1960. Translated into English by W. H. Auden and Leif Sjöberg as *Markings*, the book had a wide sale in England and

America. Here are a few of its haiku, in new translations:

Snö i april.	Snow in April.
Kardinalen sökt skydd	The cardinal sought shelter
i den vita Forsythian.	in that white forsythia.
Cikadorna skrek,	The cicadas shrieked,
luften glödde förbränd	the glowing air burnt up
deras sista afton.	their last evening.
Ännu långt från stranden	Now far from the strand
lekte havets friskhet	the sea's freshness played
i bronsblanka löv.	in bright bronze leaves.

While these are haiku, though in the past tense (haiku normally are in the present, or the present perfect), most of Hammarskjöld's seventeen-syllable poems are philosophical aphorisms and the like, not haiku.

The Afro-American novelist Richard Wright had studied R. H. Blyth's books, and wrote several hundred haiku during the last year and a half or so of his life. He died in 1960 in Paris, leaving behind a manuscript with these:

Coming from the woods
A bull has a lilac sprig
Dangling from a horn

Just enough of rain
To bring the smell of silk
From umbrellas

And in 1961 an American poet who fully understood the juxtaposition of images that occurs in many haiku, and who had studied the poetry of William Carlos Williams and other streamliners of the language, published his first book in New York City.

These are from Cor van den Heuvel's *Sun in Skull:*

> in the toy pail
> at low tide   floats
> the still ferris wheel

> a black model-T ford
> rounds the white curve
> of the heron's wing

> snow
> on the saddle-bags
> sun in skull

The freshness of van den Heuvel's movie and amusement park images, and his spare handling of the language, were not to be equalled in haiku by other Americans until almost a decade later.

HAIKU MAGAZINES IN ENGLISH

In 1963, five years after the publication of Kerouac's *The Dharma Bums* and Henderson's *Introduction to Haiku*, the first of many magazines devoted to English-language haiku began publishing. There is not space here to go into a detailed history of English-language haiku magazines. Rather, I will give a brief sketch of the major ones, with their years and places of publication, the editors' names, and a few examples from their pages. In each case I have picked poets whose work is well known to the haiku community, through publication in both anthologies and individual books of their own work. A forthcoming history of the haiku in English, and a book by each of the authors represented, are listed in Resources at the end of the handbook.

American Haiku (Platteville, Wisconsin; 1963–68) was started by James Bull and Donald Eulert. As the first all-haiku magazine in English (in any Western language, I believe), it established a number of trends later magazines would take up. Its first few issues contained work that was quite free-form; later, under and after Clement Hoyt's editorship, it would prefer haiku written in what has been called the "five-seven-five form". And it introduced many haiku poets to a broader readership. Among them:

An evening cricket;
   the trout pond reflects the glint
     of a falling star.

        Robert Spiess

Bass
   picking bugs
     off the moon!

     Nicholas A. Virgilio

As the sun sets,
   the old fisherman sorts out
     the fish he can sell.

       Sydell Rosenberg

The water deepens—
   following the dark canoe
     a pair of muskrats.

    O Mabelsson Southerd

Only scattered stars,
   till the moon wakens clusters
     of saguaro flowers.

       Foster Jewell

Not a breath of air—
   only a water bug mars
     the pine's reflection.

    Marjory Bates Pratt

Haiku (Toronto; 1967–71 / Paterson, New Jersey; 1971–76) was begun by Eric W. Amann, who wished to stress the sources of haiku in Zen consciousness, à la R. H. Blyth and the works of Alan Watts, D. T. Suzuki, and so on. Amann concentrated on the content of haiku and the spareness of its language, calling it (after Watts) "the wordless poem". He sought out new translations from Japanese, as well as from other European languages in which poets had written haiku, and published the first English-language renga, haibun, and haiku sequences. He also published experiments in "concrete haiku" (visual poems). Many of the best haiku poets of the 1970s and 1980s frequented *Haiku*'s pages:

September rains,
   —gout patients
sit in the waiting room.

    Eric W. Amann

On this still hot day,
   only the sound of soft grass
    in the beaks of ducks.

       Claire Pratt

Listening . . .
　　After a while
　　　I take up my axe again.

Rod Willmot

red flipped out
chicken lung
in a cold white sink

Anita Virgil

cleaning whelks
　　the sound
　　　of the knife.

Larry Wiggin

fog moves through
the burned out house:
gently

Jack Cain

Deep into this world
of Monet water lilies . . .
no sound.

Elizabeth Searle Lamb

New Year's Day—
taking a load
to the junkyard.

John Wills

```
GGGGGGGGGGGGGGGGGGGGGGGG
RRRRRRESRRRRRRRRRRRRRRR
AAAAAKSNAAAAAAAASNAAAA
SSNSKESSKESSSSSSNAKESS
SSAKESSSESNSSSSSAKESSS
GGGGGGGGGNAKGGGAKEGGGG
RRRRRRRRRRKESRAKERRRRR
AAAAAAAAAAASNAKEAAAAAA
SSSSSSSSSSSSAKESSSSSSS
SSSSSSSSSSSSSSSSSSSSSS
```

Larry Gates

This last, one of the series of "test patterns" by Gates, has become a classic of concrete haiku. Did you find the snake in the grass?

In 1971 Amann turned the editorship of his magazine over to me, and I continued publishing these poets along with Michael McClintock, Cor van den Heuvel, and many others, under the title *Haiku Magazine* (the simple title *Haiku* had been used for so many books it was becoming very confusing). Two more by poets whom Amann and I both published:

In the hook	buzzZ
of a wave—	slaP
the tide	buzzZ
Virginia Brady Young	*Alan Pizzarelli*

Haiku West (Forest Hills, New York; 1967–75) was edited by Leroy Kanterman. He welcomed many of the poets formerly featured in *American Haiku*. In 1968 Kanterman also helped Harold G. Henderson to form The Haiku Society of America in New York City. In its early years such poets as Nicholas A. Virgilio, Elizabeth Searle Lamb, L. A. Davidson, Virginia Brady Young, Alan Pizzarelli, Anita Virgil and myself shared our poems and our thoughts on haiku at the Society's monthly meetings. Minutes were distributed to a growing international membership. In 1971 Cor van den Heuvel would first make contact with the "haiku movement" by attending one of these meetings. And the Society sponsored annual readings and lectures, bringing such translators as Cid Corman, Donald Keene, and Hiroaki Sato, the Japanese scholar Yamamoto Kenkichi, and the haiku poet Mori Sumio to New York to address the members and the public. For some time *Haiku West*, under Kanterman's editorship, was the official magazine of the Society. Two poems from its pages:

Steady fall of rain . . .	On the gray church wall,
and the scent of lilacs	the shadow of a candle
so strong	. . . shadow of its
it becomes a taste	smoke.
Gustave Keyser	*L. A. Davidson*

Haiku Highlights and Other Short Poems (Kanona, New York; 1965–72), edited by Jean Calkins, catered to writers of small fixed forms. The magazine published hundreds of poems that resembled haiku in form only. But Calkins published parts of letters from readers, and by 1969 began attracting a few of the better

American haiku poets to write letters spelling out their thoughts. She soon invited their articles, and pieces by McClintock, Virgil, Young, and myself began to have an effect; new poets were learning and established poets were contributing to *Haiku Highlights*. Two of the latter:

rain . . . washing away
my winter footprints

Joyce Webb

A boy wading—
watching a dark snake winding
out of the river.

James Tipton

Modern Haiku (Los Angeles, California, later Madison, Wisconsin; 1969-continuing), founded by Kay Titus Mormino, has published decent work by poets of all schools, avoiding the extremes. A particularly useful feature was a column called "Random Notes from an Anonymous Haiku-Watcher", which gave news of haiku publications and activities that went unnoticed elsewhere. These two examples give an idea of the magazine's range in its early years:

the long night
of the mannequins—
snow falling

Martin Shea

Spring moon;
ferns uncurling between
the river rocks.

Lorraine Ellis Harr

Haiku Byways (later just *Byways*; London, England and other locations; 1970–73) was edited by Gerry Loose, whose haiku background was similar to that of Amann. In addition to several American and Canadian poets already mentioned, he published a number of British poets. One each by three of the best:

caught out in the snow
for a moment, I seem to recognize something
in the dog's eyes

Bill Wyatt (also known as Zengetsu Kembo)

a small ceremony
lifting stakes now thinner than
my trees come of age

Dee Evetts

white butterfly, blue cabbage
the allotment hut sags
in noonday heat

Chris Torrance

Both Wyatt and Torrance have haiku in the Penguin anthology *Children of Albion*, edited by Michael Horovitz and published in England in 1969.

HAIKU MAGAZINES: THE SECOND WAVE

By the mid-1970s a number of smaller magazines were publishing haiku regularly. Cor van den Heuvel, who had written brilliant haiku since 1961, discovered this activity in 1971, and immediately began a careful reading of all the haiku materials he could find. As he went he made note of poems he particularly liked. His work resulted in the publication of *The Haiku Anthology: English Language Haiku by Contemporary American and Canadian Poets* in 1974. The several other anthologies of haiku published before and since were all lovingly produced in short press runs. *The Haiku Anthology* was a trade paperback from Doubleday, and enjoyed wide distribution. Interest in haiku grew, and several new readers and poets became involved in the haiku magazines. Most of the magazines mentioned above and in the anthology have since ceased publication or moved, but new magazines came to the fore.

Tweed (Murwillumbah, New South Wales, Australia; 1972–79) was started by Janice M. Bostok, publishing mainly haiku, much of it by North American poets already mentioned. Here are samples of her own work, that of another Australian, and one by

Gerry Loose, who published very little of his work in his own magazine:

Pregnant again . . .   straightening up
the fluttering of moths   crow
against the window   disappearing

Janice M. Bostok   *Brian Joyce*

each
grassleaf
distinct before
the storm

Gerry Loose

With the end of 1972 *Haiku Highlights* went out of existence, but really changed editors and names to *Dragonfly* (Portland, Oregon; 1973-continuing), under the guidance of Lorraine Ellis Harr. Two samples:

The white spider
whiter still
in the lightning's flash

Geraldine C. Little

The silence
of the bat's wings
this cold night.

David Lloyd

High/Coo (Battle Ground, Indiana; 1976–82), under the editorship of Randy and Shirley Brooks, would lead the way to new poets and innovations in format during the late 1970s. In addition to haiku, the magazine featured sequences and tanka. And High/ Coo Press began a series of small pamphlets by individual authors which were sent to subscribers. The pamphlet series continues today. Here are pieces by some of the poets who became prominent in large part through the Brooks's efforts, from their magazine and the pamphlet series (all spaced as originally printed):

Stalking the cricket:
the boy's slow squat before each
                                jump

Ruth Yarrow

turning in bed
our backs
face

Adele Kenny

a diver brings up the body

the rain
begins

LeRoy Gorman

late afternoon:
cattle lie
in billboard shade

Randy Brooks

Bill Pauly

The last of these is another variety of concrete haiku, so-called, in which the typewriter becomes the tool of a visual artist, divorced from words completely. Do you see the twitch in the tail of the cat on the fence?

Cicada (Toronto, Canada; 1977–81), edited by Eric W. Amann, picked up where *Haiku Magazine* had left off. In addition to the range of the old magazine, Amann added tanka and helped promote the writing of so-called "one-line haiku", a variety inspired by the one-column format of the traditional haiku in Japanese, and by the one-line translations of Japanese haiku into

English by Hiroaki Sato. Many of these poets also appeared in other magazines, notably *High/Coo* and its pamphlet series:

after Beethoven
he gets the furnace
roaring

Raymond Roseliep

After
our quarrel,
a full moon

Margaret Saunders

Wading out—
her shadow ripples
back to shore

Betty Drevniok

Passport check:
my shadow waits
across the border

George Swede

one fly everywhere the heat

Marlene Mountain

somewhere her voice in the night whispering leaves

Clarence Matsuo-Allard

empty shopping mall
faintly
the nightsweeper's broom

Michael Dudley

spring rain
in this new mud
the worm's pink skin

Penny Harter

Frogpond (originally called *HSA Frogpond*; New York City; 1978-continuing) was established by the Haiku Society of America when it became apparent that the Society was not really providing adequate services to the many members unable to reach monthly meetings in New York. Now the Society meets a few times each year, putting on one annual program at Japan House in New York, and an annual reading at the Brooklyn Botanical Gardens in April. The magazine, presently under the editorship of Elizabeth Searle Lamb, tries to stay on top of the current American haiku scene and publishes occasional news of haiku activity outside the U.S. Haiku by members, renga, and critical articles make up its usual contents. As the membership spans a wide variety of poets, many different kinds of haiku appear in *Frogpond*'s pages. Two samples:

lightning flash dog on a chain

Hal Roth

the flick of high beams—
out of the dark roadside ditch
leaps a tall grass clump

Paul O. Williams

In 1979 a small press in Toronto brought out George Swede's *Canadian Haiku Anthology*. As the back cover says, "Canada has some of the finest haiku poets in the world." Swede includes poems by Amann, Brickley, Drevniok, Dudley, Faiers, Gorman, Pratt, Saunders, Swede, and Willmot, all represented here, and several others. Although not too many people outside of the haiku community in North America know about it, the *Canadian Haiku Anthology* is a good sampling of these poets' work, much of it not published anywhere else.

Wind Chimes (Glen Burnie, Maryland; 1981-continuing), edited by Hal Roth, is the latest entry among the better magazines that seem destined to last a while, as of this writing. It has featured some interesting translations, and is crowded with work of every school of haiku poets writing in English. A pair of examples:

Still damp
earth
the unglazed bowl

Peggy Willis Lyles

Twilight from field to tree a crow

Marion J. Richardson

Modern Haiku, begun in 1969 (see above), was turned over to Robert Spiess by its founder, Kay Titus Mormino, in 1977. As in the past, the magazine publishes a variety of poets, no particular school predominating. The "Haiku-Watcher" has been replaced by Spiess's "Speculations", a series of random observations on writing haiku. *Modern Haiku* is especially valuable for its book reviews, of which it probably publishes more than any other haiku magazine. Two of the newer poets whose poems appear in recent issues:

the ledger blurs . . .	Shiva
through the half-closed blinds	all those hands
autumn moon	all those pigeons
Chuck Brickley	*Alexis Rotella*

The "haiku movement" or the "haiku community" in English is the creation of the magazines that have published these and hundreds of other poets. Here I have sampled only the more prominent magazines; many others have come and gone after one, two, or a few issues, or publish haphazardly, but each has contributed some special flavor to the whole. They have names like *Bonsai, New World Haiku, Seer Ox, The Blue Print, Leanfrog, Sun-Lotus Haiku, Muse Pie, Brussels Sprout,* and even *Haiku Spotlight,* a weekly postcard of several haiku written in English and German, published in Japan for a year and a half some time ago. Without these magazines, and the dozens of small publishers who have brought out a total of well over three hundred individual books and pamphlets of haiku during the past twenty years, there would hardly be a haiku in English, beyond the occasional experiments of a few major authors and classroom teachers. (See Resources, "English-Language Haiku: Individual Authors", at the end of the handbook for a list of books, mostly by the poets represented in this chapter.)

6

Haiku Around the World

NEW EUROPEAN HAIKU

In the last few years the haiku has spread more and more rapidly around the world. Today there are enough haiku poets in Yugoslavia and Holland to support handsome quarterly magazines in Serbo-Croatian and Dutch, and the German haiku movement has taken over several pages of a magazine there.

The post–World War II revival of haiku on the European continent seems to have begun with the German novelist Imma von Bodmershof (d. 1982). Two of the following are from her 1962 book *Haiku*, and the third is a later revision. All have been translated with the help of Petra Engelbert:

Im grünen Wasser
das grüne Fischlein—
nur sein Schatten verrät es.

In green water
the little green fish—
only his shadow betrays him.

Der große Fluß schweigt
manchmal nur tönt es leise
tief unter dem Eis.

The great river is silent
only sometimes it sounds quietly
deep under the ice.

Gräber im Nebel   Graves in the fog
leere Nester—die Schwalben   empty nests—the swallows
kreisen im Süden   circle in the south.

Bodmershof inspired other Germans to take up haiku, and lived to see her poems published in North America and Japan. *Haiku: Časopis za haiku poeziju* ("Haiku: Magazine of Haiku Poetry"; Varaždin, Jugoslavija; 1977–1980?), edited by a committee, published articles on Ezra Pound, Jack Kerouac, and R. H. Blyth, along with a large selection of haiku and sequences, in its first issue. Subsequent issues include translations from the writings of Alan Watts, Gary Snyder, Allen Ginsberg, Imma von Bodmershof, and Harold G. Henderson, as well as Japanese poets. The magazine has the same breadth as Amann's *Haiku* and *Cicada;* translations from its pages have appeared in *Cicada* and *Frogpond.* Yugoslavian haiku vary from classical to modern in tone, as these examples demonstrate, translated with the help of Nina Zivancevic:

Ispod meseca   Under the moon
tek olistala vrba   just the little willow leaves
i sama svetli.   shedding their own light.

                    Aleksandar Nejgebauer

Dranuja kola   The wagon rattles
po poljskom putu—   on the road by the field—
žito se trese.   the grain shakes.

                    Katarina Pšak

Pod kopitima   Under the hooves
spomenika kralju   of the king's memorial
dvadesetak golubova twenty pigeons.

                    Vladimir Devidé

The Netherlands and Flanders (Dutch-speaking Belgium) enjoy a relationship much like that between the United States and English-speaking Canada, in that poets writing in the same language communicate freely across borders and join together in many activities. Thus the Haiku Kring Nederland ("Haiku Circle of Holland") and the Haikoe Centrum Vlaanderen ("Haiku Center of Flanders") work together to publish *Vuursteen: tijdschrift voor haiku, senryū en tanka* ("Flint: Magazine for . . ."; Baarn, Nederland; 1981-continuing). The magazine publishes haiku and related poems and articles by Dutch-speaking poets, along with pieces on traditional and contemporary Japanese poems. Three from the Dutch, translations made with the assistance of Wanda Reumer, Director of the Haiku Kring Nederland:

een duivepaar	a pair of pigeons
in een mist van lenteregen	in a mist of spring rain
schouder aan schouder	shoulder to shoulder

Anton Gerits

de asters bloeien.	the aster blossoms.
de dauwdruppels schitteren	the glittering of dew drops
tot na de middag.	'til after noontime.

Karel Hellemans

Over het weiland	Across the meadow
traag-bewegende tongen	the slow moving tongues
grazende koeien.	of grazing cows.

Piet Zandboer

Soon after its founding, *apropos* (Lauingen, West Germany; 1980-continuing) established a section in each issue devoted to the haiku in German. Sabine Sommerkamp, editor of the section, includes articles on haiku poems and events, as well as a selection of work by German haiku poets. Volker Schubert helped me translate these poems by a few of the poets appearing in *apropos:*

> *Fern nun die Berge.*   Far now the mountains.
> *Wie sind ihre Linien*   How their lines are
> *einfach geworden!*   become simple!

Hajo Jappe

> *Mein Gärtchen verkauft—*   Sold my garden—
> *wie anders klingt auf einmal*   now how different they sound
> *der Vögel Gesang!*   the birds' songs!

Sabine Sommerkamp

> *auf kahlem acker*   on a bare field
> *die verrostete egge—*   the rusted harrow—
> *weißglitzernd bereift*   frosted glittering white

Ilse Hensel

ENGLISH IS NOT THE ONLY AMERICAN TONGUE

In addition to the new interest in haiku in Yugoslavia, Holland and Flanders, and Germany, some new Spanish and French-speaking poets of the Americas have taken up haiku recently. One or another of the North American haiku magazines has published a few poems by each of the following three poets during the last several years.

Ana Rosa Núñez, a Cuban expatriate, published a book of haiku in 1971. Here is an example from *Escamas del Caribe* ("Fish Scales from the Caribbean"), translated with the help of Merlin Marie dePauw:

> *Ha vuelto del cansancio*   Returned from weariness
> *Mientras la ola*   While the wave
> *Se aleja despacio.*   Recedes slowly.

María Luisa Muñoz, a retired professor of music at the University of Puerto Rico, includes this poem in her collection *Miniaturas* (1982), and was kind enough to help me with the translation:

Duermen las aves,	The birds sleep,
la noche silenciosa	the night silent
baja del cielo.	descends from the sky.

André Duhaime, whose *haïkus d'ici* ("haiku from here") was published in 1981 in Québec, had this poem in the final issue of *Cicada:*

une dent en or	a tooth of gold
en sortant de chez le dentiste	going out of the dentist's office
les feuilles tombent	the leaves fall

Canada has figured strongly, as we have seen, in the growth of an English-language haiku. Now André Duhaime and coeditor Dorothy Howard have assembled a book that should be a major leap forward in the spread of haiku. To be published in 1985, twenty-five years after Henderson's *Introduction* and a decade after van den Heuvel's first *Anthology* (another is in the works as of this writing), we have *Haiku: anthologie canadienne/ canadian anthology.*

This second Canadian anthology features a good selection of work by each of over forty poets, and has two unique features. First, it is entirely bilingual; all works appear in both their original languages and in French or English translations. Although the English-writing poets outnumber the French by about three to one, several of the French selections are quite striking. Second, it includes a number of haiku by Japanese-Canadians who write in Japanese, probably a first in North American publishing. These have been translated into both French and English, making the book in part trilingual.

Haiku: anthologie canadienne includes work from over a twenty-year span, a good deal of it previously unpublished, in everything from formalist five-seven-five's to concrete haiku. Though Canada, and particularly the group of poets who have been encouraged by Eric W. Amann's *Haiku* and *Cicada*, has been a strong source of energy in the growth of English-language haiku, many of the poets represented in this anthology were new to me. I have picked a few poems by poets not yet encountered in this handbook, and present them here in the format used in the *anthologie*. The left-hand poem is in the original language; that on the right is the translation by Duhaime and Howard:

whale spray!   *une baleine souffle!*
a shaft of sunlight   *un jet de soleil*
in the bay   *dans la baie*

Nick Avis

Des corneilles craillent   Cawing crows
dans un orme desséché   in a dried-out elm
dentelle du jour   lace of light

Alphonse Piché

moment of birth new shadow   *naissance nouvelle ombre*

Ruby Spriggs

Pique-nique. La fourmi
sur la nappe quadrillée disparaît
dans un carreau noir.

Picnic. The ant
on the chequered tablecloth disappears
into a black square.

Jocelyne Villeneuve

As of this writing, the translations of the Japanese haiku to be included in *anthologie canadienne* are not complete, so I am unable to include any of them here.

INTERNATIONAL HAIKU

Today a new possibility for haiku presents itself. For some time now various European language publications in Japan have featured haiku in English, German, and so on—usually written by Westerners living in Japan. But only in the last few years has the haiku community in Japan begun to take notice of overseas efforts in the genre. The *Itadori* group (see the end of Chapter 3) led the way, developing a close relationship with a number of German haiku poets centered around Imma von Bodmershof. A few private publishers have put out polylingual anthologies of haiku in Japan in recent years. The most important nationally circulated Japanese haiku magazine, *Haiku* (published by Kadokawa Shoten), devoted several of the almost three hundred pages in its September 1982 issue to articles on haiku in the West. And a growing number of Japanese critics has become aware of the advances of Western haiku poets; some have dared to suggest that Japanese haiku will be renewed by contact and interaction with Western haiku.

In *anthologie canadienne*, in this handbook, and in the increasing appearance of haiku from several languages in Western and Japanese haiku periodicals, with translations, the haiku community has begun to share across national and language boundaries. In the meantime, poets in India, China, and North Africa have begun to write their own haiku. A truly international convocation of haiku poets seems likely in the near future—with readings in Japanese and half a dozen other languages.

Part Two

THE ART OF HAIKU

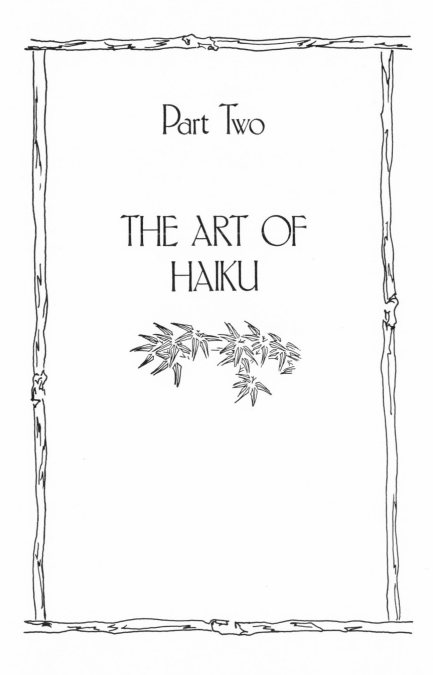

7

Nature and Haiku

HAIKU AND THE SEASONS

You may have heard that haiku are nature poems, or that each
haiku has to have a "season word" in it somewhere. Indeed, a
number of haiku have some obvious mention of a season, like
these:

> Snow falling
>> on the empty parking-lot:
>>> Christmas Eve . . .

Eric W. Amann

> Spring dawn:
> Turning toward the storm cloud,
> I lost sight of the bird.

Julius Lester

hana kuzu ni	to a mass of petals
kuchi aku koi ya	a mouth-opening carp . . .
natsu-mekite	summer-appearing

Tomiyasu Fūsei

Le banc de bois est humide,	The wooden bench is wet,
Le banc de pierre est glacé:	The stone bench is freezing:
Rendez-vous d'automne.	Meeting in autumn.

Albert Poncin

Still other haiku contain words that show the season, or at least give us a chance for an "educated guess":

> a mayfly
>> struggles down the stream
>>> one wing flapping dry

John Wills

> Vine
>> leaves pressing
>> church window

Christopher Faiers

> wind
> circling
> into
> leaves

Janice M. Bostok

In the falling snow
A laughing boy holds out his palms
Until they are white.

Richard Wright

Mayflies are named for the month in which they appear. In John Wills's Tennessee one might be able to pinpoint the week during which such an event would occur, since Mayflies tend to come out all at once, breed, and die all at once.

More subtle, the poem on the vine leaves, written in England, is a bit ambiguous. I suspect that if Faiers had seen ivy he would have told us so. More likely, it is some vine he does not recognize. The intensity of "pressing" makes me vote for summer on this one. The uninitiated reader may say that the season is totally ambiguous in this poem; to do so leaves out a range of sensation which would be available to the reader who accepts one or another seasonal hypothesis. Since summer came to my mind spontaneously when I first read the poem several years ago, and I find no contradictory evidence in the poem, I accept it. (One could just as easily say that the vine is pressing against the window to escape the wintry draft, it now seems to me, which would result in a different set of sensations—but it *would* result in sensations, and that is the point of haiku.)

Again, "wind/ circling/ into/ leaves" gives me an image of autumn. I am drawing on my own northern-latitude experience, but expect that it accords with that of Bostok's Australia. If there is some weather phenomenon that often makes leaves swirl in circles during the Australian summer, I still have not lost by lending the poem my New Jersey autumnal associations.

"In the falling snow" obviously refers to winter. Here the poem gains depth as we see the contrast between the warm palms of the boy and the cold of the snow, and see the warmth of his laughing against the cold backdrop of the snowy landscape. For many readers, the knowledge that this is the same Richard Wright, of Chicago, who wrote *Black Boy* and *Native Son*, may give his haiku added depth.

Often enough we read a haiku without picking up on its seasonal associations. But if the experience recorded in the poem has a seasonal setting we are much more likely to grasp what the poet wants to share with us if we know and respond to the fact of the season as well as to the specifics of the poem. Using the name of a season or obviously seasonal event or object in a haiku gives the reader quite a bit of information in a few words. Even if the season is not stated or dramatically obvious in the poem we can probably still "get" the seasonal aspect of the experience from most traditional haiku.

THE JAPANESE TRADITION

The haiku has a very specific, historical reason for indicating the season. Haiku originated as the starting verse, or hokku, of the longer renga, or "linked poem". Renga were written at parties, by several poets who took turns at writing successive short stanzas. The opening stanza of a renga, the hokku, had a very important function. It had to indicate when the renga was written. Some early hokku had the flavor of newspaper date lines. But subtle poets simply named objects associated with the particular time of year, thus suggesting, rather than stating, the season. The words for these objects came to be known as *kigo,* or "season words".

In the fourteenth century, one of the first great critics of renga, Nijō Yoshimoto, suggested some "seasonal topics" *(kidai)* appropriate to the hokku of renga composed at different times of the year:

First Month (lunar calendar; starts on "Chinese New Year"):
    lingering winter, remnants of snow, plum blossoms, Japanese nightingales;
Second Month:
    plum blossoms, cherry blossoms;

***

Fifth Month:
    cuckoos, "fifth-month rain" (i.e., the rain of early summer), orange blossoms, irises . . .

Yoshimoto and his friends, all of whom were serious tanka poets, thought of renga-writing as a game. Games have rules. By the time of Bashō, three centuries later, one could buy a book of rules for writing renga, and it would list the objects, mostly plants and animals, particularly flowers and birds, associated with each season. The original requirement, to specify the time of composition of a renga in its hokku, became altered to: The hokku *must* be on a seasonal topic, or kidai, and contain a season word, or kigo. As the hokku became independent of the renga and developed into the haiku this rule stayed with it, right up to the beginning of the twentieth century.

SEASON IN MODERN HAIKU

Many Japanese haiku poets of the early twentieth century grew weary of the requirement for kigo. Some simply did not bother to learn which plants and animals and household objects "belonged" to which seasons.

When these modern haiku poets were criticized by traditionalists they pointed out that the season-word lists were artificial even in those things which are very specific in time. For example, cherry blossoms flower and fall during a period of a few weeks. So in a specific area we can.pinpoint almost to the week when a poem involving cherry blossoms takes place. But spring moves northward, in the northern hemisphere, and cherry blossom time in Kyoto is followed some time later by the display in Tokyo, and much later by the famous festival in Hirosaki. Yet a haiku with cherry blossoms will be associated with the dates of their appearance in Kyoto, according to the tradition.

As the twentieth century—and the modernization of Japan—progressed, those who dropped season words also argued that much of modern life is spent indoors, in controlled environments. Or in cityscapes where relatively few manifestations of "nature" may be encountered in a day, or weeks at a time. The point of haiku is not the content of experience, but the quality of experience, and of perception. It makes no difference what experience a poet writes of, so long as it is an experience that can bring us to a new or deeper perception, and the emotion which arises from it.

I doubt if any season-word list contains Takako's "fresh-washed hair", and I would rather read the poem than the season-

word list in search of the phrase. But does not the poem seem
filled with spring sunlight:

> fresh-washed hair
> everywhere I go
> making trickles

As in reading traditional haiku with season words, where it
helps to know the season intended by the poet so that we can
fully appreciate the images and their setting, so also we can
amplify our appreciation of many supposedly "seasonless" haiku
by accepting some seasonal background that may suggest itself to
us, either from the poem, or from some experience of our own
that harmonizes with it.

Though most Japanese haiku poets today still observe the sea-
sonal cycle, and many Japanese haiku magazines open each issue
with a group of specifically seasonal poems or have a column
devoted to poems seasonally identified with the month of publi-
cation, there seems to be less tension over seasonal matters now
than during the first half of this century. The relatively few haiku
masters and editors who have ignored season words continue to
ignore them. Most Japanese people, and most Japanese haiku
poets, continue to feel that the seasonal element is basic to haiku.
Haiku anthologies and collections of haiku by individual authors
are often arranged by season, and by seasonal topics within each
season. In part, this serves an indexing function. All of Bashō's
poems on "autumn wind" will be found under that heading in
the *Bashō Kushū (Collection of Bashō's Haiku)*. In the magazines it
also provides some sense of community of spirit. Many of the
poems in a given issue will relate to the whole complex of expe-
riences that form the concept "spring" or "summer" or "autumn"
or "winter". Season pervades Japanese haiku at a deeper than
conscious level.

Western writers on the haiku have often briefly noted the sea-
son words in haiku, and then passed on to more important topics,
like Zen. But for many Japanese the seasonal feeling holds the

key to haiku art. Their position is well stated by the committee of scholars commissioned to explain haiku to the West in the book *Haikai and Haiku* (1958):

> The season implied in a season word does not necessarily coincide with the calendar season, but must be understood in a particular aesthetic association with man's feelings. The days are longest in summer, but in spring, particularly after the equinox, the lengthening of the day strikes our senses more forcibly after the short days of winter.

Thus *nagaki hi*, "the long day", is a season word of spring, not of summer. After citing additional examples, the committee goes on to say:

> Just as a *haiku* expresses the apex of an emotion, so a season word shows a particular thing at its best and most attractive. *Hototogisu* [Japanese cuckoo] is always represented as crying . . .; flowering trees and plants are conceived as in bloom . . .; the moon means the full moon, that of the fifteenth of September . . .

and so on. So we see that a season word does not merely name an object, for a Japanese reader of haiku. Rather, the reader envisions that object at its fullest glory, and the vision itself is sufficient to trigger an aesthetic experience.

Miyamori Asatarō, a Japanese scholar who tried to help Westerners appreciate Japanese literature, wrote in *An Anthology of Haiku Ancient and Modern* (1932):

> The Japanese are passionate lovers of Nature. Every feature, every phase, every change of Nature in the four seasons powerfully excites their delicate aesthetic sense. . . . cherry-blossom viewing picnics . . . are the custom among all people, high and low, young and old; the Japanese often row out in pleasure-boats on the sea or on a lake to

enjoy the harvest moon; they often climb hills for views of the "silver world" of snow; they often visit rivers in darkness to contemplate fireflies; ... On autumn evenings singing-insects kept in cages are sold at street-stalls; and townsfolk listen to them in order to hear "the voices of autumn."

Obviously, the Japanese haiku poets who abandoned the season word do not have many poems in *Haikai and Haiku* or *An Anthology of Haiku Ancient and Modern.* People who make it their business to interpret their native traditions to the outside world usually project a more conservative viewpoint than that held by contemporary artists in those traditions. Japanese who inquire about Western music will be treated to compositions by Bach and Tchaikovsky; they are unlikely to be introduced to the music of John Cage or Lucas Foss unless they happen to be talking to a serious student of contemporary music.

But just as the music of Bach and Tchaikovsky underlies and makes possible, in some sense, the music of Cage and Foss, so the tradition of contemplating nature in its specific, momentary manifestations and taking deep aesthetic pleasure in them underlies and makes possible the poems of Shūson, Tōta, and others who do not care whether or not they use season words. The Japanese haiku began with poets who looked, deeply and appreciatively, at the world around them. That world consisted mostly of what we call "nature". But the "nature" of Bashō's day also included parasols, mosquito nets, and other paraphernalia of human affairs. Even the "fulling-block", equipment used in the dry-cleaning process of earlier times, is a season word. To be sure, these pieces of equipment have seasonal associations. But only by accident have sail boats, galoshes, and garden tools avoided promotion to the season-word lists; indeed, they may appear in some exhaustive modern poetic almanacs.

Conventions arise because many people do the same thing. Many people wrote poems on frogs in the spring, when their singing was first noticed, and therefore most noticeable. Soon it was the fashion to write of frogs in the spring. People who observed—and observe—this fashion do not deny the existence of frogs in the summer. But they express their membership in a special community of human perception by writing of frogs in the spring. As a reader of haiku it seems reasonable to try to know these conventions of season, and to use that knowledge to expand the meanings of haiku written according to them. To help with that, I have included a list of traditional Japanese season words in the reference section at the back of this handbook.

When we find a Japanese haiku that does not seem to have a season word as such, it may still have a seasonal association for us. If so, we are within our rights to use that background for our own increased enjoyment, provided that we do not insist on our special interpretation to the exclusion of others. And while some more traditional Japanese haiku poets of today, and many Japanese individuals who may know little of the modern developments in haiku, can insist that without a season word a poem is not a haiku, we in the West do not have that right. A number of very serious and dedicated Japanese poets write seasonless verses which they consider to be in the haiku tradition. We cannot exclude them.

THE WESTERN EXPERIENCE

Very few documents widely circulated in the West have gone into much detail about the use of season words in Japanese haiku. So most poets who write haiku outside of Japan do not well understand the intricacies of using season words, or the interrelationships of season words (kigo) and seasonal topics (kidai). One American haiku magazine editor attempted to examine the use of possible season words in English-language haiku a few years ago; he concluded that the geography in which haiku are being written around the world varies too much to fit the confines of traditional Japanese season-word lists. Given these difficulties, non-Japanese haiku poets have generally not worried about season words.

When season seems important to a Western haiku author, it can be incorporated easily enough. But very few Western haiku poets feel they must indicate the season in every haiku in order to *make* it a haiku. With their modern Japanese counterparts, they recognize that many events which they wish to record in verse do not involve a particularly seasonal consciousness. They concentrate on capturing the kinds of moments—the sudden intimate seeings—that they wish to remember for themselves and share with others.

8

The Form of Haiku

TRADITIONAL FORM IN JAPANESE POETRY

During some pre-literate epoch, Japanese speech came to move in units averaging twelve short, simple sounds. And these groups of sounds usually had a grammatical break after the fifth or seventh sound. Here are two examples of a similar effect in English:

> I bought some candy on my way to the ball game.
> I swung at the ball and then ran to first base.

In the first example the main sense division comes after the word "candy"; in the second it comes after "ball". Although the two examples have different grammatical structures, they have similar rhythms. If we read them aloud one after the other we may notice rhythmical similarities in the pair of slightly shorter phrases, "I bought some candy" and "I swung at the ball", and in the pair of slightly longer phrases, "on my way to the ball game" and "and then ran to first base."

As Japanese poetic form evolved, poems were made by arranging the groups of sounds so that their grammatical breaks all went the same way, usually with the shorter phrase going first.

A sense of cadence was created by ending with an additional phrase of about seven sounds. Poems in this form, called *chōka* ("long poem"), have from three to over one hundred groups of about twelve sounds. The following anonymous poem from around the sixth century demonstrates the form. I have tried to approximate the effect in the translation.

> *fuyugomori   haru sarikureba*
> *ashita ni wa   shiratsuyu oki*
> *yūbe ni wa   kasumi tanabiku*
> *hatsuse no ya   konure ga shita ni*
> *uguisu naku mo*

> As winter's bonds   grant spring freedom
> in the morning   white dew falls down,
> in the evening   mist stretches out;
> on Hatsuse Plain   under the twigs of trees
> a nightingale sings!

This poem is from the *Manyōshū*, the first great anthology of Japanese poetry, collected in the eighth century A.D. Many of the poems in the *Manyōshū* are tanka ("short poem"), which have the same form as chōka, but with only two units of nominally twelve sounds each, plus the final phrase of about seven. Here is an example by the great *Manyōshū* poet, Hitomaro:

> *akikaze wa   suzushiku narinu*
> *uma namete   iza no ni yuka na*
> *hagi no hana-mi ni*

> The autumn wind   has become cooler now;
> horses abreast,   let's go to the meadow
> to see the *hagi* blooms.

Hagi is a small, pink-flowering shrub, sometimes called "bush clover" in English. We see that there is one major pause in Hitomaro's poem, after the first twelve sounds in the Japanese (at the end of the first line of the translation). Many tanka of the *Many-ōshū* have this structure.

However, by the time of the *Kokinshū*, a second anthology (collected in the early tenth century), another structure for the tanka had become popular. Many of the *Kokinshū* tanka divide near the middle of the second twelve sounds. For example, here is a poem by one of the editors of the *Kokinshū*, Ki no Tsurayuki:

> *yadori shite   haru no yamabe ni*
> *netaru yo wa   yume no naka ni mo*
> *hana zo chirikeru*

Finding shelter   among the hills of spring
slept the night;   even amid my dreaming
the flower blossoms fell.

The *Kokinshū* also has many tanka with no sharp division, or which divide somewhere else. But these two patterns became the two main structures of tanka. We can look at these structures more easily if we consider each five- or seven-sound unit as one verse-line. Here are the two tanka given above, in the usual format for tanka translations, side-by-side, for comparison:

The autumn wind	Finding shelter
has become cooler now;	among the hills of spring,
horses abreast,	slept the night;
let's go to the meadow	even amid my dreaming
to see the *hagi* blooms.	the flower blossoms fell.
Hitomaro in the	*Ki no Tsurayuki in the*
Manyōshū (ca. 700 A.D.)	*Kokinshū (ca. 900 A.D.)*

The semicolons mark the major rhythmical breaks. In the originals the breaks divide the poems 5/7//5/7/7 and 5/7/5//7/7, respectively. (In the translations I have duplicated the original word order as closely as possible, and substituted the natural English rhythms of two accented beats and three accented beats, respectively, for the natural Japanese rhythms of five and seven sounds.) During the next two hundred years the rhythmical structure of the second example above came to dominate tanka composition.

Poets of the classical era often met together for the purpose of composing and sharing tanka. By the thirteenth century it became the fashion, after some hours of deep poetic concentration on their individual works, to relax by writing a humorous renga together. The form of the long collaborative renga resembled a chain of tanka, with each poet writing a stanza of about seventeen sounds (5/7/5) or about fourteen sounds (7/7) in turn.

The haiku originated as the opening verse of a renga. Therefore the traditional haiku in Japanese lacks the formal resolution or cadence provided by the pair of seven-sound phrases at the end of a tanka. In terms of its origin, the form of the traditional haiku is incomplete.

TRADITIONAL FORM IN HAIKU

Many Western authors have fallen into the simplistic trap of saying that the haiku is a seventeen-syllable poem in three lines of five, seven, and five syllables. This has led to whole classrooms of teachers and children counting English syllables as they attempt to write haiku. But Japanese haiku are written in Japanese, which is quite different from English or other Western languages.

In fact, Japanese poets do not count "syllables" at all. Rather, they count *onji*. The Japanese word onji does not mean "syllable", it means "sound symbol", and refers to one of the phonetic characters used in writing Japanese phonetic script. In the language of the *Manyōshū* one of these characters did indeed represent one syllable, as we think of syllables. But even then, each of the onji of Japanese represented a very short sound, much simpler than most syllables in, say, English or German.

Since the *Manyōshū* the Japanese language has changed a great deal. Now it incorporates double-long vowel sounds, diphthongs, and a final consonant. In some words it takes two or three onji to write what we would consider one syllable. For example, how many syllables in *Manyōshū?* I think most of us would agree on three. But in Japanese it is counted as six onji.

Japanese onji average quite a bit shorter than most English syllables, and are much more uniform in length. Compare the following representative English syllables and Japanese onji:

English syllables: a on two wound wrought

Japanese onji: a n ka shi tsu

In Japanese the sound "tsu" takes no longer to say than the sound "a". And the Japanese probably say that "a" faster than Americans in most situations. I think most speakers of English will agree with me that "wound" and "wrought" usually take twice as long to say as "on"—or longer. Even the clipped English words "potato" and "tomato" are just barely a match for common three-onji words in Japanese like *aoi, atsui,* and *tōi.*

Some years ago I did a study of Japanese haiku recited by a Japanese actress and English translations of the same poems recited by an American speaker. They were part of the sound track of a movie, *Haiku,* produced by the Japan Society, Inc., of New York. The movie presented twenty-eight haiku and translations. Even though the translations had fewer syllables than the Japanese haiku had onji, the readings of the translations averaged almost sixty percent longer than the readings of the Japanese. Granted, some of this difference may be due to variation between the readers, but native speakers of both Japanese and English whom I questioned told me that the reciters spoke at a normal pace.

As a result of this study I concluded that an English-language translation of a typical Japanese haiku should have from ten to twelve syllables in order to simulate the duration of the original. A well-known translator of Japanese poetry, Hiroaki Sato, has also concluded that his haiku translations "must come to about . . . twelve syllables in the case of those written in the orthodox 5-7-5". Maeda Cana, a scholar who has made an extensive study of quantity in Japanese and English poems, has worked very hard at duplicating the durations and rhythmical patterns of Japanese haiku in her English translations. Her translations average just under twelve syllables each. I find it significant that two other translators agree with the finding which I independently arrived at: Approximately twelve English syllables best duplicates the length of Japanese haiku in the traditional form of seventeen onji.

The simplistic notion of seventeen-syllable haiku has obscured another important feature of traditional haiku form here in the West. Most traditional haiku have a *kireji*, or "cutting word". The kireji usually divides the stanza into two rhythmical parts, one of twelve onji and the other of five. The kireji is a special grammar word or verb ending that indicates the completion of a phrase or clause. In effect, the kireji is a sort of sounded, rather than merely written, punctuation. It indicates a pause, both rhythmically and grammatically. Some kireji also lend a particular emotional flavor to the five- or twelve-onji phrase that they end. Along with the kigo (season word), the kireji carried over from the starting verse of renga into the independent haiku.

The starting verse of a renga also had to leave room for an additional thought, to be added in the next verse. Often the starting verse was grammatically incomplete. The tendency toward grammatical incompleteness carried over into haiku—as either incomplete sentences or very clipped, almost telegraphic speech. This allows haiku poets to concentrate on image-making words as they omit much of the complex grammar that occurs in everyday conversational Japanese.

The great British student of traditional Japanese haiku, R. H.

Blyth, once suggested an ideal English parallel for the form of the Japanese haiku: three lines of two, three, and two accented beats, respectively. Blyth's intuitive suggestion, coupled with a kireji-like pause, yields a form that consists of one pentameter (five-beat) unit, plus one unit less than half as long as a pentameter line. Such a form very nearly duplicates the traditional form of the Japanese haiku using the English language in ways that are native to traditional English poetry, and therefore comfortable to native speakers of English. Such a form also results in a sense of rhythmical incompleteness in English, similar to the formal incompleteness of the traditional Japanese haiku.

Here are a few traditional Japanese haiku, with English translations that follow the two-three-two form. In each case, there is a line-for-line correspondence between the original and the translation. Punctuation in English marks the locations of the kireji in the originals:

> *furuike ya*   old pond . . .
> *kawazu tobikomu*   a frog leaps in
> *mizu no oto*   water's sound
>
>   *Bashō*

> *fuji hitotsu*   Fuji alone
> *uzumi nokoshite*   remains unburied:
> *wakaba kana*   the young leaves!
>
>   *Buson*

> *utsukushiki*   a really lovely
> *tako agarikeri*   kite has risen above;
> *kojiki goya*   a beggar's hut
>
>   *Issa*

> *kumo o fumi*   walking the clouds
> *kasumi o sūya*   even sucking the mist!
> *agehibari*   soaring skylark
>
>   *Shiki*

By Bashō's seventeenth century there was not as much emphasis on kireji as there had been in previous centuries, but haiku were permanently marked by the kireji pause. Most traditional haiku have a major pause after either the first five or the first twelve onji. Occasionally a poet uses a kireji in the middle, between the sixth and the twelfth onji, for effect, countering the normal five-seven-five movement of the traditional form. In these instances the poet plays against the expectations created by the traditional form, much as Shakespeare's occasional run-on lines in the sonnets go counter to our expectation of the sonnet. (See *kireji* in the glossary for more information.)

We can summarize the traditional form of the Japanese haiku as follows:

1. A Japanese haiku in the traditional form usually has two rhythmical units, one of about twelve onji and one of about five, the break between them often marked with a special grammatical device called a kireji, or cutting word.

2. Since the break between the two rhythmical units is equally likely to occur after the first five onji or after the first twelve, the normal rhythm of a traditional haiku *in Japanese* is five, seven, and five onji.

3. The form of traditional haiku originated in the incomplete opening stanza of a longer poem; the haiku form is therefore rhythmically incomplete.

4. Haiku often omit features of normal grammar, such as complete sentences and complicated verb endings.

This picture of the form of Japanese haiku holds until about 1900. There were some variations. The kireji waxed and waned in importance from one era to another. Poets occasionally wrote haiku with a few extra onji. For a time a seven-seven-five form was almost as common as five-seven-five, but by the end of

Bashō's career five-seven-five had become the norm. From then until the intrusion of European literature traditional haiku went relatively unchanged in Japan.

A "TRADITIONAL FORM" FOR HAIKU IN ENGLISH

It seems to me that the most pleasing form for a "traditional haiku" in English would be similar to the form of the translations presented a page or two earlier:

1. For haiku in English an overall form consisting of seven accented syllables, plus unaccented syllables up to a total of about twelve, would yield a rhythmical structure native to English and at the same time approximate the duration of traditional Japanese haiku. A major grammatical pause between the second and third or fifth and sixth accented syllables would provide the sense of division created by the Japanese kireji.

2. While Japanese are used to reading traditional texts in which rhythms are not visually identified, the Western notion of a printed poem-text incorporates the idea of a line of type equalling a rhythmical unit, or verse-line. Therefore a three-line structure of two, three, and two accented syllables, respectively, would establish rhythmical proportions similar to those of traditional Japanese haiku.

3. Since the most commonly encountered short structure in traditional English poetry is the "heroic couplet" with two five-beat lines, the two-three-two-beat structure with a strong grammatical break after the second or fifth beat, as proposed, would yield a sense of rhythmical incompleteness similar to that in Japanese haiku.

4. Grammar should be stripped to the minimum that seems reasonably natural. Complete sentences may or may not occur; articles ("a, an, and the") and prepositions should be used sparingly, but not unnaturally omitted.

I have put the suggestions for a "traditional form" for haiku in English in the middle of this chapter so that they will not be taken as the last word on the subject of haiku form. They are offered to provide a model of an English-language form that corresponds both to our sense of poetic tradition and to the quantities and rhythmical proportions of, as well as the amount of information normally contained in, traditional Japanese haiku. Those who wish to write what they might think of as "traditional haiku" in English may use them as guidelines. But since haiku have only been written in English for a few score years, it seems a bit early to call any kind of haiku in English "traditional".*

Here are a few excellent haiku by poets writing in English which happen to be in the form I am suggesting as "traditional":

*Those wishing to create a "traditional" haiku form in other languages should consider the relationship between the Japanese tradition and their own in regard to rhythmical structures, what sounds natural to their own poetic sensibilities, and so on. They should also consider the duration in time of typical Japanese haiku, as well as whether the same amount of information will usually fit into the same amount of time in both languages. For example, while German syllables are approximately as complex and long in duration as English syllables, those in the Romance languages tend to be shorter and simpler; perhaps a nominally five-seven-five syllabic form for haiku in Spanish or Italian would duplicate the length of traditional Japanese haiku. But in English and German seventeen-syllable haiku average about sixty percent longer than traditional Japanese haiku. A "haiku" in seventeen Chinese monosyllabic words would be at least twice as long in duration as a traditional Japanese haiku, and contain about twice as much information!

where peonies bloom
    the tomcat lurks and watches
        falls asleep

                    Beverly White

Jeep tracks
    over deer tracks
        in new snow

                    William R. Mosolino

as far toward the trees
as the wire mesh gives—
    the fox's nose

            Michael McClintock

a yellow leaf
stuck between screen and window
        not a word

                    Selma Stefanile

    to hear them
    walking more slowly

    leaves falling

            Gary Hotham

drop of ocean
in my navel
reflects
the Amusement Park

        Alan Pizzarelli

While the first four authors either let the reader find the major grammatical break or, in McClintock's case, indicate it with punctuation, the last two use space to indicate the break equivalent to that provided by kireji in Japanese. Hotham leaves a blank line, dividing the poem into a 2/3//2 rhythm. Pizzarelli breaks the poem into four "lines"—but, as with the mid-poem kireji of some Japanese haiku, this creates a more nearly equal, two-part rhythm, running 2/2//1/2. Compare this with the rhythm produced by the mid-poem kireji *ya* in this poem by Bashō, where the original has the rhythm 5/3//4/5:

> *kiku no hana*   chrysanthemums
> *saku ya ishiya no*   bloom . . . amid the stones
> *ishi no ai*   of the stone-yard

MODERNIZATION AND HAIKU FORM

As the modernization of Japanese culture progressed, many Japanese haiku poets remained more or less faithful to the traditional form and content of haiku. Others experimented freely. Even ignoring the extreme variations, we find many haiku with very irregular rhythms, including poems much longer than seventeen onji. Here are three examples, showing the number of onji in the originals, by Santōka, Hōsai, and Ippekirō, respectively:

matsu wa katamuite	8	the pines careen
aranami no kudakeru mama	11	the way the rough waves crash

suzume no	4	grasping
atatakasa o nigiri	9	the warmth of a sparrow
hanashite yaru	6	and letting it go

aki no hi no hinaka no no no ishi no nukumi   **17**

the warmth of a stone of a field of midday of a day of autumn*

While Ippekirō's haiku is seventeen onji long, there is no break in the run-on rhythm at all. Breaking it into the traditional five, seven, five divides a word in the middle.

We should note that most Japanese "Free-Meter Haiku" poets, in other words, those who ignore the traditional five-seven-five-onji form, have continued to write their poems in a single column the way traditional haiku are written. Thus the visual form of their poems on the page equates to one line of type in English. There is no authority for breaking the non-traditional haiku of Santōka, Hōsai, or Ippekirō into verse-lines, as I have

---

*The order of the original is exactly opposite, from autumn to warmth.

done often in Chapter 3 or above, other than my own sense of
the rhythmical structure of each original.

A few Japanese haiku poets experimented with typographi-
cally indicated verse-lines. Ōhashi Raboku (1890–1933), who
contributed haiku to Seisensui's *Sōun*, appears to have been
among the first, with the following poem published in 1931:

sara mo arōte	won't even wash
kurenu mono	the dishes
are kore to	do this, do that . . .
higurashi	evening cicada

The language of this poem is colloquial, rather than "poetic".
Tadashi Kondo suggests that if we take it as mimicking a few
snatches of conversation, and fill in the blanks, we get something
like: "He doesn't even do the dishes, and keeps telling me to do
this and that all day—until the time of the evening cicadas." In
fact, the word which literally means "clear cicada" is a pun on
phrases meaning "passing the time" and "the day closes". Some
translators call the *higurashi* the "day-darkener".

Raboku did not live long enough to follow this example with
many more, but even in this earliest use of typographic verse-
lines he demonstrates the flow of syntax visually. This princi-
ple—letting the appearance of a poem on the page be governed
by the flow of speech—is one key to the structure of most modern
poetry throughout the world today. Abandoning the worn-out
vocabulary of supposedly poetic language meant also abandon-
ing the old forms which had been fitted to it.

Takayanagi Shigenobu (1923–1983) started writing haiku in
the traditional style and form. Later he experimented with visu-
ally indicating his verse-lines, but some of his poems in this man-
ner seem to read just as well in the traditional form. For example:

mi o sorasu niji no	body-arching rainbow's
zetten	pinnacle
shokeidai	gallows-stand

is a striking poem that loses *almost* none of its force when found
in the traditional single column of type (as I once encountered it),
and read in the three verse-lines of the traditional structure:

mi o sorasu	body-arching
niji no zetten	rainbow's pinnacle
shokeidai	gallows-stand

What does Shigenobu gain by setting his poem out on the
page in the unusual manner? It is visually arresting, especially to
a Japanese, who normally expects to encounter haiku written or
printed in a single column. And the layout puts extra space
between the introductory image, of a person arching back to look
up at a rainbow, and the chilling object found at that rainbow's
pinnacle—the gibbet, which is a body-arching device in its own
right. In effect, the layout of the poem leaves the reader in doubt
as to what is at the top of the rainbow's arc for the space of time
required to find the next word on the page, much as the visual
experience stretches the capacity of the viewer. What is that thing
cutting the rainbow? Why, it's a—gallows!

Although Shigenobu experimented widely with visual for-
mats, traditional haiku rhythms lurk in many of his poems. The
following may be one of his more extreme pieces, though some
are longer:

sanmyaku no	in a mountain range's
hida ni	creases
ki	hear
ki	ing
su	clear
mi	ly
umo	the
re	bur
ru	ied
mimi	ear
ra	s

In a more normal format it would look like this,

sanmyaku no	in a mountain range's
hida ni kikisumi	creases hearing clearly
umoreru mimi-ra	the buried ears

revealing a not unreasonable variation of the traditional form: five, seven, seven. Shigenobu is playing with the reader in much the same way as e. e. cummings in his famous "r-p-o-p-h-e-s-s-a-g-r", but Shigenobu is really abandoning traditional haiku form in a superficial way, much as cummings only superficially abandons traditional sonnet form in many of his poems. Still, Shigenobu's original form makes the reader work, right up to the last phoneme, to find out just what he will say—and that work helps build the effect of the startling image, just as cummings's anagram gymnastics allow us to perceive the object in question only after the explosion of its *leap!:* grasshopper.

Another key to most modern verse structure is the desire of the poet to lead the reader's perception in a rhythm that corresponds to the poet's experience. In explaining this principle of organic form a friend once said it was an attempt to capture "the cadence of perception".

The larger point here is that many Japanese haiku poets, led by the radicals of the 1920s, 1930s, and 1940s, have refused to be stuck in the box of one or two rigid metrical patterns. Though most Japanese write their first haiku in the conservative atmosphere of the classroom in strict traditional form, even the most traditional haiku magazines publish poems that vary from that form. And the last decade has seen new interest in the more experimental poets of the years prior to World War II. More Japanese today are reading the haiku of Santōka, Hōsai, and the other free-meter poets than ever before.

CONCLUSION

In an essay published in 1912 Ezra Pound stated the case for step-
ping out of traditional poetic forms succinctly: "I believe in an
'absolute rhythm' . . . in poetry which corresponds exactly to the
emotion or shade of emotion to be expressed." Since the shade
of emotion to be expressed changes moment by moment, expe-
rience by experience, most serious modern poets find it less than
helpful to restrict themselves to rigid traditional forms. However,
many Western haiku poets first learned of the haiku as a "poem
in seventeen syllables, arranged in three lines of five, seven, five"
and began writing in that form. As you can see from looking over
the work in the chapters on the history of Western haiku, some
very striking poems have been written in this mode. There is no
reason to discard such fine poems simply because they were writ-
ten under a mistaken impression of the nature of haiku form in
Japanese. In fact, some of the "five-seven-five" poets are well
aware that the form they write in is longer than the traditional
Japanese form, but they find it still has a balance and grace that
they like, and provides a kind of challenge when they attempt to
compose a haiku.

Today in both Japan and the West haiku poets honestly differ
with one another over the definition of haiku. Many—perhaps
most—Japanese who write haiku feel that it should be written in
a fixed form. They recognize the five-seven-five-onji structure as
the norm, with occasional variations such as seven-seven-five or
the addition of one or at most two extra onji to a verse-line. Most
traditionalists allow at least this much variation.

Many of the more prominent traditionalists have paid less
and less attention to this aspect of haiku. They evidently feel that
the kind of experience recorded or built in a haiku is more impor-
tant a defining characteristic than its form. Even poets such as
Ippekirō, who reject traditional form and season words, often
write poems which have seasonal associations, and occasionally

fall into a structure near the traditional rhythm. And just as most haiku poets have gradually, if grudgingly, accepted modern objects and experiences into haiku content, they have also more and more frequently accepted modern speech rhythms and vocabulary.

The renga of Bashō's day was vital and growing largely because it built upon a rejection of the rigidities of the past as to speech and content. It was a break from tradition which ultimately renewed and sustained that tradition. The early twentieth century trends toward modern content, language, and speech rhythms in Japanese haiku resulted from attempts at again renewing and sustaining that tradition. Now that the conservatism of the war era and the despair of the immediate post-war decades is past, perhaps the tradition of Japanese haiku has resumed the normal process of growth and change. The continuity with the pre-war Humanist school of haiku, provided by the longevity and vigor of such poets as Nakamura Kusatao and Katō Shūson, and the dynamic work of poets like Kaneko Tōta emerging since the war, should help this process.

Westerners interested in haiku have only just begun to discover that not all Japanese haiku conform to the traditional structure. Ten years after the last of Blyth's books on haiku, the word finally began to reach us. Soichi Furuta's translations of Ippekirō came out in 1974, followed by Makoto Ueda's *Modern Japanese Haiku: An Anthology* in 1976. John Stevens's free-form translations of Santōka appeared in 1980, closely followed in 1981 by the anthology *From the Country of Eight Islands*, with one-line translations of Hōsai's haiku by Hiroaki Sato. Perhaps as the reading public, and Western haiku poets, become more aware of this body of work, they will come to understand haiku as a vehicle for sharing experience, rather than as a vessel for thoughts about nature. While the liquid in a vessel conforms to the vessel's shape, the most practical vehicle-designers take the shape of the contents into account.

Today's writer of haiku, East or West, is free to imitate the styles of the old masters or to look to the more modern works of our immediate predecessors and contemporaries for models. While American haiku poets warred over "traditional" versus free-form American haiku throughout the 1960s, in the 1970s each camp acknowledged that there were poems of outstanding worth in both styles. Now anyone can write a haiku in the style that fits the needs of the particular poet, moment, and perception. And write another in a different style the next time.

9

The Craft of Haiku

THE SENSES, THE IMAGE, AND HAIKU

"I sense, therefore I am!" Descartes might better have said. Our first route to experience is through the senses. Our experiences give rise to emotion. Our language captures this connection very well, for when we talk of our "feelings" or say that something "touched" us we apply to our inner mental state words that literally mean having a physical sensation of the outer world.

We store our experiences in the mind as mental images. In the rest of this book the word "image" means words which name objects or actions that cause sensations from which we form mental images, or the mental images themselves. An image is the language equivalent, or the mental equivalent, for a physical sensation or a set of sensations.

Vivid, clear writing gives the reader clear images. This results in a kind of vicarious experience, in which the reader pictures what the writer's words show, hears what they sound, feels what they touch, and so on. If a writer captures the images of an experience that produced emotion, then the reader—if comprehending and sympathetic—will have a similar emotion based on experiencing the images provided by the writer.

The haiku is the quintessence of this kind of writing. One of Buson's simplest haiku presents a single image, only slightly elaborated:

botan chitte	peony falling—
uchikasanarinu	dropped overlapping
nisanpen	two or three petals

The peony is a rich, vibrantly colored flower. Its petals fall, and as they do, they overlap one another, two or three of them. The lushness of the petals, even as they fade, contrasts with the falling. By focusing on the interval between the life and death of the peony blossoms Buson gives us both.

Some haiku seem to contain only one essential image, like Buson's poem on the peony petals. But depth, a chill down the spine, usually comes from perceiving some relationship, which implies two or more things relating to each other. Sometimes that relationship is between something stated and something unstated, as in the following poem by Elizabeth Searle Lamb, with its contrast between our usual state of going through the world blind, and then suddenly

> pausing
> halfway up the stair—
> white chrysanthemums

Most haiku, either directly or by implication, present two objects, actions, or states of being. Usually there is little grammatical connection between the things presented, and sometimes the mixture of contrasts and unities is abrupt and startling.

To use a photographic metaphor, I call one method of doing this the "zoom-lens effect", in which there is a rapid shift of focus, of space and distance. This haiku by Penny Harter is a good example:

> in the meadow
> the cow's lips
> wet with grass

Here the eye jumps from the meadow directly to the lips of the cow. And on those lips we see the dew-wet grass—a close-up of one minute portion of "the meadow".

Harter's poem is a special case of the more general phenomenon in haiku, particularly Japanese haiku, in which an object and its action appear in a setting. The poet must be careful to avoid merely providing a background. The setting itself becomes an image to interact dynamically with the other, more sharply focused image. Here is an example by Kaga no Chiyo (often called Chiyo-ni, "Nun Chiyo", 1703–1775):

hirou mono	things picked up
mina ugoku nari	all start to move
shiohigata	low-tide beach

First we are in close, actually feeling the rough shells in our hands, the sudden startled movements. Then we look up, across the broader expanse of water. Our surprise and delight in this small squirming in our palms is tempered by the breadth of the beach and sea, and our own smallness as we, too, wriggle in the grip of forces we do not understand.

While setting and an object or action in the foreground often interact in a haiku, many haiku contain two foreground images. These images act like the poles in a spark gap. The sparks jump back and forth faster than the mind can follow. A Canadian haiku poet and critic, Rod Willmot, uses the term "resonance" to describe these relationships. Here is an example by Penny Harter:

> snowflakes—
> dust on the toes
> of my boots

Do not read this as a metaphor! The "dust" is really dust. And when you reach into your closet for your boots to go out in the first snow of the year, your thumb probably marks a shiny spot right on the toe. The dust reminds us of the time that has passed since we last wore our boots in the snow. The momentary phenomenon of snowflakes echoes against the whole round of the seasons. And dust as the emblem of time reminds us also of our origin and end. Haiku are as simple as life and death.

Kenneth Yasuda says that "what, when, and where" are the three elements of haiku. Usually the image itself is the what, while it implies the when and the where. For example, in this haiku by John Wills

> the moon at dawn
>   lily pads blow white
> in a sudden breeze

we have the time of day plainly stated; and "lily pads" gives a fair hint as to the time of year. "Lily pads" also tells us that we are on a lake, pond, or some slow-moving part of a river, giving us an impression of place.

The when and where show up in some parts of this haiku, but the what fills it entirely. To the opening image in the first line, the second and third lines add a beautiful and complex image that builds as it moves from word to word, line to line. The moon suggests roundness, mirrored immediately in the potential of day and its round light, the sun. And the moon suggests also the dark of the night sky where we normally expect to see it. The roundness of the lily pads echoes the roundness of the moon, though their dark color and the darkness of the water at dawn relate to the darkness that recedes as day comes on. But moving through the lines we discover the flipped-up white undersides of the lily pads, as strange a sight in its dark surroundings as the moon's light is at dawn. We see the blowing in the lily pad's action, then in the last line feel the temperature and pressure of the sudden

breeze against our bodies. Does the chill arise from the seen res-
onance, or from the breeze that unexpectedly caresses us? Both.
This poem aptly demonstrates another principle of haiku, first
mentioned so far as I know by Robert Spiess, who says that usu-
ally "the better haiku poets use multiple sense imagery". One
might wonder how many senses can be involved in a single, short
haiku. The following haiku by Anita Virgil may give us a start at
an answer:

walking the snow-crust
not sinking
sinking

When I ask a class of elementary school children to tell me all the
senses in the first line of this poem they say: movement (muscle
sense), balance, sight, hearing, temperature, touch, smell (it
smells different when there is snow on the ground), and some
suggest adding taste, for the snowflakes they catch with their
tongues—though that seems stretching it a bit. The second line
adds no new sensations, but the trepidation it implies sharpens
some already present in the first line. The third line adds the
organ, or visceral sense, that "feeling in the pit of the stomach"
when the elevator suddenly goes down. Omitting the snowflake
catchers, I count eight senses! (We should not fail to note the
shape of the words on the page, resembling the shape of the
snow-crust where something has broken through it.)

This poem also demonstrates the rightness of recording the
objects and events that cause sensations in the order of percep-
tion, as suggested by Harold G. Henderson. Probably Anita Virgil
was not fully conscious of all the sensations involved in this
"walking the snow-crust" experience when she had it. Yet by
recording the experience in words that name its actual objects and
events, and by choosing and ordering her words to correspond to
the sights, sounds, and physical reality of the experience, she has
made it possible for us to re-experience it, and even perhaps to
imagine parts of it that she had hardly noticed.

In the best haiku the author tries to share the experience itself, so that the reader may share in that experience as directly as possible, and not be limited to the author's response to it.

THE LANGUAGE OF HAIKU

The brevity of haiku forces a deeper, more disciplined approach to language than any other kind of writing. As William Carlos Williams wrote:

> There's nothing sentimental about a machine, and: A poem is a small (or large) machine made of words. When I say there's nothing sentimental about a poem I mean that there can be no part, as in any other machine, that is redundant.

Brevity, and the consequent stripping away of the unnecessary, provide haiku with several advantages not always found in longer kinds of writing.

Brevity encourages drama. We create drama by raising questions in the minds of readers that can only be answered by further reading. Often the "resonance" between images in a haiku raises just such questions, which may be answered in part,

> A boy wading—
> watching a dark snake winding
> out of the river.
>
> *James Tipton*

or not at all:

> *natsukusa ni*   in summer grass
> *kikansha no sharin* a steam engine's wheels
> *kite tomaru*   come and stop
>
> *Yamaguchi Seishi (b. 1901)*

Brevity requires that the poet leave out unneeded grammar words and connectives. For example, the lack of connectives allows the images of the following haiku to resonate with each other:

> *meigetsu ya*   harvest moon . . .
> *keburi haiyuku*   smoke goes creeping
> *mizu no ue*   over the water

> *Hattori Ransetsu (1653–1707; disciple of Bashō)*

As the haiku gives us the moon first, we look up at it, enjoying its fullness and brilliance. Then we notice the smoke spreading over the water, and see the moon striking down through it. Connecting the moon with the rest of the poem grammatically would have destroyed the effect, for we would not have seen the moon for itself, with the interaction coming gradually into our consciousness.

Punning provides a means of expanding meaning common to all languages. In the following pre-Bashō hokku the pun in the translation duplicates that of the original:

> *toshi kurete*   the year giving out
> *hito mono kurenu* people give me nothing—
> *koyoi kana*   this evening . . .

> *Yamazaki Sōkan (1458–1546)*

The opening line is a standard expression which would usually be translated "the year closing". However, when the second line echoes back the sound *kure-*, root of the verb "to give", the meaning of the first line suddenly expands. In contrast to the people Sōkan knows, who will not be giving him presents during the New Year's celebration, the year "gives out" right up to the very end. Perhaps a little ruefully, Sōkan honestly remarks on his situation, being a monk, having given up family connections and the presents that go along with them. But he also smiles at the year's gift to him; the poem is a sort of humorous prayer of thanksgiving. However, not all punning in Japanese poetry is simple or intended for humor.

Grammatical ambiguity, in which a word or phrase serves two different grammatical purposes at once, appears in the most famous hokku of all, Bashō's

furuike ya	old pond . . .
kawazu tobikomu	a frog leaps in
mizu no oto	water's sound

The second line ends in a form that may signal the end of a sentence, or may continue on without a break in meaning into the last line. Read the first way, we have "old pond . . . a frog leaps in" and then the result, "water's sound". But when we notice the second alternative the meaning shifts to this: "old pond . . . a frog leaps in water's sound"—in other words, "old pond . . . the sound of the water a frog leaps into". In a plain prose statement this latter meaning would be the only interpretation, but placing the statement into the traditional form of the haiku causes an enjambment between the verse-lines that opens the meaning. The enjambment makes "a frog leaps in" seem at first a complete sentence, then part of a larger grammatical whole.

Generally, haiku poets avoid wide-open ambiguity. Without a fairly well-defined concrete image there is not much for the reader to build on. But occasionally risking the border of out-and-out vagueness produces startling results, as in this widely praised haiku by L. A. Davidson:

> beyond
> stars beyond
> star

Examples of literary allusion in haiku appear in Chapters 2 and 3. This method of expanding meaning is used frequently in Japanese haiku, but often eludes Western readers, or even modern Japanese, who may not have the literary background necessary to appreciate many allusions. However, Nakamura Kusatao has a poem with an allusion that most of us will understand immediately:

sora wa taisho no	sky the Beginning's
aosa tsuma yori	blue—from the wife
ringo uku	getting an apple

With his allusion to the Genesis story of Adam and Eve, Kusatao both records a lighthearted impression of his and his wife's innocence, and jokingly suggests that they are about to fall from that state.

Another way to capitalize on reference to earlier work is allusive variation, common to haiku in both Japan and the West. Sometimes a poet will paraphrase the haiku of another, changing just enough to shift the images and their relationships without making it hard to see the resemblance between the new poem and the earlier one on which it rings changes. For example, the following haiku by Jack Cain first appeared in *Haiku* magazine (Toronto) in 1969:

an empty elevator
opens
closes

The poem was included in Cor van den Heuvel's *Haiku Anthology*, published in 1974. In 1976 the magazine *Bonsai* published this haiku by Frank K. Robinson:

the elevator
opens . . .
      vacant masks
. . . closes

When an elevator opens we half expect to see a crowd of people standing in it. There is some air of mystery about an opening elevator. But here the elevator opens to reveal seemingly empty people. When we add to Robinson's poem the prior knowledge of Jack Cain's haiku, we discover that elevators may be empty in more than one way. Cain's elevator seems to be going up and down looking for passengers and not finding any. The poem has a certain sense of loneliness, what the Japanese call *sabi*. Robinson, however, supplies us with an elevator already full; it is the people in it who appear empty. The focus of "the empty elevator poem" of which these are two variations has shifted from the almost personified elevator to the depersonalized humans in the elevator.

Though one occasionally stumbles across a frank simile in pre-modern hokku, the use of simile and metaphor seems to have increased in recent decades, perhaps due to Western influences. The best similes in haiku, as in any poetry, strike us because they are both *apt* and *unusual*. Here is an example by Tomizawa Kakio (1902–1962):

tōten ni	wintry sky—
botan no yō na	like a peony
hito no shita	one's tongue

When I first read this poem two conflicting images struck me. I saw people sticking their petal-like tongues out to catch snowflakes. And I thought of a tongue, round, red, and lush, hidden in the mouth like a peony bud beneath the snow. Either way, the simile creates a sensuality that dramatically contrasts with the wintry sky.

Like similes, metaphors were occasionally used in the older hokku, but modern Japanese haiku poets seem to have been more successful in creating depth and mystery through metaphor. In Chapter 3 we encountered examples by Kaneko Tōta and Katō Shūson. Here is another, by Mori Sumio (b. 1919):

kari no kazu	a number of geese
watarite sora ni	migrating—in the sky
mio mo nashi	not even a wake

Sumio has commented that although the wild geese, particularly their migrations, have long been a subject of literature, one does not see them so often in Japan anymore. The careful selection of words in this haiku creates several overtones. "A number" suggests that he could see a specific number—the geese were not "countless", as they perhaps had been in the past. Sumio also noted that he did not just say a "line" of geese, because he did actually look at each one. Once this particular group has passed there are no more. *Mio*, not an everyday word, literally means "water-tail"; Sumio was very conscious of borrowing the word from the water and putting it in the sky. But in this sky there is no wake—the geese go, leaving no sign of their passage.

Synesthesia, a special variety of metaphor in which the author writes of one sensation in terms of another, occurs in haiku now and then. Perhaps this is not so much a technique of haiku as an unusual sensory perception that sometimes finds its way into haiku. Psychologists have verified the common observation that the senses interact with one another, that one may have an impression of colors while listening to music, for example, or of smells while seeing a movie, and so on.

Bashō's haiku exhibit synesthesia more often than do any other poet's, so far as I know. One of his more famous poems illustrates a subtle mixing of the sensations:

sazanami ya	rippling waves
kaze no kaori no	with the wind scent
aihyōshi	beat together

Studying the sight and sound of the rippling waves, Bashō gradually becomes so attuned to the rhythms that he feels the harmonic beating of the waves in the scent and push of the wind.

The pathetic fallacy—a kind of metaphor or personification in which human actions, thoughts, or emotions are attributed to other than human beings—appears occasionally in humorous haiku, especially those written before Bashō. For example, from the old haikai-no-renga master Sōkan:

te o tsuite	hands to floor
uta mōshiaguru	offering up a song
kawazu kana	the frog . . .

Frogs traditionally "sing" in Japanese poetry, but here the "hands together" and "offering up" suggest an even closer parallel to human activity and motivation.

Onomatopoeia dramatically unifies a poem and the experience it represents. R. H. Blyth distinguishes three types of onomatopoeia in haiku: direct representation of sound; representation of movement or of sensations other than sound; and "the representation of soul states".

Words represent sounds fairly often in haiku. Many words are onomatopoetic, such as *chickadee, swish, screech, whistle*, etc. The trick in writing onomatopoetic haiku is to avoid using too many words that sound like what they mean individually, and find combinations of words that sound like the aural image in toto. Buson does this very nicely in the following poem on "fulling blocks"—a sort of mallet used to dry clean clothes. In Buson's day it was not uncommon to hear the fulling blocks of one's neighbors long into an autumn evening.

ochikochi	here and there
ochikochi to utsu	here and there beat
kinuta kana	fulling blocks

The original's alternating *k* and *ch* sounds, plus the irregular rhythm in the first line of the poem, suggest the syncopated effect of two neighbors beating their clothes, not quite in time with each other.

The Japanese may be especially sensitive to Blyth's second kind of onomatopoeia. They have a large number of adverbial phrases in which a basic sound repeats, indicating the character of a motion or the way in which something happens. Issa is a master at using these, as in

ŏbotaru	a huge firefly
yurari yurari to	wobbling, wobbling
tŏrikeri	passed by

They say Issa made several versions of this poem before settling on the one given here. He worked hard for his simplicities.

On the "representation of soul states" Blyth says, "This is always indirect, unconscious, spontaneous. Great poetry depends chiefly for its effect upon this factor." Here are two of his examples, in new translations. The first is by Issa, the second by Santōka:

hito chirari	people scattered
konoha mo chirari	the leaves too scattered
horari kana	and spread ...

azami	thistle
azayaka na	brilliant
asa no	morning
ame agari	rain finished

In Issa's poem the repetition of rari, a perfect tense ending, emphasizes the finality of the desolation. In Santōka's the assonance, the ah-sounds (i-sounds in the translation) repeating, gives the joyful tone.

Alliteration, or consonance, occurs so much in Japanese haiku that finding an example outstanding enough to warrant singling out from the others is difficult. The last two examples give an impression of the frequency of repeated consonant sounds. And the following poem could easily be presented as an example of Blyth's third type of onomatopoeia. I cannot reasonably translate it into English and reproduce the effect of the alliteration in the last line, so I hope you will study the sound of the Japanese transliteration. This haiku appears in the early autumn portion of Bashō's *Narrow Roads of the Interior,* with the title:

tochūgin   Hummed on the Road

aka-aka to	redly redly
hi wa tsurenaku mo	the sun relentless but
aki no kaze	the autumn wind

The *aka-aka* of the opening line—the heat—explicitly echoes in the *aki ... ka ...* of the final line—the cold. The result is a sort of synesthesia in which two aspects of the same sense become confused, finally yielding one almost overwhelming sensation of *temperature.* Bashō presents this same poem in another context with the following preface:

> Journey's sadness and calmness combined, languid autumn at last somewhat arrived; as might be expected, chafed by the sound of the invisible wind increasingly sad—ah, still, as it commingles with the lingering heat ...

THE WRITTEN HAIKU— VISUAL ASPECTS

Traditionally, the Japanese print haiku in magazines and books in one vertical column of writing, as in the example at the right. This equates to one horizontal line of type in Western languages, thus:

old pond ... a frog leaps in water's sound

A few Japanese haiku poets, notably moderns influenced by contact with Western literature's typographically indicated verse-lines, have experimented with organizing their haiku, traditional or otherwise, into what correspond to Western visual verse-lines. (See

古池や蛙飛こむ水のをと

Chapter 8.) But most have continued presenting their poems in print in the traditional single column.

However, there is a traditional Japanese equivalent for the visually organized metrical structure of modern Western poetry. When a Japanese poem, particularly a short haiku or tanka, is presented in calligraphy, it is often spread out horizontally, rather than in a single column. Though the syntax of the poem is seldom ignored, the breaks from one column of writing to the next often do not follow the formal verse-lines of the poem. They may be arranged specifically to fit a certain visual situation, to accompany a drawing perhaps, or to accentuate a particularly interesting character in the writing. Or they may make some alternative rhythm in the poem more noticeable.

Among the numerous calligraphed examples one might choose, the following poem by Issa recommends itself. Making the horizontal line of romanization our equivalent for the vertical column of Japanese writing, the poem appears in printed works this way (I have added space to show the breaks in the traditional form, which are not indicated visually in the original but would be felt by the reader familiar with the haiku genre; the translation is extremely literal):

niwa no chō   ko ga haeba tobi   haeba tobu

garden butterfly   as baby creeps flies   creeps flies

But in a calligraphed scroll including a sketch of his cottage, Issa arranges the poem somewhat like this:

niwa no chō
ko ga haeba
tobi
haeba
tobu
ie mo Issa

garden butterfly
            as baby creeps
                  flies
                        creeps
                              flies
                                    house too Issa

Granted, Issa spread the poem across the scroll for visual balance and harmony with the drawing of a cottage (the final line indicates that both the calligraphy and the drawing are his), but he also shows the relationship of writing to speech. Here the movement of the baby and the movement of the butterfly, both in fits and starts, suggest the presentation of each verb independently. Issa has written to build a sort of visual onomatopoeia, making the visual and aural rhythms together reflect the rhythms of the original motions that inspired the poem. Spreading the words out tells the reader how to hear the words, the pacing and emphasis.

Since the late 1960s a number of English-speaking haiku poets have constructed each poem "from scratch". They attempt to document visually the precise rhythms they wish to impress upon the reader's ear. While most of their haiku still appear in three lines, there is more freedom within that pattern, as in these examples:

in the hot sun
    still   swinging
      this empty swing

Elizabeth Searle Lamb

factory whistle
            the fried egg
            left staring

Raymond Roseliep

she dresses

under her arm
the moon

LeRoy Gorman

Several poets have experimented with other presentations:

on this cold
      spring 1
2 night 3 4
      kittens
      wet
      5

Marlene Mountain

a milkweed seed

        blowing across the darkening lake

                Cor van den Heuvel

the drip

echoes
unknown
before

the cave

William J. Higginson

As shown in Chapter 5, The Haiku Movement in English, a fair number of North American haiku poets have also experimented at the borders between haiku and concrete, or visual, poetry. It is easy to see that poems can present visually, as well as aurally, images suggested to the mind by words.

In a movement seemingly in the opposite direction, several North American haiku poets have experimented with writing their own haiku in one line. Some of them knew that Japanese haiku are traditionally presented in one column of type, or simply felt that the particular poem they were working on needed to appear in one line. Some have used extra space between words to indicate rhythmical breaks, in effect really breaking their poems into two or three verse-lines, regardless of the horizontal format, while others have perceptions that want no pause, such as these:

Before we knew its name the indigo bunting

Peggy Willis Lyles

a warm wind tickles the dark between my toes

Geraldine C. Little

And still others present in one compact line a group of words so constructed that the reader is virtually forced to observe a line-break, though none is indicated, as in this example:

at dusk hot water from the hose

Marlene Mountain

REVISING HAIKU

Bashō, referring to the craft of haiku, said "On tongue-tip turn a thousand times." Evidently he followed his own advice. When the poem that marked his turn away from the superficial, humorous haikai of his day to the rich and dignified style of his major works first appeared, in 1680, it read this way:

kare-eda ni	on a barren branch
karasu no tomaritaru ya	a raven has come to settle . . .
aki no kure	autumn dusk

The final version, first published in 1689, reads:

kare-eda ni	on a barren branch
karasu no tomarikeri	a raven has perched—
aki no kure	autumn dusk

One wearies of finding Western commentator after Eastern commenting that there is no difference in meaning between the two versions. Granted, the basic images are the same. But the shift from -*taru ya* to -*keri* achieves four distinct improvements, any one of which would have been worth the effort.

First, Bashō slightly shortened the extremely long middle line. The first version of the poem has five, ten, and five sounds per line, respectively. It was written during a period when Bashō was seriously questioning many aspects of the haikai tradition, and several of his poems written then have irregular structures. (Such irregularities as an extra sound in a line were quite common with many poets at that time, however.) An intermediate version of the poem—in which only one sound was changed—was printed with an annotation (perhaps by an editor) that shows concern about the excessive length. Clearly, though, since the ultimate version is only shortened by one sound, this was not the major consideration.

Second, while there is little difference in actual verb tense, the change from -*taru ya* to -*keri* gives the second line a stronger sense of finality. Some indication of Bashō's desire for this may be seen in the intermediate version. It has -*tari* instead of -*taru*, yielding a grammatical formation not different in meaning, but sounding a bit like a noun instead of a verb.

Third, replacing the kireji *ya* with the kireji -*keri* dramatically changes the tension between lines two and three. *Ya* has somewhat the same effect as an ellipsis. There is a turning from one image to another, but the connection between them is not specified. -*Keri* also does not specify the connection between the parts of a haiku, but it closes an action, and what follows, if anything, is distinct and separate. It does not represent a turn, but a break.

Fourth, changing from *-taru ya* (or *-tari ya*) to *-keri* also greatly alters the sound structure of the poem. Even in the first version, the dark *k*-sound predominates. Shortening the overall length of the poem and adding another *k*-sound, in a more dramatic kireji, increases the harshness of the poem and its psychological effect on the reader. (Though the verb root and meaning do not essentially change, I have replaced "settle" with "perch" to somewhat duplicate this effect in my translation of the final version.)

Whether Bashō revised this poem to bring it closer to his perception of an actual event, or to bring it closer to some ideal, we do not know. We do know that in his day the writing of hokku on classical subjects in Chinese painting was fashionable. This is a poem on the subject "cold crow and barren tree". Bashō was a minor student of painting in a rough, Zen-inspired style; he painted more than one picture on which he wrote out this poem. An early version has the poem next to a flock of birds, six or seven of them sitting on branches in various poses, and a later version has the poem and just one bird—in both cases Bashō's own painting and calligraphy. Yet several writers have debated whether we are to understand one "crow"* or many, while ignoring or dismissing the importance of the revisions this poem underwent. When a great master continues tinkering with a poem this short over a period of nine years, and even tries it out in conjunction with another medium a number of times, perhaps the possibility of improvement is important to him.

Among modern American writers there is a similar example of minute revision of a haiku over a period of years. Though not as fine a poem as Bashō's *kare-eda ni,* this poem was also very important to its author's development. But few students of his

---

*I use "raven" in my translation to draw, for the English-speaking reader, on the legacy of Poe, since Bashō draws on the traditional combination of barren images in Chinese painting. The *karasu,* a large, black bird native to Asia, is neither a crow nor a raven.

work have understood, or even looked at, the successive revisions of Ezra Pound's famous "metro poem".

In the issue of *Poetry* magazine for April 1913 it reads:

In a Station of the Metro

The apparition   of these faces   in the crowd :
Petals   on a wet, black bough .

In the September 1, 1914 issue of *Fortnightly Review* Ezra Pound's essay "Vorticism" tells, among other things, how he came to write this poem. He explicitly credits the technique of the Japanese hokku in helping him work out the solution to a "metro emotion"—and he quotes the poem this way:

The apparition of these faces in the crowd :
Petals, on a wet, black bough.

The main effect of the change is to smooth the rhythm, making the poem less choppy. Grammatically, little has happened; the only difference besides closing up space is the substitution of a comma for space, an interchange fairly common in poetry today, usually going the other way.

But Pound wrote another version of the metro poem—the one most of us are familiar with. In *Lustra*, published two years after the "Vorticism" essay, the poem appears this way:

In a Station of the Metro

The apparition of these faces in the crowd;
Petals on a wet, black bough.

Most readers notice the absence of the comma after the word "petals". More important, at the end of the first line Pound changed the colon to a semicolon. A colon tells the reader that one thing restates another in a different way, or that the first simply introduces the second, making one a metaphor for the other. A semicolon shows that two statements are independent of each other, though they may be related. Thus in the final version of "In a Station of the Metro" both "faces" and "petals" should be understood as real, physical objects, each a core image that stands out against its own background. By revising the poem Pound turned an otherwise sentimental metaphor into a genuine haiku. Our sense of the Paris commuters as delicate, vulnerable life builds, now that we see them come up out of the dark underground into a world of falling petals and spring mist. This is a haiku that Shiki would have been proud to write, and it foreshadows the brilliant juxtapositions of Pound's *Cantos*.

These revisions by Bashō and Pound involve subtle shifts of inflection and punctuation. A more common problem for beginning writers of haiku, particularly Westerners, is reducing a potentially dynamic pair of images to a flat simile or metaphor. This usually occurs if one writes a grammatically complete sentence. For instance: "Begging for dinner/ the curl of the cat's tail/ is her meow." This made-up example uses the striking resemblance between the cat's body language and her voice—uses it metaphorically. The metaphor limits the reader to hearing the "meow" in the shape of the cat's tail. Reading the poem carefully, we do not have a meowing cat at all. Rather, she curls her tail *instead* of meowing. However, in most instances of this kind the writer seems to want the reader to see one image and hear the other.

How much stronger this poem becomes when we remove the metaphor by deleting "is":

> begging for dinner
> the curl of the cat's tail
> her meow

Here we both see the curling tail and hear the meow. Further, we now see the begging in the tail and hear it in the meow. Thus the opening line becomes particularized in the following images, rather than merely serving as a weak introductory phrase.

Revising haiku is not limited to changing the grammar or

removing words that do not sharpen and present the image. Imma Bodmershof published one of her haiku this way in 1962 (translations made with the help of Volker Schubert):

Rückkehr aus Sonne und Schnee   Come back out of sun and
                                             snow
ich tappe zur roten Glut.   I grope toward the ruddy glow.
Ist hier mein Zuhaus?   Is this my home?

By 1975 it was revised to this:

Rückkehr aus Sonne und Schnee   Come back out of sun and
                                             snow
ich tappe zum Herd   I grope toward the stove
ist hier mein Zuhaus?   is this my home?

At first glance the initial version might seem preferable—a "ruddy glow" seems a stronger image than simply a "stove". But, as the German haiku poet and critic Hajo Jappe has pointed out, a person stumbling into a house snow-blind is unlikely to see anything so subtle as the glow of the coal stove. If we take our time with the later version, we find the heat of the stove before catching sight of it, which is truer to the experience, as well as a more interesting combination of sensations. The revision also makes the poem a bit briefer. (I think it could use more pruning, as could many German haiku, which so far tend to be written in the seventeen-syllable format, and therefore are as long as English-language efforts in that form.)

Sometimes one changes a poem to achieve a different image, and therefore present a different experience. This poem by Michael McClintock was first published in *Haiku Byways* in the spring of 1971:

> rowing downstream;
>   the red leaves   fall
>   in my lap

Later the same year the poem appeared in his collection *Light Run*
as:

rowing downstream
red leaves   swirling
behind me

Here McClintock has dropped a rather melodramatic image to
move to one that seems more natural, and yet carries more
motion. We may note that when one rows downstream one faces
upstream, and that "behind me" may be taken to mean behind
the boat. The leaves swirl behind him, seeming to float upstream.
Thus the red leaves, symbolic of decay and death for all their
bright color, swirl on in the wake of his passage; but he is going
downstream, as they are, some faster and some slower, but all
going downstream.

Bashō, Pound, Bodmershof, McClintock, all worked to clarify,
to make their poems increasingly accurate to their perceptions
and to the experiences they hoped to give their readers. The craft
of haiku comes to this: The language must be utterly clear,
stripped of all impediments to sharing.

10

Sharing Haiku

SHARING HAIKU PERSONALLY

By now you are probably ready to start composing haiku, if indeed you have not composed some already. Earlier I said, "The central act of haiku is letting an object or event touch us, and then sharing it with another." When we want to share something with a friend or family member who is right there with us, we usually point to the object, or possibly re-enact the action, that we want to share. An experienced haiku poet might well compose a haiku and recite it on the spot. If the person we wish to share with is not present, perhaps a haiku written or typed as part of a card or note can be left as a message or mailed to the absent person.

Haiku poets, when writing to each other, frequently include a recently composed haiku, perhaps at the beginning or end of a letter. In the course of writing this book I received a number. L. A. Davidson, then Recording Secretary of the Haiku Society of America, closed a business letter to me with

> after all these lighthouses
> still drawing them crooked

which caused me to remember that the Davidsons take their sail-
boat out at almost every opportunity, and she has been drawing
lighthouses for some time. There is a broader expanse of time
here than found in most haiku, but the wry tone suggests a sen-
ryu quality too (see Chapter 15, Beyond Haiku). By closing a busi-
ness letter with this allusion to her own avocations—the sea and
drawing—she personalized the letter and gave me a chuckle. It
was a delightful light touch at just the right place.

Early last spring I received a note from Elizabeth Searle Lamb
acknowledging receipt of a package I had sent her. She headed
her note with this haiku:

> a plastic rose
> rides the old car's antenna—
> spring morning

How appropriate to respond to a shipment with mention of a
vehicle and the season in which the goods were received. While
I do not generally like plastic flowers, this one endeared itself to
me immediately.

A few years ago Cor van den Heuvel sent me a Christmas
card on which he had written this poem, immediately one of my
favorites:

> the little girl
> hangs all the ornaments
> on the nearest branch

Speaking of Christmas cards, when I was working on this
handbook's first draft a number of my friends received letters that
ended with a haiku I had composed during the first week of
December that year:

> a yellow paper
> zig-zags to the floor
> bare trees

In this short image I tried to capture the sense of a writer at work and the passing of the seasons going almost unnoticed. Friends who knew that I was working hard to meet my publisher's deadline would understand if I was not answering their letters or getting out my Christmas cards as quickly as usual.

This sort of personal sharing is the ideal use of haiku. We give a friend, in a few words, a capsule image of how we are, what is going on in our lives, how we feel about "things".

VARIETIES OF PUBLICATION

Writing a haiku and sending it along to one or a few friends in a letter or handwritten cards is one thing, but to pick one and have it printed on a number of cards, or perhaps a letterhead, is another. A few years ago one of America's finest haiku poets sold note paper with some of his haiku printed on them, one to a sheet. They sold fairly well in the little shop that he and his wife ran. I can imagine someone delighting in taking this poem by John Wills as a springboard for writing a short note to a friend:

> keep out sign
> but the violets keep on
> going

If you happen to come up with a few particularly noteworthy haiku a local quick print shop can help you to put them on any number of cards, letterheads, or note papers.

The idea of having poetry around, visually, in our daily lives has been a major feature of East Asian culture for centuries. Today in Japan one can find haiku and other traditional poems in lovely calligraphy on everyday objects, and on a variety of scrolls, cards, and specially printed papers made for display. While famous masterpieces by ancient poets often find their way onto such objects, one of my favorite examples is the following poem, which was given to me by a Japanese friend on a thin towel of the kind used in Japanese kitchens, and often as bandanas and headbands by Japanese laborers. The poem is by a woman of Hokkaido, Japan's northernmost island, who makes a living selling her poems on towels, poem cards, and the like:

> *waga kokoro*   as my heart
> *takayuku toki ya*   goes soaring off—
> *momochidori*   ten myriad birds
>
> *Ogawa Yoshino*

Takayuku, "goes soaring off", is associated in the old poetry with the *hayabusa,* a peregrine falcon, a brave bird given to solitary, lofty flights. The phrase *momochidori,* "ten myriad birds", means "hearing something that sounds as though a hundred thousand ... small birds had swarmed together to make a concert"—according to one Japanese season word guide. So, the author's heart—for which read spirit—goes soaring off like a falcon as she hears the cacophony of chirps from a flock of small birds. The contrast is especially striking when we consider that it appears on a towel, one of the more common instruments of everyday life.

One of the major satisfactions in writing is having people tell you how much they enjoyed reading your work. A local form of publication—putting your writing where the people who see you every day, week, and month will see it—frequently brings more satisfaction than national exposure. In a school environment this can mean bulletin boards (in the hall, preferably, and at a level where one's peers can read it), and sheets printed and distributed by some readily available and inexpensive means, such as spirit or stencil duplicators. Often among a small group of friends one or another will have access to inexpensive copying in modest quantities. And if it costs a little bit, so much the better—people will concentrate on selecting a few good poems for publication, rather than papering the walls of the world with every weak attempt.

Recently, one public use of haiku has puzzled, amused, and sometimes pleased commuters in cities like Boston, Philadelphia, and Cleveland, where advertisement-sized placards with short poems on them were placed among the ads on buses. Several of the poems used were haiku, which probably provided a momentary respite from the rat race for a few riders who looked at them long enough to figure out that they were not selling anything. Poetry on the buses may have been a short-lived fad; I have not heard anything about it for a year or more. But it may break out again soon in your community, and if you are writing haiku you might submit some. The placards usually give an address to send comments and inquiries to.

There are a number of magazines that publish haiku in the English language. They are "little magazines"—little not so much in size as in circulation. Some that were active in the 1960s and 1970s are mentioned in Chapter 5, The Haiku Movement, and more have undoubtedly started up (and others ceased publication) during the interval between my writing and your reading this. The easiest way to keep up is to get a list of haiku magazines that is updated each year. In English the best such list appears in *The International Directory of Little Magazines and Small Presses*, published and updated every summer. This guide lists some four thousand magazine and book publishers who specialize in every conceivable subject from agriculture to Zen. They are indexed by geography and subject—the current edition lists more than twenty-five places to publish haiku. For any writer interested in that first step beyond local publication, *The International Directory* is a must; it is listed among the resources at the end of this handbook. (Editors or publishers who would like to be listed in the *Directory* should write to the publisher for a listing form.)

Haiku poets who write in languages other than Japanese or English may also find magazines that publish haiku in their own languages, beyond those few mentioned in Chapter 6, Haiku Around the World. Major university libraries, teachers, national and local arts councils and writers' organizations may help you locate them. Ask around. If you do not find any magazine to your liking, start your own. And bear in mind that several haiku magazines published in English are receptive to work in other languages, especially if provided with an English translation. Some editors will take the trouble to put a notice in their magazines inviting readers who speak your language to write to you, which could perhaps lead to translation and publication of your work.

In addition to magazine publication, many haiku poets have published books of their works. Some have waited until they published a number of poems in magazines, which gave them the reassurance that someone else thought their haiku worth publishing, before trying book publication. Others, disdainful perhaps of the bickering about haiku that sometimes erupts in the magazines, or not caring to "submit" their work to the individual judgments of a few editors, have published books on their own to give to friends or persons who they thought would be interested. Some of these books were published by presses that have a special interest in haiku. Some were published by the authors themselves, perhaps with the help of a friend or two. And some were published by cooperative efforts among a group of persons who respected one another's work and contributed time and money toward mutual publication. Most of the more serious publishers of haiku in English are also listed in *The International Directory* mentioned above.

Several books by English-language haiku poets represented in this handbook are listed with the Resources at the back of this book, with their publishers. Book publishers, like magazine editors, come and go. It is a good idea to check the current *International Directory* to see if they are still in business before sending work to one. In the meantime, not too many serious book publishers will be interested in publishing your haiku if you have had none of them in magazines; for the new haiku poet the magazines are a good place to begin publishing beyond your local area.

Even if you wish to publish yourself, and thus retain artistic control over your books, you can use some information. First, you should know the work that is getting published. Subscribing to some of the haiku magazines will help you find that out. Second, you will want to do the best job of publishing your own work that you can for the money you can afford to spend. Often the difference between a good-looking (and well-reviewed) book and a sloppy-looking (and not-reviewed) book is the knowledge and care that went into producing it, rather than the cash expended at the print shop. *The International Directory* lists a number of books on how to publish your own in the front of the current edition, so I will not go further into it here. But I heartily recommend studying a good book or two on the subject before proceeding. The money spent now will save several times its value in cash later, not to mention the time not wasted and the misunderstandings avoided.

Poetry readings have become very popular in the United States during the past decade or two. A poetry reading at a school or public library can usually be set up by a poet or a group of poets simply by asking the librarian and leaving some samples of the works that will be read. It is probably better to have a small group of poets read, rather than one poet alone, if the library does not have a tradition of sponsoring poetry readings. If each poet who is to read has two or three friends come the group will have a respectable audience. Also note that if you plan to give a reading you should *practice* reading your poems out loud! At first, perhaps, in front of a mirror; then in your home for family and eventually a few friends. Unless you have had experience reading your own work in front of an audience it can be pretty frightening. I know school teachers who, despite performing every day in front of class after class, "freeze up" in front of an audience of a dozen strangers when they try to read their own poems.

HAIKU CLUBS AND
ORGANIZATIONS

Writers often feel most comfortable sharing their work with other
writers. Literary history abounds with examples. Even the most
isolated writers often correspond with several others. Many writ-
ers enjoy banding together in groups that can easily meet once a
week or month to share and discuss one another's work, and per-
haps the work of other writers whom they admire. Such groups
may be organized on a fairly formal basis, with officers and by-
laws and so on, or may be as simple as the housewives or stu-
dents who get together in someone's kitchen or dorm room every
so often. If you and a neighbor are both interested in haiku, or
writing of any kind, you can start a group of two—it will proba-
bly grow.

Often a local group will meet in a municipal or branch library,
or will post notices of their meetings there. Y's and adult educa-
tion centers may serve as focal points for more or less formal writ-
ing workshop groups; ask librarians, English teachers, anyone
you can think of who might be interested in writing or know peo-
ple who are, about activities near you.

In Japan there are hundreds of haiku clubs, each usually serv-
ing members in a particular geographical area, publishing a
monthly magazine and often annual anthologies of members'
haiku and articles on haiku. In Europe and the Americas, where
the geography is broader and the population of serious haiku
enthusiasts thinner, there are relatively few clubs that have as
much activity as a typical Japanese haiku club. But there is at least
one group in the United States that functions in many, if not all,
of the ways of a Japanese haiku group. The Haiku Society of
America, Inc. was founded in 1968 in New York City. Today it
has a few hundred members, scattered all over North America,
Europe, and Japan, and publishes a quarterly magazine. The

HSA, as it is known to members, has no paid staff, so correspondence is slow, but it will respond to queries with a helpful information sheet about haiku and haiku activities. The HSA is listed among the Resources at the end of this handbook. In addition to the Haiku Society of America, Inc., there is now a Museum of Haiku Literature in Tokyo, with an International Division that tries to keep up with developments world-wide. And there are haiku organizations of one kind or another in some European countries. I have listed all that I know of as this book goes to press in the Resources at the end. (Directors of haiku societies in languages other than Japanese are welcome to send me pertinent information for possible inclusion in future editions of *The Haiku Handbook;* see my address at the beginning of Resources.)

BEYOND HAIKU CIRCLES

In this chapter mass-circulation,"slick" magazines and large commercial publishers have not been mentioned. Haiku is slowly growing in the West, but no individuals have been able to attract enough attention to their own work to interest a major commercial publisher. And the editors of magazines outside the haiku community generally know so little about haiku that what they do publish in the genre is often cause for embarrassment. The haiku used by such magazines tend to be "cute"—and are viewed by their editors as fillers, not as literature.

But the times are changing, and I hope that books of high quality haiku by Western authors will increasingly find their way into bookstores, and eventually into the lists of the largest publishers. Who knows, perhaps quality haiku—and other poetry—will someday grace the mass media.

In the meantime, I will continue to share what I write with my family and a few close friends, and send haiku that seem to strike a responsive chord with them to haiku magazines, and perhaps even put together a collection of my own, when I think I have enough good ones. I hope you will do the same.

Sharing with one's family, friends, and perhaps a public audience, is one of the main purposes of haiku. But it is not the only one. The last chapter, The Uses of Haiku, takes up where this chapter leaves off.

Part Three

TEACHING
HAIKU

11

Haiku for Kids

JAPANESE POEMS FOR AMERICAN SCHOOL KIDS?

Why use Japanese poems? Because many Japanese poets remain in the "child mind" that sees things as they really are:

kugibako no	the nail box:
kugi ga minna	every nail
magatte iru	is bent

Ozaki Hōsai (haiku poet, 1885–1926)[*]

There are no metaphors, personifications, or other "literary devices" in this poem. A metaphor or similar technique, no matter how apt, would momentarily distract us from the object itself by referring to something *outside* the here and now experience. Hōsai gives us no confusion of focus, only direct seeing of real things. The Epic Aroma of Thunderous Meters?—replaced, by a

---

[*]Uncredited translations are my own. See Resources at the end of this handbook for works quoted.

subtle onomatopoeia that makes words more like things than like thoughts.

The "words-as-things" approach works even when the rhythms take on human concern and metaphor shows the human-eye-seeing almost as much as the-thing-seen, like this:

> dadadan dadadan dadadan dadadan dan dan
> dan dan dan dan dah dah dah

> night wind licking the Kurashio crawls over the field &.
> three bonfires blaze.
> cra-ra-rackling.
> swinging flames.
>   dan dan dan dan
> boys leopard skins round their waists.
> drumsticks carving the wind &.
>   dan dan dadadan . . .

> *from "hachijo rhapsody"*
> *Kusano Shimpei (b. 1903)*
> *tr. Cid Corman and Kamaike Susumu*

I sense a directness here unlike much of anything in English after Chaucer until William Carlos Williams rammed us back into life, present, intense. Things not so much described as presented.

The most romantic of early twentieth century Japanese poets writes directly from the experience of his senses:

> came to
> a mirror shop
> what a jolt—
> I could've been
> some bum walking by

> *Ishikawa Takuboku (tanka poet,*
> *1885–1912) tr. Carl Sesar*

as did the earliest Japanese poets we know:

> The sound
> Of the gourds
> Struck for the pleasure
> Of the courtiers
> Reverberates through the shrine.

> *Anonymous tanka, before 800 A.D.*
> *tr. Donald Philippi*

The Japanese have always been keen observers of all nature, including human nature:

> "What's this for?"
>   Says the carpenter
> As he cuts it off.

> *Anonymous senryu, ca. 1800*
> *tr. R. H. Blyth*

as are today's Japanese schoolchildren:

Daddy

> Daddy is going to his office.
> I waved my hand "Goodbye."
> Daddy waved his hand too.
> My younger sister said,
> "Goodbye."
> He waved his hand again.
> Mommy said, "Goodbye."
> He didn't wave his hand.
> Why?

> *Kamiko Yoshiko, age 6*
> *tr. Haruna Kimura*

Japanese folk poetry, like that of other peoples, arises from daily life. The feelings of the moment, of the only time we ever truly know, now, come directly through in poems like this:

> Fog clings
> To the high mountain;
> My eye clings
> To him.

> *Anonymous dodoitsu, early 20th century*
> *tr. Eric Sackheim*

Having studied Japanese poetry seriously, I do not want to muddy the considerable differences among the various genres. But I think there is an important unity in Japanese poetry, and we would do well to capitalize on it, rather than dote on the superficial formal characteristics of one poorly understood genre such as the haiku. So, why use Japanese poems in the American classroom? Because they come directly from the experience of the poets, and usually steer clear of the metaphorical cover-up so characteristic of much popular Western poetry.*

Because of the directness and intensity of many Japanese poems, readers and hearers can understand them easily (unless they happen to name unfamiliar objects). Any response a child or adult makes to them cannot be called "wrong"—most of these poems do not require esoteric explanations. Teachers are freed to help children find their own understandings of these poems, just as they must find their own understandings of the world, which also requires more paying attention than esoteric knowledge.

---

*The main exception to this statement is the so-called "Court Poetry". Typical of our involvement with Asian literature, the most indirect kind of Japanese poetry has got most attention from Western scholars—e.g., Brower and Miner's *Japanese Court Poetry*. Most of Arthur Waley's work in Japanese literature also deals with the Court Poetry and the culture that produced it.

The haiku and its companion genre senryu* demonstrate these unique characteristics of Japanese poetry at their most intense concentration. In them metaphorical thinking, seeing something as having the qualities of something else and using that perception as a *descriptive* technique, seldom appears. Often things and events do illuminate one another, but never one at the expense of the other. Haiku and senryu depend for their effect primarily upon the single significant image clearly and directly presented, or upon a striking juxtaposition of two such images. Haiku are almost never philosophical or didactic in intent; senryu often are, but the better senryu teach in the same way parables teach, with pictures from life. And the best haiku seem to come from a mind as clear as a mountain spring.

Over ten years ago, when I began visiting schools to lead writing workshops, I was reluctant to use haiku in the classroom. The lack of readily available quality translations gave me pause. Also, I felt that the word "haiku" had been so contaminated by the number of sentimental five-seven-fives produced in schools that I did not want to be associated with the term in that environment, though I had edited *Haiku Magazine* for a few years. Finally, I did not wish to be drawn into discussions of "the haiku form"—terminology which I believe has been mainly responsible for many Westerners' poor understanding of the haiku genre.

These problems kept me from presenting haiku to American schoolchildren for almost a year, unless cornered by the expectations of some schoolteacher or administrator. When so cornered, I usually fell into the pedant's last resort, declaiming what a haiku is not.

However, the appearance of *The Haiku Anthology: English Language Haiku by Contemporary American and Canadian Poets* in 1974 helped me to find a way to circumvent the bull without being gored on the horns of misunderstood terminology. The fol-

---

*The Glossary at the back of this handbook gives definitions for all the names of Japanese poetic genres used in this chapter.

lowing is the diary of the first happy haiku day in my Poets-in-the-Schools career, with added examples from other days, other schools.

MY FIRST HAPPY HAIKU DAY IN SCHOOL: A DIARY

Today will be different. I will simply present the haiku itself. By presenting the poems themselves, and helping children to see how they are constructed, I will give them the *experience* of haiku without causing the confusion that using the *word* "haiku" would bring about. (It is important to pick poems that do not require explanations of the words or images; having a book with excellent haiku written by members of the students' own culture makes this easier.)

First class: Immediately after walking in, I wait for their full attention, then explain that I am about to read a number of very short poems. The poems are so short that if they miss one word they will miss the whole poem. I also say that they can respond to the poems in any way they want to, that there is no correct or incorrect response, and that I will pause at the end of each poem for them to laugh, cry, giggle—whatever they want to do. I then read them about thirty-five poems from *The Haiku Anthology*. I choose those with extremely clear, sense-appealing images, some quite traditional, like:

> Snow falling
> on the empty parking lot:
> Christmas Eve . . .
>
> *Eric W. Amann*

I also deliberately mix in a number that seem quite mysterious, whether through choice of image, juxtaposition, or use of language, and carefully include several with modern, city images, such as:

> Moonlit sleet
> In the holes of my
> Harmonica
>
> *David Lloyd*

> In the laundermat
>   she peers into the machine
>   as the sun goes down.
>
> *Sydell Rosenberg*

> the old barber
>   sweeping hair
> into the giant bag
>
> *James Tipton*

> an empty wheelchair
> rolls
> in from the waves
>
> *Cor van den Heuvel*

> The silence
>   in moon light
>   of stones
>
> *Virginia Brady Young*

I try to pick a number that rely on senses other than sight, or on more than one sense:

> Under ledges
> and looking for the coolness
> that keeps touching my face.
>
> *Foster Jewell*

crickets . . .
then
thunder

Larry Wiggin

In all of this, I read very slowly, concentrating on careful enunciation and giving full weight to both punctuation- and line-break-indicated pauses, leaving space between poems for response. The reading goes over well, the children laughing, squirming, or wide-eyed at almost every poem. The thirty-five poems take only seven to ten minutes.

After reading the poems, I tell the kids that these poems are all made up of "images"—and without further explanation *I ask them to tell me what images are.* Very quickly, as I write their responses on the board, we have several senses listed, and such phrases as "in your mind", "thinking about pictures", and "in your imagination" come out. I pounce on this last, immediately writing IMAGINATION out across the blackboard in foot-high capitals. Then I say, circling and underlining the letters as I go,

"Imagination is 'I'   **I M A G Ⓘ N A T I O N**

in the 'country'   **I M A G Ⓘ N A T I O N**

of 'images'!"   **I M A G Ⓘ N A T I O N**

The aptness of this mnemonic shocks even me.

I go on to ask where images can come from and, after a little prodding, I get them to agree with me that there are basically three sources:

1.	the senses	images within the range of *here and now* vision, hearing, touch, and so on.
2.	the memory	images *stored in the mind*, whether from personal experience or from books, movies, etc.

3. the fantasy   images *invented in the mind*, usually by
                       combining material from the senses and/
                       or the memory.

I also point out that I am making a distinction between the words
"fantasy" and "imagination". While "fantasy" refers only to
those new images invented in the mind, I think of "imagination"
as referring to all mental images.

All this, and only twenty minutes have elapsed since the start
of the lesson! And, more important, each child seems to be
actively following the whole thing, delighting in the poems, more
than half of them contributing to the lively discussion and giving
examples of new thought in its most joyful mode.

It is important for me to remember that all this discussion,
covering topics that could well be the subject of a seminar in a
graduate school writing program, arose spontaneously *from the
children* and from me in a live atmosphere of curiosity, high
energy, and delight. I must keep in mind for the future that the
particular details of the discussion, of the terminology, have to
arise from the children, and that any guiding hand I supply must
come from honest interaction with their minds *as equals*, or I will
sap the energy of this interchange. I was writing *their* words on
the board.

To the writing. To make sure that everyone has a real working
knowledge of what an image is, I suggest that we make up a
poem containing two images which connect in some strange way.
Asking anyone to call out an image, I get "The Washington Mon-
ument", which I put on the board as I wonder where we could
possibly go with that. I ask for another image to pair with that,
one which will "draw sparks" from it. Given as good as asked,
and with a war whoop I present their handiwork to them on the
board:

                    The Washington Monument
                    The Lincoln Tunnel

Asking the kids what makes this a good poem produces imme-
diate answers like "They're both presidents' names." "One goes
up, the other you look at the inside."

Overjoyed at their understanding, but still wondering if **we** can cool it a little bit and get a more or less straight haiku-like poem from the class, I ask them for images that are not major landmarks, and momentarily two of the quieter kids respond:

> a desert island
> a single flower

At this point I know it is time to shut up and let them write. I encourage them to write anything, so long as it is just images.

Here are a few of the more haiku-like images that resulted from working with four classes of fourth and fifth graders that first day:

> The big eyed owl hooing in the dark.

> Big skinny frogmen looking for treasure divers.

> A man with so much hair you can't see his head
> A bag with a head in it

> An old jukebox
> A funny record

> An overweight dinosaur
> A flattened out archeologist

> Reading a book
> Remembering what it was about

> A cactus plant.
> A dark pink flower.

As with any lesson plan used frequently, I have deliberately varied my approach somewhat through the day, and of course each class has its own personality to add to the mix. Trying the same basic approach with sixth graders in another school produced work like this:

> The tired old doctor
> The dusty girl

> The sound of a light bulb
> when it's off.

And I took the same plan to a middle school, where working with seventh and eighth graders produced these:

> The fire flickering in the distance
> consuming
> everything in sight.

> old leather wallet
> luxurious apartment

Of course, some of the poems quoted above would not qualify as haiku according to a strictly traditional view of the genre. But many would. More important in terms of a teaching objective, children have been actively engaged in using highly imagistic language, and doing so with a reasonable understanding of what they were doing—with pleasure.

In each of these classes several students wrote lists of images or more complex, layered images. I did not discourage them as long as they *were* writing images, not wanting to interfere with the energy of the writing and with their pleasure in it.

I should note the two remaining features of each session on writing images. First, I—as writer/teacher—write when my students write. This helps them to understand that writing is an adult activity (and therefore one they are more likely to value and wish to participate in), and gives them a sense that they are colleagues with the teacher instead of workers under the direction of a classroom foreman. (I do, usually, write something down quickly and then move around the room quietly helping the occasional student who cannot think of anything to write. This often simply involves pointing to some thing in the room or out the window, and asking them if they can capture that image in words.) Second, since the poems are short, there is usually time for everyone to read at least one aloud. I ask them to circle or star the one they like best, and have each person read one, beginning with volunteers, and moving to the shyer ones after others have read theirs. If students are painfully shy, I will sometimes read theirs to the class myself—often theirs are among the best. Somewhere in the middle of the reading I will usually read one I have just written, if I think it will not take up so much time as to prevent us from hearing all of the students.

ANOTHER POET'S APPROACH

Poet Ron Padgett noticed one particular feature of many classical Japanese haiku, and communicated his excitement about it to a group of students. Here is how he describes the experience:

> I explained to the students that there were haiku I liked, and that what I liked about them—among other things—was the way they often surprised you at the end. There would be two lines, usually about nature, and then a final line which at first didn't seem to have anything much to do with the first two lines. To demonstrate this I drew two straight parallel lines across the blackboard: these represented the first two lines of the poem. "Make them about nature, make them 'pretty' or 'nice' things about nature." Under these I drew a third line. "Make this last line a complete surprise, something that has *nothing* to do with the first two lines." I also told them to forget about counting syllables.
>
> The extemporaneous examples I then made up gave the kids a strong slant down which they slid into their own poems. A greater variety of examples at this point would have lent a greater variousness to the results.
>
> Here are some of the haiku written by fifth graders during that class period:

Silent are the trees
blowing in the wind
Donald Duck drowning in Lake Erie

Flowers in the garden
They are beautiful
Time for bed

It's raining out
the rivers overflow
and I'm listening to the radio

Little red roses
popping out of the ground
a car blowing up

It is summer
The river is flowing
My friend has blond hair

Perhaps the assignment worked so well because its simplicity and economy suggest the simplicity and economy of the haiku. In any case, the kids took great glee in setting up the first two lines so they could detonate them in the last line.

In the haiku parody I wrote during that period, I seemed to be trying to detonate all the bad haiku I had read and the tedious way haiku had been taught. I took line- and syllable-counting to its extreme: "First: five syllables / Second: seven syllables / Third: five syllables"—count 'em.

Kids are very good at pleasing their teachers, as thousands of bulletin boards full of five-seven-fives attest. Like the kids, I get more excitement from writing about my friend's blond hair or a dark pink cactus flower than from examples such as "Sweetly blows the wind / through the beautiful flowers / of the spring garden."—which is better than most of what inhabits those bulletin boards. If our students are to become excited about haiku it will help if we are also excited about it. But it will help more if they find the haiku exciting in itself, because it gives them a chance to express and share their own perceptions, which perhaps we should accord the courtesy of receiving, rather than trying to impress our own upon them.

12

A Lesson Plan That Works

*by Penny Harter**

SHARING A CONCERN

Most teachers would have a hard time doing what Bill did in the lesson presented in the last chapter. Mainly, they would not have the background in haiku that he acquired through several years of study. That background, and his experience as a writer in a classroom, rather than a teacher, also allowed him to jettison the "haiku objective" when something else equally interesting was going on. His main purpose was to get kids to write and think in

*Poet and fiction writer Penny Harter has taught writing in many public schools in New Jersey over the past several years. Asked to help high school teachers present haiku, she came up with this lesson plan, since used in two districts.

terms of images, and he was not too concerned with whether or not the products of his sessions were indeed haiku.

But what of the teacher who does want students to learn what a haiku "really is"—and be able to write some? I have tried to work up a lesson plan that any teacher can use, at almost any grade level. I have also developed and used media in many of my lessons, so I worked out ways that media could be effectively incorporated into the lesson plan.

I had an opportunity to test the results of using my lesson plan in regular senior high school English classes. To demonstrate the effectiveness of using this plan I also gave the students tests on cognitive knowledge of haiku and skill at writing haiku both before and after the lesson. These tests resulted in a number of verses which were then given to Bill to judge anonymously, and without knowing which had come from pre-tests and which from post-tests. Obviously, very few of the pre-test efforts resembled haiku. However, not only were a large proportion of the post-test efforts recognizable as haiku, several of them were of publishable quality. Here is a sampling of the results; remember, these are not written in a workshop situation, but in a test! I am not normally in favor of asking for this kind of creative effort in a testing situation. In this case I explained to the students that we were testing the lesson plan, rather than them individually. The students did not receive grades as a result of this test.

Lavender flowers
against the sky—
petals soft as air.

Butterfly floats
through the air.
Cloudy autumn sky.

The old fisherman
mending his nets
throughout the night.

A white night
shadows of snow
on the ground.

Wet sand
tumbling back
into the sea.

Seagulls flying
over ruined sand castles
carried by the wind.

Hitchhiker   A boat
He turns as I speed past   on the water
Driving alone   after the hurricane

A baby cries at the window,
a hearse passes by.

Discarded blossoms litter the path
An old woman sweeps.

The students who received this lesson also did well on the cognitive parts of the test, both when it was given the following day, and when it was given again three weeks later.

The teacher whose classes I taught in this experiment has since adopted my lesson plan and regularly teaches haiku to her creative writing students. She has also begun writing haiku herself, and both she and some of her students have had their haiku published by reputable haiku magazines. The poems written in her classes were sent to the magazines as regular submissions, and were not identified as student writing.

I am not sure that publication of writing by students should be the goal of every literature class, but publication certainly does suggest that the students learned to appreciate the genre they were studying. The editors who have accepted work from such students have given them grades that will mean something to those students long after the memory of a particular quiz or test grade has faded.

A HAIKU LESSON

The following lesson plan gives complete instructions for a forty-five-minute class in haiku. You may modify the lesson to suit your own needs and ways of presenting material.

Read your students the very short poems that follow. Read slowly, concentrating on careful enunciation and sufficient

pauses for line breaks, without making the reading unnatural.
Pause for a longer time between poems. The reading of these will
take about five minutes. Tell them to just listen and enjoy, using
their imaginations. These poems are so short that every word
counts, and if students miss one word they may miss the entire
poem. When you pause at the end of each poem, students may
want to laugh, cry, giggle . . . or just have a quiet feeling inside,
of joy or sorrow, of humor or horror.

> Billboards . . .
>   wet
>   in spring
>   rain . . .
>
> *Eric W. Amann*

> Holding the water,
>   held by it—
>   the dark mud.
>
> *William J. Higginson*

> someone's newspaper
> drifts with the snow
> at 4 a.m.
>
> *Jack Cain*

> Broken kite, sprawled
>   on a sand dune, its line caught
>   in the beach plum . . .
>
> *Elizabeth Searle Lamb*

> Sunset dying
>   on the end of a rusty
>   beer can . . .
>
> *Gary Hotham*

A Hallowe'en mask
  floating face up in the ditch,
    slowly shakes its head.

Clement Hoyt

Fallen horse—
flies hovering
in the vulture's shadow

Geraldine Clinton Little

Autumn twilight:
  the wreath on the door
  lifts in the wind.

Nicholas Virgilio

(All from *The Haiku Anthology: English Language Haiku by American and Canadian Poets*, edited by Cor van den Heuvel (Doubleday, 1974), as are others not attributed to students.)

After reading these poems, tell the students that the poems are all made up of images, that the images create the emotions they had as they listened to the poems. Then ask the students what they think an image is. Write their responses on the blackboard. These responses will probably include "pictures, in your mind, in your imagination". Try to get as many students as possible to tell you something about the poems, and what they think an image is. After getting several responses on the board, tell the students that—in writing—an image is a group of words which presents an object or objects, and possibly some action, that appeals to the senses. The things named in an image can be seen, touched, heard, smelled, or tasted; or the reader may get from an image a sense of temperature, pain, or movement.

There are more than five senses. Here is a haiku showing the sense of movement, as well as a number of others. How many can your students find in it?

walking the snow-crust
not sinking
sinking

Anita Virgil

Write down the senses, starting with "movement", as they say them. If there are any responses that you or members of the class do not understand, let the student responding explain. Accept and record on the board all answers that seem to have valid explanations. (I have no trouble accepting "smell", for example. See the discussion of this poem in Chapter 9, The Craft of Haiku.)

Now ask where images come from. Again, write their responses on the board. When you have responses that seem to fit the categories "here and now", "memory", and "fantasy" or "made-up in the mind", point out that these are the three sources. "Imagination" will probably come up—point out that "imagination" has the word "image" in it, and can refer to all three categories.

One of the powers of poetry, of haiku especially, is to create emotions by connecting two or more images together in new and strange ways. Read aloud these two examples of poems that do this, written by students:

the little bird
hopping
across the parking lot

empty fish tank
bubbles

Ask the students what two images come together in each of the poems you have just read. One way of expressing these is: (1) A bird hopping across asphalt instead of grass. (2) A tank full of water, with bubbles to give fish air—when there are no fish.

Now ask students to write some of their own. They can remember some images, or take some images from something right here and now, or make some up. If anyone asks what to do just encourage them by saying something like: "Just go ahead and write a few poems like the ones we've been talking about." Write some yourself—in a workshop the leader leads by going ahead. If the students see you writing (1) they will realize that you are serious, and (2) they will be a little less likely to bother you with unnecessary questions. Besides, writing yourself will distract you from worrying about those who do not start right away, but need some time to shift gears from taking in to putting out. It is okay if a few do not start writing right away. When they see the others writing they will get to it.

Allow about five to seven minutes. Then ask some to read one or two of theirs aloud. Have them point out the images in their own poems, noting whether they have one or two, or more. They should be particularly conscious of images that are alike, or contrast sharply. If you feel the need, you may underscore the use of two contrasting or similar images with the following examples:

Into the blinding sun . . .
the funeral procession's
glaring headlights.

Nicholas Virgilio

Muttering thunder . . .
the bottom of the river
scattered with clams

Robert Spiess

in the hotel lobby
the bare bulb of a floor lamp
shines down on its distant base

Cor van den Heuvel

All of these poems are haiku. There are a few more things about haiku that students should know. The haiku presents the event in an image, SHOWS us what happened, does not tell us about it or tell us what emotion to feel. "I was sad / when I saw / the dead cat." is not a haiku. This is:

> dead cat . . .
> open mouthed
> to the pouring rain
>
> *Michael McClintock*

It shows us the cat, and that makes us feel the sadness.

All of these poems tell of some *specific* event or observation. Haiku are not generalities.

Remind students that a haiku is short, usually fewer than ten words. It should not rime, usually, for that makes it sound like a sort of nursery rime, and takes our attention away from what the haiku has to show us. Occasionally a haiku will rime, and if the sound of the riming does not detract from the meaning of the poem that is okay. But deliberate riming usually makes the writer choose a word that is not accurate to the image, which is more important than getting in any particular sound.

You and your students may have heard that a haiku has to have seventeen syllables. Traditional Japanese haiku have usually contained about seventeen *onji*. But an *onji* in Japanese is not the same thing as a syllable in English. *Onji* are all quite short, and take about the same length of time to say, like the syllables in the English word *po-ta-to*. But in English syllables vary greatly in length, and some are quite long, like *wound, plough, cough,* or *wrenched.* In English haiku usually have fewer than seventeen syllables, though some poets do write them that way. And haiku in English are usually written in three lines, though they have also been written in one, two, or more than three lines.

Point out that haiku poets usually avoid similes or metaphors.

If we say "smoke rises like a twisted snake into the sky" we are using a simile; if we say "a twisted snake of smoke rises into the sky" we are using metaphor. In either case, a person hearing or reading this is likely to make a picture of a snake in the mind's sky, and that is not what the poem is really talking about. A haiku poet might say something simpler, like "Smoke rises, twisting, into the sky."

Tell students that in classical Japanese haiku one is required to indicate the season by a special word called a *kigo*, or "season word". Using "deer" or "moon" or "night of stars", for example, would indicate that the events of the poem took place in autumn. Haiku in English often show the season, but so far American, Canadian, and other poets writing in English have not tried to agree on a fixed set of season words, perhaps because the seasons vary more over the range of geography in which people speak English than they do in Japan.

Finally, tell students that the traditional Japanese haiku grew out of the *haikai-no-renga*, or comic linked poem, in which two or more poets would participate in an add-on, pass-around image game. Poets would gather to have *renga* parties. On the way to the party each poet would compose a *hokku*, or starting verse, in case he should be called upon to begin the *renga*. The starting verse had to contain references to the season and the place of composition. This explains the "here and now" feeling of most haiku. If the poet was not asked to begin the *renga* his *hokku* would be lost. But in later times some *hokku* were published independently in collections of *haikai-no-renga*. These became the first independent haiku.

Now have students try to write some more haiku. Remember to have them ask themselves these key questions as they write each one:

1. Is it brief?

2. Does it present one or two clear images, with no metaphors or similes?

3. Does the image, or do the images coming together, create an emotion in the reader *without* telling the reader what emotion to feel?

Finish the lesson by inviting whoever wants to to read their haiku to the class. Perhaps ask them to pick what they think is their best, and read it.

USING MEDIA TO TEACH HAIKU

The teacher who is comfortable with them can use a number of school media in addition to the chalkboard in the haiku lesson above. For example, write individual haiku to be used as examples on acetate with appropriate markers and show them on a screen with an overhead projector. Be sure to vary which poems you use from time to time, or, if you wish to make a permanent set of transparencies, obtain permission. Making a permanent copy of published material to use over and over again is a copyright violation. Many authors will be glad to grant permission if you ask in advance. They can usually be contacted through the publisher of the book in which their work appears, including this one. Or you can write the author or the editor of a book directly. (The address of the author of this handbook is listed at the beginning of Resources at the back.) An opaque projector can be used to show pages from books.

You might want to make up a transparency showing some of the Japanese words in the lesson plan.

A striking way to use media in teaching haiku has produced excellent results for me. I often use a group of twenty to thirty slides, most of them color photographs taken on vacations and the like, at the end of the lesson where I ask the students to continue writing haiku. These slides of objects, scenes from nature, and some of animals and people, provide the students with moments, objects, or events to write about. The writing is done simultaneously with the showing of the slides, not afterward. I tell the students that they are going to see a number of slides that will be full of things for them to write images from. There will be some slides that give a single image (for example, close-up shots of water in a stream), and some that bring two or more images together (like a cat on a windowsill watching a bird at the feeder). I show the slides, going through the whole set once so they can decide which ones they might like to write about. Then I go back to the beginning and proceed more slowly, stopping for a longer time on the five or six that several class members want to write about.

The students can write about any slides they wish to along the way—or about any other images they have in mind. I go back and forth through the whole set of slides a number of times. During the first showing, in particular, both the students and I usually comment on which pictures are especially striking, and would make good subjects for haiku. I encourage them to notice the slides which bring together two usually related objects in new ways. And occasionally students will read aloud what they have written.

At the end of the class I encourage any who wish to do so to read their haiku aloud. This may be done with the lights still partially out, to help everyone recall the slides, and to lend an air of informality and even anonymity to the readings.

If you do not take pictures yourself, you can often find colleagues who will be glad to lend you slides of their own. It is a good idea to specify that you want pictures of natural and/or interesting objects, and that if they have a strong center of attention they will be better for your purpose.

Another way to provide visual stimulation, other than projection media, is to find some large-format books with pictures that could serve the purpose. Some Sierra Club books, for example, have very good pictures. You can walk slowly around the room, showing pictures to a few students while the others are writing images from their memories or fantasies. Gradually you can cover the whole room this way, so that all will have a chance to work out of their own images in their minds and from the pictures you show them. (This also gives you a good excuse for moving around the room, and you can see how people are doing as you go around.)

If you find the lesson takes longer than you expected, you can do it without the pictures one day, and then remind the class of the haiku on another day and show pictures for them to write to at that time.

Classroom media should be used by teachers who are comfortable with them. They should be used unobtrusively, so that they seem a part of the natural flow of the lesson. Do not break the lesson up into several small segments of different media, hopping from one to another. Use the transparencies where they are convenient to you. If you half-darken the room for them, then it will be easy to slip into the darker conditions ideal for showing slides. There is no need to come back to full lighting in the middle of the lesson, between the last transparencies and the slides, if you use both. However, full lighting is needed for the chalkboard work at the beginning of each lesson.

RESULTS

As the examples from my lessons show, students can learn to write haiku. More important, they will learn to write strong, interesting images through these methods. It is not hard to show, in a short story, for instance, examples of sharp images, and note how they help to set the scene, move the action, or portray character. You do not have to tell the reader that a person who is standing biting a fingernail and tapping a foot is nervous.

Writing haiku can have many functions in life as well as in the classroom. Several of these uses for haiku form the subject of the final chapter of this handbook. But the important thing about writing haiku is that it makes us look at things, hear things, notice the touch and taste of things in ways that will connect us with the world around us, and help us articulate and share our experiences and perceptions with the people around us.

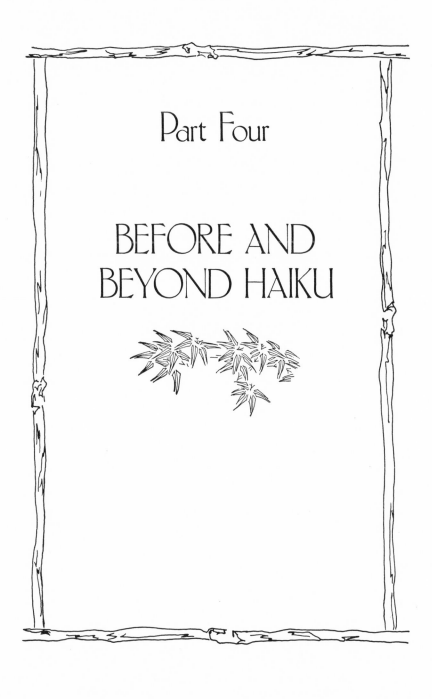

Part Four

BEFORE AND BEYOND HAIKU

13

Before Haiku

TRADITIONAL JAPANESE POETRY AND TANKA

A variety of genres makes up the whole of traditional Japanese poetry, each with its own characteristic content and formal structure. As in other traditional poetries, the content of each genre is almost as "fixed" as the form. In English poetry the name "ballad" suggests not only a certain metrical pattern but a certain type of content, for example, a story. In Japanese the word *dodoitsu* refers to a folk-song of work or love in a meter of seven-seven-seven-five onji (approximately), and so on.

In the beginning of Chapter 8, The Form of Haiku, I described the origins of tanka rhythm in the chōka, and presented examples of the two main stanzaic patterns, the five-seven / five-seven-seven pattern common in the *Manyōshū*, and the five-seven-five / seven-seven pattern that became prominent later on. But the tanka differs from other genres of Japanese poetry as much by content as by form. If the sonnet was the typical vehicle for the love poetry of Italian and English courtiers during the Renaissance, the tanka served a like function during the five centuries of the Nara and Heian Periods in Japan (taken together, roughly

700 to 1200 A.D.). However, while the sonnet seems usually to
be a poem in praise of an unattainable love, the tanka was the
main form in which notes were written and actually sent from
lover to lover, expressing desire or gratitude. The tanka was (and
is) also used to express appreciation of nature—in fact this was
among its first uses. Here is an anonymous example from the
Manyōshū:

ō-umi ni	on the great sea
shima mo aranaku ni	there are no islands
unabara no	on surging waves
tayutau nami ni	of the ocean plain
tateru shirakumo	stand white clouds

But from the late seventh century the *Manyōshū* records tanka
like this, written by Princess Nukuda, "thinking of the Emperor
Tenji":

kimi matsu to	waiting for you
waga koioreba	in longing . . .
waga yado no	making the blinds
sudare ugokashi	of my house move
aki no kaze fuku	autumn wind blows

And the *Manyōshū* also contains a number of examples of tanka
exchanges, or notes sent back and forth, often between lovers.

As the lives of the courtiers became more and more refined,
particularly after the capital moved from Nara to Heian-kyō
(present-day Kyoto) in the latter part of the eighth century, liter-
ature and the arts became the main means of expressing refine-
ment. Ivan Morris, in *The World of the Shining Prince: Court Life
in Ancient Japan*, notes one of the main features of the culture that
produced *The Tale of Genji* in these words:

> . . . Their civilization was, to a quite remarkable extent,
> based on aesthetic discrimination and, with the rarest of

exceptions, every gentleman and lady was an amateur performer in one or more of the arts.

Among the arts poetry was essential. The composition, exchange, and quotation of poems was central to the daily life of the Heian aristocracy, and it is doubtful whether any other society in the world has ever attached such importance to the poetic versatility of its members. . . .

While the aristocratic society of Heian-kyō put great store in refinement, a combination of knowledge of the art of the past and ability to create art on the spot, it also lived close to nature. The tanka in praise of nature continued, but natural imagery now more than before became the vehicle for expressing human concerns. Two major poets of the *Kokinshū*, an anthology compiled early in the tenth century, provide examples:

omoikane	thought unendurable
imo-gari yukeba	and going to her place
fuyu no yo no	the winter night's
kawakaze samumi	river-wind so chill
chidori naku nari	the plovers are crying

Ki no Tsurayuki

With the affair on my mind, went on a visit; from the road seeing the burnt-over fields, composed:

fuyugare no	thinking
nobe to waga mi o	myself a withered
omoiseba	winter field,
moete mo haru o	though burning, still one
matamashi mono o	who would await the spring

Lady Ise

Both poems compare features of the winter landscape with their authors' feelings. Tsurayuki's passion drives him out into the chill wind of the river; his unendurable thoughts of his lover rise from the heat of his passion just as the cries of the plovers rise from the cold of the wind. And Lady Ise's vision of the winter fields reminds her of her love-wracked body; her passion has consumed her so that she almost wonders if she would have entered into the relationship had she known the force of it beforehand. She burns with it, and wonders if she will be rejuvenated in the spring, like the fields burnt-over to stimulate spring growth.

TANKA REFORM AND OTHER GENRES

This short survey cannot give even a hasty impression of the shifting currents throughout several centuries of tanka composition. From the *Kokinshū*, completed about 914 A.D., to the *Shinzoku kokinshū*, completed in 1439, there are twenty-one imperial anthologies, with a total of about 33,000 poems, virtually all tanka. And the anthologies represent only the best-known and most fashionable works of their eras; just a portion of all the courtly tanka composed throughout the period made their way into these collections.

All through the long history of Japanese poetry tastes and styles have shifted, become more or less static, and then shifted again. Social, political, and economic factors have played a strong role in this process. But so have certain poets, who from time to time came on the scene and turned their backs on the fashionable concerns of their day to write in new ways. And new genres arose to challenge the supremacy of the tanka, once synonymous with *waka*, "Japanese poetry".

In this survey of the tanka I will mention only one more "court" poet, the Priest Saigyō (1118–1190), before skipping to modern developments in the genre. According to Earl Miner, the Japanese love the Priest Saigyō best of all the court poets. He also had perhaps the least to do with the court. I do not mean that Saigyō did not grow up in the court tradition. His family was renowned for military prowess, and he became a captain of guards in the highest levels of the court. He also served one of the most powerful families at court, and learned the art of poetry from the very best poets of the time. He left the court at the age of twenty-three to become a Buddhist monk. The aristocracy were shocked. He was young, gifted, and well placed. But instead of building this combination into a brilliant political career, he took the discipline of his military background and the art of poetry with him into the life of a religious.

Saigyō also literally left Heian-kyō to live, for various periods of time, in one religious retreat or another, and to travel more widely than any other poet of his time. In his travels Saigyō looked at the humble people, whose lives were unimaginable to those caught up in the brilliance of the court. He depicted their lives and their surroundings in ways that at first shocked, but later changed the sensibilities of the rest of the court poets. And though his poetry is deeply imbued with Buddhism and classical learning, not since the *Manyōshū* had a poet so sincerely celebrated nature for its own sake. The compilers who began working on the *Shinkokinshū* little more than a decade after his death included more of Saigyō's poems than any other poet's.

In viewing the activities of the common people, Saigyō can be almost brutally objective, as when he sees "divers in the open sea taking abalone":

iwa no ne ni	going toward
kataomomuki ni	the rocky bottom
namiukite	through waves
awabi o kazuku	diving for abalone
ama no muragimi	the head fisherman

Though his Buddhist understanding decreed it a sin to take the life of any creature, and many of his poems on clamming, shrimp

fishing, and the like lament the sinful nature of the work, Saigyō
maintained sympathy for the workers.

This tension, between the demands of Buddhism to give up
all attachment to the world and a love of the deep richness of life,
pervades much of Saigyō's poetry. He states it openly in his most
famous verse:

kokoro naki	even heartless
mi ni mo aware wa	my body must know
shirarikeri	how touching:
shigi tatsu sawa no	snipe rise from the marsh
aki no yūgure	in the autumn nightfall

The point is that no matter how much one—Saigyō—may seek
to extinguish one's feelings, the simplest observation of nature
will deeply move precisely the sort of person who tries to "aban-
don this world of illusion". Little wonder that Bashō loved so well
the verses of Saigyō, the traveling poet whose skill was only
exceeded by his dedication to Buddhism and his empathy with
nature.

The tanka, once the characteristic poetry of the aristocracy,
continues down to the present day. But only under the pressure
of European influence in the nineteenth and early twentieth cen-
turies did it flare up with a brightness that could again compare
with the great ages of the *Manyōshū*, the *Kokinshū*, and the *Shin-
kokinshū*. As the political and economic power in Japanese society
shifted from the aristocracy to the warrior class, and more grad-
ually to the rising "townsmen", literature also changed. Renga
replaced tanka as the dominant poetic genre, and later developed
into the haiku and senryu in turn. Literature became more pop-
ular in tone, and the refinement of the court was replaced by the
wit of the town.

Where courtly tanka poets had used natural imagery to
express their passions the townsmen used similar imagery in a
sort of tanka-*manqué*, called *kyōka*, to present the funnier sides of
their love life. In the latter part of the eighteenth century books

and special collections of wood-block prints with kyōka were published to suit the taste of the times. The old tanka and Chinese styles of painting did not die away. But, as has happened a number of times in Japanese literary history, the new vulgar take-off arose for a while to equal its staid ancestor in social, if not artistic, importance.

Utamaro, one of the great artists of the wood-block print, made several series of prints which had kyōka incorporated into them. Here is an example from a book called *Momochidori kyōka awase,* or "many-bird kyōka contest":

sadamenaki	fickle one
kimi ga kokoro no	with the heart of a
mura suzume	village sparrow
tsui ni ukina no	suddenly scandals
hatto tatsuran	will start to take off

Aya no Orinushi

The pen name fits the verse; Aya no Orinushi means "Master of Leash-Weavers". Perhaps the author's wit will be powerful enough to prevent the "sparrow"—and the scandals—from taking off.

Kyōka never achieved the staying power of senryu, which seemed to penetrate every tavern and teahouse for several decades. But the relationship between tanka and kyōka parallels that between haiku and senryu. The popular tone of kyōka mirrored the rising self-consciousness of the common people. However, only in the modern era has the tanka, with all its seriousness and passion, become the property of the mass of the Japanese people.

THE MODERN TANKA REVIVAL

Masaoka Shiki (1867–1902), who almost single-handedly preserved the haiku from oblivion in the face of the Western literature pouring into Japan in the late nineteenth century, tried to perform a like service for the tanka. While Shiki had advocated a clean pictorial style in haiku, and admitted modern images and modern sensibility, his main inspiration for the tanka reforms he proposed was the simplicity of the *Manyōshū*. The *Manyōshū* had been an anchor for several attempts at tanka reform earlier, but Shiki tended to write tanka even simpler and less romantic in tone than his own haiku.

Even when Shiki gives us a portrait of himself in fatigue— and no doubt pain—the language is excruciatingly spare, devoid of romance, almost chill in its objectivity:

cha   *tea*

yo o komete	crowding night
mono kakiwaza no	weary with the work
kutabire ni	of writing things
hi o fukiokoshi	blew the fire to life
cha o nomi ni keri	and drank some tea

Saitō Mokichi (1882–1953) never knew Shiki, but came upon a collection of Shiki's work, *Take no sato uta* ("Songs of a Bamboo Village"), and decided to become a poet. Mokichi was a great student of the *Manyōshū*, and completed a five-volume work on the most famous poet in it, Kakinomoto Hitomaro. What he admired in the *Manyōshū* was the immediacy of its images and the sincerity of its feelings. He tried to apply these principles to his own, modern tanka, some of which retain the objective tone advocated by Shiki:

tsuchi no ue ni	over the ground
yamakagashi asobazu	the grass snakes have quit
nari ni keri	taking their leisure
irihi aka-aka to	the setting sun can be seen
kusawara ni miyu	red-red in the meadow

In contrast with poets like Shiki and Mokichi, who worked to make tanka regain the freshness of the *Manyōshū*, several poets took up the more emotional strand of tanka history typical of the Heian era and mixed it with Western Romanticism. Their tanka are often powerful statements of emotion, and have a broad appeal. Two poets of this group are best known in Japan.

Yosano Akiko (1878–1942) was a major figure in the Romantic movement at the turn of the century. Her first book of tanka, *Midaregami* ("Tangled Hair"), gained wide notice, and she married the editor of the most important tanka magazine of the movement. In addition to her work as a writer, she had a strong interest in women's welfare, and founded a women's college. Here is one of her tanka:

uta ni kike na	hear the poems:
tare no no hana ni	who would deny the red
akaki inamu	of a field's flowers?
omomuki aru kana	how delicate this is—
haru tsumi motsu ko	a girl with spring desire

Ishikawa Takuboku (1886–1912) was one of the younger poets attracted to the magazine published by Yosano Tekken and Yosano Akiko. His difficulties in gaining literary recognition, and his economic problems, contributed to a deeply Romantic spirit. As his health grew worse his work continued to exhibit a spirit of adolescent depression. After his death at the age of twenty-six his poems, in both tanka and free-verse form, became the strongest single influence on modern tanka for several decades.

Early in his writings Takuboku discarded the convention of having his tanka printed in one column, preferring instead to specify a three-column structure; he also did not care whether he limited himself to the nominal thirty-one-sound length of traditional tanka. Yet almost all of his tanka actually contain the traditional meters or a close approximation to them. In his last collection he added Western-style punctuation. But the real innovations in Takuboku's work are the modern diction and the breadth of subject matter, as compared to the tanka of old. Takuboku's main subject is himself, his own emotional states. And love, the usual subject of emotion-laden tanka, does not take a primary place in his work.

The following examples, one from earlier and one from later work, illustrate something of the range of moods in Takuboku's tanka:

hosoboso to
sokora kokora ni   mushi no naku
hiru no no ni kite   yomu tegami kana

> faintly
> around here around there   insects cry
> coming to the noonday moor   ah the letters to read

yaya tōki   mono ni omoishi
terorisuto no   kanashiki kokoro mo———
chikazuku hi no ari.

> thought it   a rather distant thing
> the sadness   of a terrorist's heart———
> lately it's getting close.

TANKA IN THE WEST

Occasionally, since the growing interaction of Japan and the West, an Occidental poetaster has chased the elusive spirit of tanka through counted syllables, usually with little success. But in the last decade or so three New World poets have gone deeply into the Romantic world from which Akiko's and Takuboku's tanka came, and have come back with examples their Japanese forerunners might well be jealous of. An example by each of the three poets will demonstrate their unity with the tradition of Japanese Romantic tanka:

hungry
without money—
after awhile
stopt pretending
ate a parsnip

Michael McClintock

Alto en la cumbre   High on the summit
todo el jardín es luna,   the garden is all moonlight
luna de oro.   the moon is golden.
Más precioso es el roce   More precious is the contact
de tu boca en la sombra.   of your lips in the shadow.

Jorge Luis Borges   *translated by Alastair Reid*

this summer night
at the magazine rack
fingers
desperately
turning

Sanford Goldstein

Some might argue that we do not need the tanka in the West, given our strong tradition of the personal lyric. The best response to such assertions is creation of poems that work for the writer, and perhaps for readers as well. I see no reason to ignore the possibilities, and leave the subject with one of my own:

drove past
the apartment house
she lived in
my five-year-old
sweetheart

AN INTRODUCTION TO RENGA

Japanese scholars point out that question and answer poems, composed by two persons, appear in the earliest documents of Japanese history and literature. But the society that made aesthetics the core of life and raised the tanka to subtle and refined heights of artistry, Heian-kyō's aristocracy, really originated and brought to bud the first of the kinds of collaborative poems called renga.

In each of its traditional manifestations renga composition can be described thus: A group of poets, usually three or more, meets to compose a long poem of several short stanzas. They may take turns according to some planned order, or volunteer their contributions, one stanza at a time. Formally, the stanzas resemble the two parts of a later tanka, composed in rhythms of about seventeen and fourteen onji, alternately. A typical renga from the thirteenth through the sixteenth centuries is fifty or one hundred stanzas long; several are considerably longer, with a length of one thousand stanzas not extremely uncommon.

The point of renga writing is *not* to tell a story in a logical progression. Each stanza must move in some new direction, connected to the stanza just before it, but usually not to earlier stanzas. When reading a renga we do not discover a narrative sequence, but zig-zag over the different imaginary landscapes of the poets' minds, much as a spaceship coming out of polar orbit might flash now over ice and snow, now over teeming cities, now over green forests, ultimately to splash down into blue ocean. As readers we should enjoy the flow of sights, sounds, and insights as they tumble past. Indeed, "enjoyment" is a key word in early descriptions of renga by the first poet to codify the rules of the game.

Nijō Yoshimoto (1320–1388), the first of the great compilers of renga rules, and an important tanka poet, said "As renga has no ancient models prescribed from the beginning, it should simply be an entertainment, arousing current emotions." Apparently others agreed with Yoshimoto, for he was the first to collect an anthology of renga, though the genre had flourished for over a hundred years when he was writing. Renga was considered a pastime, a thing of the moment. Most renga were not preserved, so we do not know much about the early history of the genre.

What we do know comes mainly from the writings of Yoshimoto and later scholars who extended his work. In several documents, written over an active lifetime as a major poet and the leading student of the renga master Kyūsei (also called Gusai, 1284–1378), Yoshimoto set out what he felt were the important features of renga. These include elegant images, usually associated with the seasons; the ways in which poets link one verse to another; and a unity made up of variety, in which the poets work together to give the poem a harmony of movement and mood similar to that of a piece of classical music.

In one of Yoshimoto's early works he lists, month-by-month, a number of objects which express "the heart of the seasons"; a few of them are mentioned in Chapter 7, Nature and Haiku. Yoshimoto particularly recommends these as topics for the starting verse, the hokku, of a renga. Once past the opening stanza, the rules of renga multiply.

RENGA LINKING—BASHŌ STYLE

While the detailed rules of renga composition shifted from era to era, the main challenge of renga has always been making one verse connect with another. The art of linking verses in renga reached its peak in the work of the Bashō School. A number of historical factors led to the haikai-no-renga of Bashō and his followers.

The seventeenth century haikai grew out of a sort of doggerel renga practiced by the same court poets who invented renga. Some scholars feel that the haikai (the word means more or less "funny", but is often understood as "vulgar") actually was the first kind of renga. They point out that renga writing originated in the relaxed aftermaths of contests in tanka composition, and was a comparatively informal way for the poets to put aside the seriousness of waka and play a game together. In time the loose style of renga subsided to be replaced—at least in theory—by the ideals of poets such as Yoshimoto. Thus, for a few hundred years the serious, or *ushin* (literally "with heart/mind") renga gained the upper hand, and the vulgar *mushin* ("heart/mind-less") renga, or haikai, occupied the same place in Japanese poetry that the limerick had in Victorian English literature.

Between the time of Yoshimoto (1320–1388) and Bashō (1644–1694), the rise of the middle class progressed to the point where wealthy merchants routinely mixed with samurai and priests. And they began to participate in learning and the arts in greater numbers and with greater influence.

In the decades before Bashō haikai underwent many changes, including a descent into quite tasteless vulgarity of content, and the loss of any sort of standards of formal structure. While most of the literary products of the time have little value in themselves, they set the stage for a flowering of literature in the Genroku Era (1688–1704) that has been called the Japanese Renaissance. During this era, Ihara (or Ibara) Saikaku (1642–1692) virtually invented the modern Japanese novel, Matsuo Bashō perfected the haikai, and Chikamatsu Monzaemon (usually known as just Chikamatsu; 1653–1724) wrote a body of plays for the kabuki and jōruri (puppet) theaters that most scholars consider a rival to Shakespeare's.

The art of these three writers, and of dozens of others who wrote extremely well but are overshadowed by these three geniuses, owes much of its strength to the economic and social upheavals that preceded them. For their art spoke of and to the lives of the townspeople of Osaka and Edo (now Tokyo), and put Japanese literature back in touch with colloquial language and actual experience, as opposed to the almost total dependence on the images and vocabulary of the received tradition which had dominated the courtly literature for several centuries.

Bashō and others of his generation devoted their lives to bringing sincerity into haikai. They did not try to restore the canons of the old ushin renga. They accepted much of the broadened subject matter achieved in the previous century, including many objects and events from the daily lives of the common people which certainly would not have found their way into the court poetry. And the members of the Bashō School, in particular, strengthened the process of linking one stanza to another. They also wrote their haikai in the popular, shorter, thirty-six-stanza format called *kasen*.

The linking techniques of the Bashō School depend mainly on the images of the stanzas, and on the psychic archetypes and actual situations from life which the images represent. Though linking through allusions to earlier literature is not uncommon, it was not considered to be more important than other kinds of linking. (Literary allusions formed one of the primary foundations of linking in the older renga.)

According to the writings of Bashō's disciples, the following pairs of stanzas demonstrate linking by "scent" or "fragrance" (*nioi* or *kaori*):*

    tips refreshed   a pine in evening shower
    a Zen monk   is stark naked   cooling

                    * * *

    rice shoots lengthen   in a soft breeze
    a convert   starts by going over   Suzuka Pass

---

*Each stanza is given here as one horizontal line, with extra space in the line indicating the metrical structure of the original. The indented stanzas consist of two verse-lines in the original, usually of seven onji each; the others have three verse-lines in approximately five-seven-five onji.

Though nothing in any stanza overtly refers to the other in each pair, one feels a unity, a magnetism between the stanzas. Of the latter example a group of Japanese scholars says:

> The frailty of young paddies swayed by the slightest breeze . . . is matched . . . with the mood of uncertainty of a priest, who, having only lately entered a religious order and shaved his head, has donned the black robe of a novice, and is now crossing a desert mountain range.

They also note that the last stanza, composed by Bashō, may call to mind the following tanka by Saigyō:

suzukayama	Suzuka Pass
ukiyo o yoso ni	the world indifferently
furisutete	cast off
ikani nariyuku	how will it come out?
waga mi naruran	what will become of me?

But knowing Saigyō's poem is not essential to appreciating either the stanza for itself or its connection with the previous verse, though we may be sure that Bashō had Saigyō's tanka in mind.

A stronger, but still indirect, connection between stanzas is called "echo" *(hibiki)*:

> an orphaned crow   in sleep-perplexing moon
> the thief-   challenging lances'   sound deepens night

Here the disturbed order of things in the orphaned crow's sleeplessness resounds in the clatter of lances as a thief, one of society's cast-offs, runs for his life through the shadowy alleys of night.

Another example of "echo":

> in azure sky   the waning moon's   daybreak
> in the autumn lake   Mt. Hira's first frost

The moon seems almost not there, fading in the light before sunrise. The frost appears like vapor reflected on the still lake, and awaits the vaporizing rays of the sun. Tranquillity and expectancy mix in each stanza.

"Reflection" *(utsuri)* seems a bit more subtle than "echo" in terms of narrative, but implies some sort of shift of location. Here is an example of "reflection" with a comment on the stanzas by one of Bashō's disciples:

> water chestnut leaves   coiling and turning   a teal cries
>   a prayer-drum calls out   in mountain shadow, frost

> Coming upon the water chestnut's leaves at the water's edge and the cry of a teal or the like is reflected in hearing the prayer-drum of the mountain shadow.

The following verses demonstrate a less obvious connection, as well as the shift of locale characteristic of "reflection":

> in snow-sandals   walking Kamakura   spring hills
>   yesterday distant   Yoshiwara sky

Each of these stanzas has a feeling of time and timelessness. The poet of the first walks the hills around Kamakura, the former capital of a military ruler, still wearing winter sandals even though spring has come. The second poet lets go of the problems and pain of yesterday under the sky of the entertainment district on the outskirts of Edo.

The nuances of difference among these and other methods of linking verses in haikai easily elude one. But we can readily see that in most cases the connections are impressionistic, rather than logical or narrative. These examples also clearly show how the haikai of the Bashō School incorporate images as lovely as any from the earlier ushin renga right along with such vulgar topics as a thief in the night and the pleasure district.

Since most Japanese readers, let alone readers from other cultures, require extensive notes to understand classical renga, and such explications are beyond the scope of this book, no complete Japanese renga will be offered here. However, the example in the following section will give the reader a good impression of the texture of many Japanese renga. A number of classical Japanese renga and Bashō School haikai have been published in English translations, often with extensive explanations of fine points of composition and background. Some of these appear in books listed in the Resources section for this chapter at the back of the book.

RENGA AROUND THE WORLD

Relatively few Western poets have tried to write anything resembling a Japanese renga. But since the late 1960s some North American haiku poets have made attempts at it, and renga increasingly find their way into American and Canadian haiku magazines. Thus the West has reversed the historical process in Japan, where renga grew up as a game, and resulted in the detached hokku or haiku as a serious literary genre after many centuries of development. Most Westerners who have tried renga first learned to write haiku and later tried to learn the process of linking haiku-like images into renga.

While many Japanese renga have been and continue to be written in one continuous meeting of a group of poets, Westerners have had difficulty with this aspect of renga. One reason is that few towns or cities in the West boast more than a handful of possible renga poets, while in Japan at the peak of Bashō's career one might find a group ready to write haikai in almost any village. Another may well be that when poets begin writing with the ideal of creating striking individual poems it is difficult for them to shift gears and write verses that fit well together into a renga. Some of the attempts at renga parties which I have attended with American haiku poets ended in miserable failure, for each poet wanted to write nothing but the most brilliant verses, and discussions always seemed to center on whether a particular verse was "good enough" to be used in the poem, rather than on whether it *fit* the poem. In one instance, four of the finest American haiku poets took several hours to come up with five stanzas of renga. Then they gave up and went home.

These poets failed because they did not consider the two most important aspects of renga as a whole: The smooth movement from stanza to stanza. And constructing stanzas that fit the overall design of the poem as it grows. The American poets would have done well to preface their meeting with a passage from the essay "In Praise of Shadows" by one of Japan's greatest modern novelists, Tanizaki Junichirō. In it he speaks of various aspects of Japanese culture, especially architecture. This excerpt has been translated by Thomas J. Harper and Edward G. Seidensticker:

> We value a scroll above all for the way it blends with the walls of the alcove, and thus we consider the mounting quite as important as the calligraphy or painting. Even the greatest masterpiece will lose its worth as a scroll if it fails to blend with the alcove, while a work of no particular distinction may blend beautifully with the room and set off to unexpected advantage both itself and its surroundings.

In effect, many American would-be renga poets have been too preoccupied with the possible beauty or defects of the scroll to look at the way it did or did not blend with its surroundings.

A number of moderately successful renga have been completed by Western authors who live at some distance from each other, and write renga by correspondence. For the past decade or so there have probably been at least a few such efforts in progress at any given time, and a number have been published in magazines. Some of these renga-by-mail have been international efforts, involving Japanese and American authors together, usually writing in English.

Japanese students of renga often write solo renga, usually as practice exercises, and a few Western poets have tried this also.

Octavio Paz, the well-known Mexican poet, has written one rather engaging example in Spanish, as have several haiku poets writing in English. Western efforts at solo renga have not amounted to much as yet, however.*

To date, the most substantial work in renga written in a Western language has been done in Japan. Tadashi Kondo and his wife, the American artist Kris Young, invited friends to gather at their home in Tokyo over a period of several months during 1980, 1981, and 1982 to write renga. It may be significant that few if any of the participants, besides Kondo, had much previous experience with haiku. The dozen thirty-six-stanza renga produced at their gatherings will be published in a pamphlet soon in the United States, and we may expect additional interesting renga to follow.

The relaxed atmosphere of these gatherings can be felt in Kondo's letter to me describing the process of making the renga. Here are some excerpts:

> We did not have any written format or order to follow. . . . Once in a while we stopped to talk about linking technique, structure, or aesthetics. One of us would start talking or asking about them, then we would exchange our opinions. Naturally I referred mainly to Japanese classic renga . . . but I always tried not to impose the whole framework of Japanese renga, because I was interested in finding what we might be able to produce when writing renga in English in Tokyo in the 1980's with international backgrounds. The core of Japanese renga was formed by a

---

*Paz's solo renga, called "El día en Udaipur" ("The day in Udaipur"), can be found in Spanish and English in his book *Configurations*. Some American examples appear in Hiroaki Sato's *One Hundred Frogs*. See Resources.

court poet in Kyoto in the fourteenth century. Some rules are relevant and others are not in the twentieth century, especially when we are trying an international renga.

I like the analogy of the renga structure to that of Noh; the idea of the structure consisting of three phases of beginning, development, and finale. I thought we could apply this basic structure. It would be like the form of classical music. . . .

Knowing about the rules of the positions of the moon, flowers, and so on, may not spoil an international renga, but it would cause more trouble than help to try to impose those rules. . . .

We would give comments on each other's stanzas after they were made. Sometimes we had to think or wait an hour or so until a decent one came out. . . . The gatherings were always in a casual and friendly mood. . . .

So we discussed many of the verses until we were satisfied. We spent a lot of time trying to help organize what one wanted to say, and to search for how to put it in a brief phrase. . . .

"Eleven Hours" is the only renga we intended to finish in one session. Philip, who had been working . . . in Tokyo, found a new job [in] Kyoto. . . . We wanted to try a farewell renga party in one session. We did not expect it to take that long. Tim came after Philip made his second stanza. When we finished, everyone was tired but happy for the success. We decided to call it "Eleven Hours" to celebrate the success, although we could call it "Morning Wind", which I like very much .

Here, then, is an English-language renga written in Tokyo one night in March 1981, by Philip Meredith (English), Tadashi Kondo (Japanese), Robert Reed (American), Kris Young (American), and Timothy Knowles (Welsh):

Eleven Hours

morning wind
blowing away the rain clouds
swaying willow buds   *Philip*

a group of children
getting on a tour bus   *Tadashi*

almost catching
never being caught
three boys and a duck   *Robert*

shadows deepen
the old man locks the gate   *Kris*

crows gathering
in the branches
the sky darkens   *Philip*

in from the cold
the choir practices   *Timothy*

chat over beer
steam rising
from lake trout   *Tadashi*

the cook opens the back door
to look at the snow   *Robert*

cat tracks
crisscrossing
the alley   *Kris*

locking up the night club
blinking in the dawn   *Philip*

don't forget your briefcase, dear
it's cheese, pickled onion
and a little surprise   *Timothy*

five minutes by bike
to the station   *Tadashi*

the old woman
is not there today
sweeping in front of her house   *Robert*

plum petals
and sheets of white pills   *Kris*

steam on the mirror
waiting for the bath to cool
squeezing a spot   *Philip*

tight jeans, latest style
chosen with care   *Timothy*

disco horror
and takenoko*
swinging in town   *Tadashi*

one girl crying as she sings
a kindergarten graduation   *Robert*

a nameless cap
and three left mittens
the lost and found box   *Kris*

a chipped mug of hot sweet tea
a moth pats at the window   *Philip*

uncurled, stretching
tail twitching a little
leaves the room   *Timothy*

thirteenth night moon
over her home   *Tadashi*

*Literally, "bamboo shoot"—slang for wildly dressed youth.

a mother and daughter
part a flock of pigeons
leaving the shrine   *Robert*

reading her fortune
she stifles a laugh   *Kris*

returning by train
a purple beach bag
plump pink toes   *Philip*

an old yellow snapshot
found between the leaves   *Timothy*

the cottage roof
leaking, the drips
measure the night   *Tadashi*

lying down in the sunlight
on the floor   *Robert*

my head
cradled on your arm
drifting into sleep   *Kris*

brushing by the banks
the boat creaks and moves downstream   *Philip*

a summer storm
drives the boys
to shelter   *Timothy*

bamboo pinwheel
the colors of a rainbow   *Tadashi*

brand new
little red
puddle-hunting boots   *Robert*

three in the afternoon
grandmother knitting by the window   *Kris*

switching on the lamp
faces in the wallpaper
logs shift in the grate   *Philip*

the mother wakes
as her child dreams   *Timothy*

This is one of the best renga in English I have read. In particular, the twists and turns of these last six stanzas stand out. The summer storm and boys of one stanza suggest the pinwheel and rainbow of the next. They, in turn, shift to smaller children playing outside—different from the earlier boys, who were seeking shelter. Then we see a grandmother in the afternoon sunlight, knitting by the window where she can keep an eye on the little one in red boots. Time moves on, and grandmother sees images of the past in the gathering dusk. Finally, the logs shifting in the grate awaken mother, and her child dreams on, ending the renga on a pleasant note, gently looking to the future. It is as though Philip, who is about to leave Tokyo for his new job in Kyoto, was thinking of his years in Tokyo and his friends there, and he is consoled by Timothy, who suggests that he consider the possibilities of the future, much as a dreaming child.

When Masaoka Shiki came on the scene in the late nineteenth century, he said that renga was not literature, but that haiku could be revived. And he did a good deal to revive it. Perhaps, now that increasing Western interest in all aspects of haiku is beginning to gain notice in Japan, even the renga will be revived through the interaction of Japanese and Western authors. Certainly Tadashi Kondo and Kris Young, and their guests, have begun to show the way.

14

Haiku Prose

THE JAPANESE HAIBUN

Japanese haiku poets have not always stayed within the confines of haiku and renga. As we saw in Chapter 2, The Four Great Masters, Buson created a sort of free-verse long before the *vers libre* of modern European poetry. He also wrote a number of haibun—short essays in prose with hokku (that is, haiku) mixed in. Bashō did his most important work in the haibun.

A few poets in Bashō's day wrote humorous, or haikai, prose. Bashō took this haikai prose and wed it to the great tradition of the poetic diary, adding new depth to the playfulness of haikai in prose as he had in verse.

Here is a short haibun by Bashō. Note the relationship between the prose and the verse; the hokku could very well stand independently, but it also completes and deepens the description of Bashō's surroundings. "Raku" is an old name for Kyoto, and "Rakushisha" means roughly "House of the Falling Persimmons"; Kyorai is one of Bashō's closest disciples. I am indebted to Tadashi Kondo, who stayed two years in the present Rakushisha on the site of the original, for bringing this haibun to my attention and helping me translate it.

Record of Rakushisha

Raku's What's-his-name Kyorai has this cottage in the thicket of Shimo Saga, foot of Arashiyama, close to the stream of Ōigawa. This area has the convenience of tranquility, a place to clear the mind. That Kyorai's a lazy fellow, grasses high in front of the window, a number of persimmon trees spreading branches wide—June rains leaking in, tatami and shōji smell moldy, no place fit to sit down. This sunshine, however, this is the owner's hospitality.

> *samidare ya*   June rains . . .
> *shikishi hegitaru*   poem card torn away
> *kabe no ato*   trace on the wall
>
> *Bashōan no Tōsei*

Even in this short piece, we can see the shifting tone, from the traditional humorous opening to the formal and sincere praise of the location's virtues. Then a few words expand on the humor connected with the owner. He is too lazy to cut down the grass around the place, or prune his fruit trees. Everything is wild and run down. But the rains of June (the original says "Fifth-month rains", referring to the lunar calendar) have cleared for the moment, and the sunlight streams in, lighting up the interior. Actually, Bashō is praising the isolation of the place, and appreciates the beauty of its wildness. And he notes that the previous resident, probably Kyorai himself, was a person of taste, as indicated by the marks where poem cards had been attached to the wall. Finally, he signs with his pen name of the time, which means "Peach Green of Banana-Plant Hut" and shows his familiarity with other simple living arrangements.

From this example we can see the characteristics of haibun, as Bashō practiced it. Here is a list, based on the observations of Makoto Ueda, a scholar and admirer of Bashō's work:

Characteristics of Haibun

1. Written in prose, usually concluded with one or more haiku.

2. Brief.

3. Abbreviated in syntax; grammar words, sometimes even verbs, are omitted.

4. No explanation of the haiku; the connection between the prose and the haiku is often like linking in renga.

5. Imagistic; relatively few abstractions or generalizations.

6. Objective; the writer is somewhat detached, maintains an aesthetic distance, even when describing himself.

7. Humorous; while seriousness and beauty concern the writer, a haibun usually demonstrates the light touch.

As Ueda says, "It is up to the reader to grasp the meaning of the prose, and then of the haiku, and to go on to discover the undercurrents of meaning common to both."

Bashō's short haibun, of which there are more than sixty, cover such subjects as places (like Rakushisha), people he meets, and the events of his daily life. He also wrote five travel journals, and an extended diary in the haibun style. The longest of these, *Narrow Roads of the Interior (Oku no hosomichi)*, stands beside Lady Murasaki's *Tale of Genji* as one of the great classics of Japanese literature. Fortunately, this work has been translated into English with something of the compression and brilliance of the original by Cid Corman and Kamaike Susumu, under the title *Back Roads to Far Towns* (which is listed, with other books containing translations of Japanese haibun, in Resources at the back of this handbook).

Like Bashō, Buson also wrote a number of haibun, of which the following is the last, written a few months before he died. Buson, in his late sixties, was invited on an excursion by a younger disciple. This is slightly longer than the usual short haibun, and demonstrates the renga-like movement of such longer pieces as Bashō's travel journals. Uji is southeast of Kyoto; a few footnotes explain allusions that Buson's readers would have understood.

Uji Visit

South of Mount Uji, deep in the mountains, to Field-Moor Town called to gather mushrooms, young companions ahead greedily competing for the spoils, I, lagging behind, with heart serene searched through nooks and crannies, found five pine mushrooms about the size of small hats of sedge. Such splendid ones, how is it that Uji's Chief Councillor of State, Lord Takakuni,[1] stopped writing, honoring us with the marvelous information on flat mushrooms, but finished without adding the auspiciousness of pine mushrooms?

> *kimi miyo ya*　　look, Sir—
> *shūi no take no*　mushrooms for gleaning
> *tsuyu gohon*　　five dewy ones

On the highest summit, dwellings visible; called High Ridge Village. They resort to scooping trout[2] as an occupation, a means of making a way in the world. Thatched cottages built in the clouds, a broken bridge[3] verging on the water—that people live even hanging beyond the earth—in spite of itself the visitor's heart chills.

---

[1]Said to be the author of *Gleanings and Stories from Uji*.

[2]*Ayu*, sometimes translated as "sweetfish".

[3]Alluding to a poem by Tu Fu, with the lines:

> broken bridge　no plank walkway
> fallen willow　fresh wild branches

ayu ochite	trout falling
iyo-iyo takaki	taller and taller
onoe kana	the ridge-peaks

Said to be Rice Landing, where the Uji River makes its most rapid channel; water and stone fight each other in rushing waves, the high billows like flying snow resemble clouds whirling. The sound reverberating in mountain and valley confuses human speech.

a silver jug suddenly dashed   crystal fluid spatters
armored cavalry rushes out   swords & spears resound
four strings one sound   like tearing silk

—remembering the magnificent poem in which Po Chü-I makes a metaphor for the lovely sound of the biwa.

kinu o saku	the silk-tearing
biwa no nagare ya	biwa's current—
aki no koe	autumn's voice

"Uji Visit" begins in a lighthearted vein, with Buson's pleasure in finding some excellent mushrooms that the younger people, rushing ahead in eagerness, missed. The work Buson alludes to, *Gleanings and Stories from Uji,* apparently a sort of travelogue, suggests a typical outing in which a small group goes for a day of sightseeing in the countryside. Buson gently pokes fun at his companions and then at Lord Takakuni, both of whom missed the pine mushrooms. The hokku underscores this by showing how fresh-looking they are in the dew. The pointed crowns of the pine mushrooms prepare the reader for the next section's opening image.

With the peaks of High Ridge Village the emotion shifts to awe at the hardiness of the high villagers, and respect for their tough way of life. The wildness of the environment and the fragility of the works of man show in the graphic description and the reference to Tu Fu's poem. As the trout "fall"—come down river in the autumn—Buson feels more and more the height of the peaks and the wildness of the place.

As the fish come down they carry Buson with them, linking us to the next place, a rapids in the lower portion of the river. Here a cacophony of images blends to convey the turbulence of white water and rushing sound. Direct quotation of lines from the great T'ang Dynasty poet Po Chü-I picks up and expands these images through layers of metaphor. The pieces of the "silver jug" and the spattering fluid restate the billows and froths of the rapids, the resounding swords and spears of the cavalry expand the "fight . . . in rushing waves"—and then we find that Po Chü-I was speaking of the sound of a stringed instrument, a sort of lute! Now Buson shifts all the passion of his description of the rapids, through Po's lines, into the striking image of tearing silk. Using this image to open the hokku brings all of the images connected with it in metaphor into the hokku as well. He links these images to the river itself by calling the biwa's sound a "current", and then carries them all further into the final phrase, "autumn's voice". In both Chinese and Japanese traditional poetry "autumn's voice" normally refers to the sounds of rustling leaves and singing insects. Here Buson gives the somewhat hackneyed phrase new and powerful meaning.

For those familiar with the Chinese poets, as Buson's contemporary readers no doubt were, Po Chü-I's poem contains rich associations. The poem is "Biwa Visit" (*P'i-pa Hsing*) and describes how one night Po and a friend went out in a boat to enjoy the moon and some wine together. Po Chü-I had been sent away from the capital to this outpost, and was trying to make the best of the circumstances. He and his friend were about to return to shore, having no music to complete the aesthetics of the moment, when they heard beautiful music—played in a style one might expect at the capital—coming from a nearby boat. Po Chü-I describes the conclusion of the playing thus:

a silver jug suddenly dashed   crystal fluid spatters
armored cavalry rushes out   swords & spears resound
song gathering to the end stroke   with care struck
four strings one sound   like tearing silk
eastern skiff & western boat   still   without words
simply see in the river's heart   the autumn moon   white

At this point Po Chü-I comes to fully realize how deeply he has missed the rich pleasures of life in the capital.

As a cosmopolitan, city person, Buson too knows the "pleasures of the capital" and would like to continue experiencing them. But he also takes pleasure in the natural surroundings of the country. In his hokku at the end of "Uji Visit" he combines all the elements of pleasure in the season—the sounds of leaves and insects, the roar of the rapids—but he also recalls in Po Chü-I's poem the pleasures of art, of life itself. Perhaps conscious that he is at the end of his own life's autumn, he has built into this short haibun humor and lighthearted gaiety, a sense of the hardships of life, and awe in the face of nature's beauty and power. He has praised a poet whose works he loved, and made a poem in which that poet's genius joins his own in a celebration of art and nature together.

Probably the second most important extended haibun, after Bashō's *Narrow Roads of the Interior*, is Issa's best-known work, *My Spring (Ora ga haru)*, an autobiography in haibun form. Cast as the diary of one full year when Issa was well along in life, it reveals the full range of his delicate joy in family life and his grief at the deaths of his children. It is a long work—too long to excerpt effectively here. An English translation is listed in Resources.

In the twentieth century Japanese haiku poets have continued to write occasional haibun, usually in a light, humorous style. The energy and taciturnity of the best haibun style, as found in the passages quoted above, have influenced modernist writers of prose poems, based mainly on French models by Charles Baudelaire, Arthur Rimbaud, and Stéphane Mallarmé. As we might expect, these works take on the colorings of their surreal, often despairing forebears, and do not usually exhibit the lightness that characterizes the traditional short haibun. A decent English translation of some of this work, with an excellent introduction, is listed in Resources.

HAIBUN IN THE WEST

Relatively few Western writers have written anything resembling haibun. Perhaps one of the earliest examples is a passage from the *Days (Meres)* of the Greek poet George Seferis (1900–1971). In Volume I, covering the years 1925–1931, the following entry appears; the English translation has been made for this book by Manya Bean:

1 January 1931

I hear a dialogue without seeing the faces:

—How is Mrs. R.?
—She passed away.
—Died! The poor "girl"!
—No matter, we'll all get there. I have my brothers and I bury one each year; and one year, one along with my mother, who was run over by a car in Kozane.

Not Given
For the lady
who searched in the field
for goldfish.

This dialogue has the quality of some of the lines quoted in the opening section of T. S. Eliot's *The Waste Land*, which Seferis admired and translated into modern Greek. His little poem in haiku form, though it sounds more like a dedication than a poem, relates to the prose in much the same way that the hokku of Bashō's "Record of Rakushisha" relates to its prose. The prose has the tone of everyday banter, the second speaker deliberately countering the first's incipient emotionalism with dry irony, while the poem seems to have a gentle humor.

The density of image, event, experience piled up on one another in Bashō's *Narrow Roads of the Interior*, Buson's "Uji Visit", or Issa's *My Spring* has rarely been achieved in English. Occasionally Jack Kerouac has it, and puts it together with haiku, as in this passage from his novel *Desolation Angels*, first published in 1965. This section was written in 1956:

> Meanwhile the sunsets are mad orange fools raging in the gloom, whilst far in the south in the direction of my intended loving arms of señoritas, snowpink piles wait at the foot of the world, in general silver ray cities—the lake is a hard pan, gray, blue, waiting at the mist bottoms for when I ride her in Phil's boat—Jack Mountain as always receives his meed of little cloud at highbrow base, his thousand football fields of snow all raveled and pink, that one unimaginable abominable snowman still squatted petrified on the ridge— Golden Horn far off is yet golden in a gray southeast— Sourdough's monster hump overlooks the lake— Surly clouds blacken to make fire rims at that forge where the night's being hammered, crazed mountains march to the sunset like drunken cavaliers in Messina when Ursula was fair, I would swear that Hozomeen would move if we could induce him but he spends the night with me and soon when stars rain down the snowfields he'll be in the pink of pride all black and yaw-y to the north where (just above him every night) North Star flashes pastel orange, pastel green, iron orange, iron blue, azurite indicative constellative auguries of her makeup up

there that you could weigh on the scales of the golden
world—
The wind, the wind—
And there's my poor endeavoring human desk at
which I sit so often during the day, facing south, the
papers and pencils and the coffee cup with sprigs of alpine
fir and a weird orchid of the heights wiltable in one day—
My Beechnut gum, my tobacco pouch, dusts, pitiful pulp
magazines I have to read, view south to all those snowy
majesties— The waiting is long.

> On Starvation Ridge
> little sticks
> Are trying to grow.

Kerouac is sitting in a fire-lookout station on top of Starvation
Ridge in the northern Cascades, just south of the border between
the state of Washington and British Columbia. It is near the
beginning of the two-month stay he has signed up for, and
already he feels lonely. Passages of description, like this one, and
of memory jogs, philosophical introspection, and the inane word-
music of just trying to crank up the writing machine, chase one
another around through the forty-seven short "chapters" of
which this is number four, entire.

Words filling the void, companions few: "The wind, the
wind—" and a fresh sprig or two of alpine fir, a wilting flower,
gum and tobacco his only substitute for the booze and other
intoxicants left behind with civilization. Kerouac had finished
writing *On the Road*, which would come out the following year,
and had yet to start *The Dharma Bums*. He had hoped to write
while he was up there, and to seek a deepening of the religious
impulses he felt. "The waiting is long." And the little sticks on
Starvation Ridge are at too high an altitude to grow very much,
though they try. We might compare Kerouac's attitude toward
this landscape with Buson's toward that of Uji.

A movement like the renga linking technique in Buson's "Uji Visit" occurs in the extended haibun *Behind the Fireflies*, by Hal Roth. Roth combines haiku written on the spot today with his own short prose descriptions of events during one of the bloodiest days of fighting in the American Civil War. To these he adds direct quotations from accounts by eye-witnesses to and participants in what Northern historians call "The Battle of Antietam", which took place at Sharpsburg, Maryland. The following passage represents five pages from the book, with asterisks indicating page breaks:

> waves of summer heat
> cows huddle
> beneath a sycamore

*

The Union attacks focused upon the high ground surrounding a small white structure on the Sharpsburg ridge, the Church of the Brethren.

"Under the dark shade of a towering oak near the Dunker Church lay the lifeless form of a drummer boy . . . flaxen hair and eyes of blue and form of delicate mold. . . . His lips were compressed, his eyes half open, a bright smile played upon his countenance."

Private J. D. Hicks, USA

*

> around and around
> the little white church
> a boy chases his sister

*

As the battle on the Union right dwindled in the exhaustion of both sides, fresh brigades crossed the creek and engaged Lee's center where a sunken country lane provided natural fortifications for the defenders.

Again, the advancing lines with colors unfurled, with polished bayonets flashing in the sunlight; again, the rattle of muskets, the acrid, billowing smoke; again, the violence of artillery shaking the green, rolling hills.

*

through hazy stillness
a brass cannon points
at two lovers

Roth makes effective use of renga and haibun techniques in this work, but instead of roaming a diverse landscape or mindscape, he bears down on the two realities of the "Battle of Sharpsburg", as Southern historians call it, and the present peaceful park on the site of that battleground. One could, in fact, read through all the even-numbered pages of the book and gather a fairly full, if brief, picture of that 17th of September, 1862, when a field of corn and soldiers was cut down by cannon fire, and a country lane was paved with bodies dressed in blue and butternut. And one could read all the odd-numbered pages to find an idyllic sequence of haiku on a summer day in the park, almost any park. Read straight through, however, *Behind the Fireflies* zigzags only so far as the alternating teeth of a rapidly closing zipper, the teeth, if you will, of life and death. For the feeling person, reading this book leads directly to a deepening sense of the strangeness of war, and perhaps its futility, as earlier caught in another battlefield haiku, from Bashō's *Narrow Roads of the Interior*:

summer grass—
those mighty warriors'
dream tracks

LIVING—NOT EMOTING

In these few examples of Japanese and Western haibun we have seen a wide variety of events, thoughts, and feelings: Bashō's pleasure of place; Buson's enjoyment of an excursion and reflections on the hardships and joys of life; a brief conversation overheard by Seferis and his even briefer but many-layered response to it; the intensity of Kerouac's isolation in a grand natural setting; the juxtaposition of past horrors with the present pastorals found in a park by Roth.

All of these writers have taken the outer, specific objects and events of the here and now, and mixed them to a greater or lesser degree with the shared past and personal inner life, arising now in direct quotation from or allusion to history or literature, now in a choice of metaphor. In some pieces, like those by Bashō and Kerouac, the present reality dominates. In Roth's the present is very much with us, but serves as a foil for the more insistent past. And in those by Buson and Seferis the past soon shifts the present into some almost timeless space.

Like haiku, haibun begins in the everyday events of the author's life. These events occur as minute particulars of object, person, place, action. The author recognizes that these events connect with others in the fabric of time and literature, and weaves a pattern demonstrating this connection. And if this writing is to be truly haibun, the author does this with a striking economy of language, without any unnecessary grammar, so that each word carries rich layers of meaning.

The concision of haibun yields another benefit. Such precise, taut language creates an aesthetic distance that undermines our tendency to self-satisfaction or self-pity. The writer focuses on the action of living, rather than on the "liver". Bringing the spareness of haiku poetry to prose gives us the best of autobiography and familiar essay—the actions, events, people, places, and recollections of life lived—without weighing them down with sentimentality, perhaps the greatest enemy of art and life.

15

Beyond Haiku

SENRYU—THE HUMAN COMEDY

Like haiku, the senryu* originates in haikai-no-renga. But the senryu begins in the middle stanzas of the renga, not in the hokku, or starting verse. Just as renga poets practiced composing hokku, they also practiced linking stanzas. Called *tsukeai*, "joining together" or simply "linking", the game of someone supplying one stanza and someone else adding a second had been around since *Manyōshū* times, when two poets occasionally composed a waka or tanka together. As renga grew in popularity more and more poets practiced the art of linking stanzas in pairs. Books on renga commonly discussed pairs of stanzas in isolation, yielding the examples of linked pairs in Chapter 13, for example. The earliest anthologies of renga contained mainly pairs of stanzas. In all of these instances, the emphasis was on the connection, the tsukeai, between one stanza and another.

---

*The Japanese word *senryū* is properly romanized with the long sign over the *u*; accepting it as an English word, I have dropped the long sign. It is pronounced somewhat like the English phrase "send you" with the *d* replaced by a flipped, Spanish *r*.

Since the inner verses of a renga often involve humor, concentrating on tsukeai tends to produce humorous verses. As the samples in Chapter 13 indicate, the inner stanzas of renga frequently deal with human events and actions. While many of the inner stanzas have a seasonal feeling, many do not. Since season words usually contribute no humor in a renga, and the point of practice linking eventually became humor, the season word disappeared from tsukeai, which came to be called *maekuzuke*, "joining to a previous verse". In time the *maeku*, "previous verse", became less and less interesting in itself, merely providing a pretext for the new *tsukeku*, "joined verse". Eventually the maeku was dropped altogether.*

Here is a pair of linked stanzas from the first renga anthology, the *Tsukubashū* (1356), edited by Nijō Yoshimoto:

hitomaro ni nite	resembling Hitomaro
uta ya yomuramu	reciting some songs!
kaki no moto o	beneath a hedge
nagaruru mizu ni	in the flowing water
naku kawazu	a singing frog

Lord Tamesuke (b. 1263)

The humor here is not just in the comparison of the great *Manyōshū* poet, Hitomaro, with a frog. *Kaki no moto* means "beneath a hedge" and is a homonym for Hitomaro's surname, Kakinomoto.

---

*Authorities disagree on the meanings of *maekuzuke*, *maeku*, and *tsukeku*. Some, like R. H. Blyth, indicate that *maekuzuke* means "joining in front of a verse", with the *maeku* added in front of the challenge verse, or *tsukeku*. This view would have the completed *maekuzuke* result in a verse in tanka form, five-seven-five-seven-seven. With Hiroaki Sato, Sugimoto Nagashige, and others, I accept the conceptually simpler transcription for *maekuzuke*, "joining to a previous verse"; thus the *maeku* is the challenge verse, written first, and the *tsukeku* is added after it. This seems to better reflect the growth of *maekuzuke* from renga.

This example, and the other linked pairs in the *Tsukubashū*, came from actual renga of a hundred or more stanzas. Yoshimoto selected them as particularly good examples of linking technique. The point of this pair is the strong connection between them, both in harmony of meaning and in the pun skillfully built in by the author of the tsukeku. Here the tsukeku makes active use of the material of the maeku, and without the maeku it would have much less impact.

By the end of the seventeenth century, about the time of Bashō's death, the game of maekuzuke had become detached from renga composition. Maekuzuke became particularly popular through contests at teahouses and wineshops. A "selector" or "marker" left a group of maeku off at the shop, and customers would add their tsukeku. Then the marker would collect the customers' efforts, select the best, and publish them in a *mankuawase*, "collection of ten thousand verses". The authors of the tsukeku paid a small fee for participating, and from these fees the selectors made their profit and distributed prizes.

A new sheet of mankuawase chosen by a particular selector appeared about every three weeks during the height of this activity, throughout most of the eighteenth century. As there were several selectors (including some of Bashō's foremost disciples), and estimates indicate that only three percent or so of the submitted verses were included in mankuawase, we can imagine that a great many verses were written. I have seen two examples of mankuawase; one, dated 1768, included about 120 poems selected from about 500 entries, and the other, dated 1770, had 284 verses drawn from about 10,500. (Those sending poems to the editors of today's literary magazines might well remember these odds!)

The participants in this massive poetical activity were mostly tradesmen, merchants, and other members of the middle class in Edo, now Tokyo. Their tastes were not as refined as those of the noble and priestly classes who had dominated Japanese poetry before them, and the subject matter of their verses frequently reflected the sort of conversations one might expect to find in the teahouses and wineshops where they wrote. The following verses from 1770 illustrate. By this time the maeku had been reduced to one seven-sound verse line, with a repeat sign, giving an effect like this:

| *mutsumashii koto* | friendly indeed |
| "   "   " | "   "   " |

Here are two of the several tsukeku written to this maeku:

okusama no	in the letter
otsukute fumi ni	his wife is writing
uta ka iri	maybe a poem
miken kizu	a forehead scratch
kono hō sawagu	from there the uproar of
ikkachū	one whole house

The first of these examples contains polite prefixes in the Japanese which make it clear that the author speaks of some superior's wife—perhaps alluding to the nobility of old, or, more probably, to the rumors going the rounds about some boss's wife. In either case, there is the unmistakable suggestion that the wife is sending a love poem to someone other than her husband. The second verse contains a pun, *miken*, meaning both "unknown" and "forehead"; thus the activities of the returned husband are broadcast to the world, and he all unsuspecting.

In both of these instances, we can easily see how the "friendly deed" of the maeku was interpreted by the authors of the tsukeku. But the tsukeku may be read entirely by themselves, without reference to the maeku, which has now become a rather unnecessary title. In typical mankuawase, in fact, the three or four maeku were printed only once each at the beginning, and then simply indicated by a symbol such as an asterisk or circle in front of each tsukeku for those who wished to know which maeku had inspired the responses.

SENRYU STANDS ALONE

In the meantime, between 1750 and 1776, some eighteen vol-
umes of an anthology of renga verses were published in a series
called *Mutamagawa*. Where earlier renga anthologies contained
pairs of linked stanzas (tsukeai), *Mutamagawa* had anonymous
single verses. In tune with the times, the editor Keikiitsu (1694–
1761) selected verses with a good deal of humor, in both the
fourteen- and seventeen-sound forms. Here are a few samples;
remember, each was originally written as a stanza of renga, but
is now presented as a solo verse:

shindai no	the fortune's
ana wa yane kara	gap—in the roof
miete kuru	shows up
mushiba no ryōji	cavity in treatment
shita e hi ga sasu	on my tongue the sun shines
ryōrinin	the cook,
nitateru uchi ni	while boiling,
gojūnen	fifty years
yoi ga sameru to	as the high fades
akai ka ga tobu	red mosquitoes fly

While renga were written throughout the eighteenth century,
most publishing activity revolved around single renga stanzas
taken out of the contexts in which they had been created, and
around maekuzuke. Karai Senryū (1718–1790) was the best
known selector of maekuzuke. In 1765 his student Goryōken
Arubeshi started publishing a series of anthologies called *Haifū
yanagidaru* ("haikai-style willow barrel"), containing tsukeku
culled from the thousands of verses published in Senryū's man-
kuawase. From the very first volume of *Yanagidaru*, Arubeshi
decided to include only verses which could be understood on
their own; the maeku were omitted.

Yanagidaru established the seventeen-sound form of the tsu-keku as a solo work, and helped spread Senryū's fame as a selector. Since the names of the selectors were more important than those of the authors of the tsukeku, the genre was anonymous. Eventually all such verses came to be called senryu in honor of the most energetic selector. A few of the verses published in one or another of the first twenty-four volumes of *Yanagidaru*, assembled from Senryū's selections for mankuawase, follow.

Senryu are almost always humorous, mainly concerned with human nature, sometimes with a light touch:

> *akarumi e*   into the light
> *hikizutte deru*   dragging along
> *shitatemono*   the tailoring

Sometimes sharper:

> *haribako o*   as he searches
> *sagasu to nyōbo*   the needle-box his wife
> *tonde deru*   comes flying

While we may need the light to sew by, we do not want all of our possessions pried into.

Some senryu do not have the immediacy of haiku, but lapse into aphorism, like this:

> *kōkō no*   when one wishes
> *shitai toki ni wa*   to show filial piety
> *oya wa nashi*   parents gone

Some senryu seem indistinguishable from haiku, except perhaps for a self-conscious turn of phrase:

> *inazuma wa*   the lightning
> *kumo o egutte*   gouges the clouds
> *dokka yuki*   and goes somewhere

While "lightning" is a season word—associated with August, which is the beginning of autumn by Japanese reckoning—this senryu differs from haiku on the topic, such as this one by Bashō's disciple Kikaku:

inazuma ya	the lightning . . .
kinō wa higashi	yesterday in the east
kyō wa nishi	today in the west

A Zen-inspired commentator might say that Kikaku does not wonder where the lightning comes from or goes to, but accepts it, while the senryu writer questions. I suspect that Kikaku simply expresses his curiosity more subtly, and the real humor of the senryu lies in the contrast between the casualness of going "somewhere" and the force of "gouges", which almost personifies the lightning.

HAIKU OR SENRYU?

To some purists only the absence of season words and kireji divides senryu from haiku—although the "lightning/gouges" poem above has both season word and kireji. Others note that senryu tend to focus on the humor in a situation, and do not always speak of the specific here and now, while haiku usually do. Human concerns, though not absent from haiku, dominate senryu.

The question of what is a haiku and what a senryu is further clouded when we compare certain poems by "haiku poets" with some senryu. For example, in this pair, which is the haiku, which the senryu?

sekkyō ni	by sermons
kegareta mimi o	soiled ears to
hototogisu	a cuckoo
machiwabiru	to waiting-weary
mimi e kaeru no	ears only the voices
koe bakari	of the frogs

Masaoka Shiki wrote the first of these about the "sermons", the bland haiku and conventional theories, of his contemporaries. His followers immortalized it by naming their haiku magazine *Hototogisu*, "cuckoo". But the poem resembles senryu more than haiku in both intent and treatment, despite the fact that the Japanese cuckoo is noted for its song, and has none of the connotations associated with the English word.

The second poem above, an anonymous senryu from a hundred years before Shiki's haiku, exactly catches a lover who has been waiting a long time, straining to hear any sound that indicates an approach. But the frogs keep croaking. If the author recognizes the irritation of the one who waits, he also does not become involved in it himself, but merely records its cause. While the subject matter here is senryu, the treatment is haiku.

The original selectors of maekuzuke were renga poets. Although they certainly recognized the differences between the hokku and the interior verses of haikai-no-renga, they considered all these works parts of the same branch of literature. But as renga faded from popularity and senryu came to be composed independently from challenge verses, people tended to see haiku and senryu as different genres. Today's haiku poets usually concentrate on an aesthetic appreciation of the world; senryu poets focus their attention mainly on the humor in the human condition.

Some Japanese will stoutly deny that haiku occasionally resemble senryu, or will claim one or the other as the higher, more satisfying art. But when we examine the poems themselves, several hokku by Kikaku, some by Bashō, and many by haikai-no-renga poets before them seem more senryu than haiku. Since we call these people haiku poets today, their hokku are all called haiku. And the anonymous verses of the mankuawase, as well as the new verses based on that tradition, are called senryu.

Today Japanese poets who write senryu write without the stimulus of any challenge verses. And there are magazines that publish only senryu. Here is a modern senryu which may be compared with a haiku we have already seen:

okaeri no	arrived home
kaban isshō ni	with the briefcase
dakitsukare	embraced
tsuma dakana	to hold my wife
shunchū no jari	treading spring noon's
fumite kaeru	gravel going home

Whether we feel love in the lumps of a briefcase in the middle of a hug or in the crunch of gravel on our way to get a hug, it is still love. When we come home late or leave lunch too quickly we have an opportunity to notice our affection for one another—if, like the anonymous briefcase-carrier or Kusatao treading the gravel, we can be poets and record the moment. Kusatao's haiku is the finer poem, dealing in loss and anticipation, and manifesting these in the heat of the sun, the crunch of the gravel. But the spouses hugging the briefcase and the senryu poet who records that hug are not to be scorned either.

SENRYU IN THE WEST

The Japanese senryu has been relatively unknown in the West. But early translators of Japanese hokku presented work by several pre-Bashō poets as well as by Bashō and later poets. Thus many of the hokku and haikai first seen in the West exhibited the playful, often witty characteristics of haikai-no-renga before Bashō added depth and seriousness to the genre. This, and Chamberlain's use of the word "epigram" in connection with the hokku, led Westerners to emphasize wit, and pay less attention to capturing real experience, when they composed their own poems on Japanese models. People familiar with both Japanese haiku and senryu find many such poems closer to senryu than to haiku.

These examples from Chapter 4, Early Haiku in the West, might well be called senryu:

> The train was coming;   Among her twenty rouges
>   I had a kiss all ready: she searches for a full pot:
>   the train left . . .   turned to stone.
>
> *Jean Baucomont*   *Rainer Maria Rilke*

Examples abound of senryu-like poems written by Westerners who thought they were writing haiku. When the Committee on Definitions of the Haiku Society of America completed its work in the early 1970s, they included the following as one definition of senryu: "Loosely, a poem similar to haiku which does not meet the criteria for haiku." Although I was a member of that committee, I do not like suggesting that a senryu is a failed haiku. In the hands of those who set out to write a senryu, such as one-time editor of *American Haiku* Clement Hoyt, a senryu "relies on *a point of wit* instead of provocation by contrast, as does the haiku." (From his article "Haiku and Senryu"; his emphasis.) A senryu of his may help to establish the point:

> While the guests order,
>   the table cloth hides his hands—
>   counting his money.

Like Hoyt, American poet Sydell Rosenberg writes both haiku and senryu, and is best known for the latter. For example:

> Library closing—
>   the sleeping wino wakes up
>   holding a shut book

And why not? The wino's eyes also were shut. From one point of view the wino has usurped the library, or at least the book, by not reading it. From another, the purpose of the library has been expanded, so it is now a more useful place, and more human.

There is a perverse steadfastness in human nature, which forms the core of this poem by Virginia Brady Young:

> In a tight skirt
> a woman sweeping leaves
> into the wind.

Occasionally humanity's steadfastness, its insistence upon its own nature, reaches cosmic proportions. Michael McClintock has dutifully commemorated this fact, especially as it refers to haiku, in the following senryu, which seems a fit place to close our discussion of the genre:

> the old pond:
> all the little croaks
> keep on frogging

For those who wish to pursue the Japanese senryu, a few books in English are listed in Resources. Most of the English language haiku magazines also publish senryu, in part because many Western editors have a hard time distinguishing between senryu and haiku, and partly because it is not always easy to place a poem in one genre or the other. Many poems, both Japanese and Western, can be read either way, like Virginia Brady Young's leaf-sweeper.

FROM RENGA TO HAIKU SEQUENCES

In Japan poets early discovered that they could collect short lyrics in groups that worked together by subject, theme, language, and so on. Before Petrarch or Sir Philip Sidney celebrated their loves with extended sonnet sequences, Ōtomo no Tabito (665–731) and his son Yakamochi (716–785?) wrote tanka sequences in praise of wine and a garden, respectively, which are recorded in the *Many-*

Ōshū. Each of the tanka in these groups presents a different aspect of the subject itself or of the poet's thought on the subject. While an order that "makes sense" may appear here and there in these "sequences", many of the poems could be taken in any order without loss of impact.

By the time of the *Kokinshū* (completed about 905) a new way of ordering poems, particularly tanka, had come into use. In the *Kokinshū* itself, and in many later anthologies, poems are placed so that certain relationships between them add to the reader's enjoyment. Often poems by contemporaries appear next to others much older. Reading one of these anthologies is like reading a dialogue with continuously changing participants from many eras. And as in a good conversation, many different topics and themes arise, shift, and fade away as they are replaced by others.

This method of ordering a large number of tanka probably had a great deal to do with determining the ideals of renga composition, where the poets create a fabric of shifting images and themes that pleases them in the act of composition itself. Not surprisingly, Iio Sōgi (1421–1502), the greatest master of classical renga, was the best known scholar of the *Kokinshū* and its tanka in his generation.

In anthologies of renga individual hokku were collected in seasonal sections. The editors who assembled these hokku ordered them in ways similar to the carefully built relationships in the tanka anthologies. In the meantime renga became more stilted. Masaoka Shiki concentrated on haiku and tanka, publishing diaries with sequences of tanka or haiku on a particular topic, and independent sequences as well. Shiki also decreed the death of renga—prematurely—and the combined effect seems to have spurred the creation of haiku sequences among modern poets.

Today Japanese haiku poets distinguish between two types of haiku sequences. One is the *gunsaku*, that resembles the earliest tanka sequences in which one subject or theme is examined from many angles. Kaneko Tōta's haiku on the green bear, toward the

end of Chapter 3, Modern Japanese Haiku, are from a group such
as this. While the poems come in a particular order, simply
because writing and reading them must proceed in time, each is
really quite free to stand alone, and one might easily suggest
another order without disturbing the meaning of any one haiku
or of the group taken together.

The other type of sequence, called *rensaku*, contains haiku
which are not intended to stand alone, and which gather meaning
from the context of the whole sequence.

The conscious use of rensaku technique in composing haiku
sequences seems to have been borrowed from the practice of
some modern tanka poets, particularly Saitō Mokichi (1882–
1953), noted for a long series of tanka dealing with the final ill-
ness and death of his mother. Quoting a few pieces from such an
extended work would not give the effect, but Mokichi creates a
full-fledged psychological narrative using very realistic tanka to
present a series of vignettes.*

Japanese haiku poets have rarely produced anything
approaching narrative haiku sequences, but the rensaku mode, in
which individual haiku become in effect stanzas of a longer
poem, flourished in the 1930s and 1940s. A particularly strong
example was written by Tomizawa Kakio (1902–1962) while he
was serving in the engineer corps of the Japanese army. He had
been drafted in 1926, and spent from 1937 to 1940 in China,
attaining a battlefield commission as lieutenant. Kakio had gained
some notice as a haiku poet before he went to China, but spent
quite a while there writing little or nothing. Eventually he came
upon an oil lamp, intact, in the city of Teian. Soon, during a with-
drawal, he was forced to leave the lamp behind. After losing it,

*A good translation of Mokichi's entire tanka sequence, "Mother
Dies", appears in Sato and Watson, *From the Country of Eight Islands;*
see the introduction to Resources.

he wrote the following rensaku for his eldest daughter, Junko. I have used the step-down tercets of William Carlos Williams, with an adaptation of his "variable foot", to preserve the original integrity of the haiku stanzas while indicating the wholeness of the composition taken as a single work. The short preface suggests that the poem replaces the lamp itself as Kakio's gift to his daughter.

Junko! A little Chinese lamp Papa picked up!

     the setting sun
         brushes the chimney
             of a Chinese lamp
     soon in the lamp
         the battlefield's deep
             gloom comes!
     the light's small
         while alive my
             shadow is thick
     foot steps
         clop-clopping
             in the lamp
     gun shots
         splat-splattering
             in the lamp
     lighting up
         just like Junko
             the little lamp
     this lamp
         being a small thing
             makes one think!
     awakened from
         the straw: a little
             chilly lamp

One commentator notes that Kakio's homesickness is shown in his "unique sensations and illusions". If we look at the order of the haiku stanzas, these sensations and illusions fall into an unalterable dramatic structure. This is a psychological history of Kakio's relationship with the lamp, which begins with simple physical perceptions, but soon involves his own body image and some of the most dreaded sensations of war. Coming out of the macabre and self-pity, he thinks how his daughter's face lights up with a smile, then realizes that the lamp has brought him out of the war for a moment. Finally, the poet discovers his reawakened spirit in writing this piece on the lamp, which accounts for the joyous shout in his preface.

WESTERN SEQUENCES AND NARRATIVES

Many Western poets have written groups of haiku exploring various aspects of one subject or theme. One of the more successful early practitioners of the haiku sequence in Europe was the Spanish poet Antonio Machado. Here are the first two sections from a nine-section sequence in his *Nuevas Canciones* (*New Songs*, 1917–1930):

from Apuntes	*from* Sketches
I	I
Desde mi ventana,	From my window—
¡campo de Baeza,	the fields of Baeza,
a la luna clara!	in the clear moonlight!
¡Montes de Cazorla,	The mountains of Cazorla,
Aznaitín y Mágina!	Aznaitín and Mágina!
¡De luna y de piedra	Of moon and stone
también los cachorros	also, the whelps
de Sierra Morena!	of Sierra Morena!

II
Sobre el olivar,
se vió a la lechuza
volar y volar.

Campo, campo, campo.
Entre los olivos,
los cortijos blancos.

Y la encina negra,
a medio camino
de Úbeda a Baeza.

II
Over the olive grove,
seen like a barn owl
to hover and hover.

Fields, fields, fields.
Among the olive trees,
the white farmhouses.

And the black oak,
halfway along the road
From Úbeda to Baeza.

The sections of *"Apuntes"* do not all contain the same number of verses, and several of the verses do not resemble haiku, although all are highly imagistic. But those quoted above and many others seem a cross between haiku and *siguiriya*, the short lyric outburst characteristic of Andalusian song so dear to Federico García Lorca. While the *siguiriya* typically deals with love between man and woman, in these verses of Machado we see his love of the countryside. Aside from the namelessness that hovers over the olive grove (the moon? the spirit of the place?), the language is more direct, more strictly presentational than that of Kakio's rensaku on the Chinese lamp. But the verses within each section of *"Apuntes"* do not seem to have a fixed and necessary order like that of Kakio's sequence. In terms of the Japanese classification, we would call *"Apuntes"* a long poem containing, among other things, a number of gunsaku haiku sequences portraying the region of Baeza, southern Spain.

When the poet and scholar Robert Hayden's book *The Night-Blooming Cereus* came out in 1972 it contained the following haiku sequence:

Smelt Fishing

I
In the cold spring night
the smelt are spawning. Sportsmen
fevered crowd the lake.

II
Thin snow scatters on
the wind, melting as it falls.
Cries for help for light.

III
Who is he night-
waters entangle, reclaim?
Blank fish-eyes.

Hayden's fame as a poet will continue to rest on his great evocation of the horror of the slave trade in "Middle Passage" and the compassion of such poems as "The Whipping", written well before this small group of haiku. But Hayden put as much skill and passion into these small pieces of a gripping narrative as he did into any other poem he wrote. In the first haiku the dampness and cold of the spring night contrast vividly with the heat of animal activity—two kinds of animals. Next the cold and the dampness deepen as thick snowflakes land. There is a sudden commotion of fishermen's cries through the wind-blown, wet snow. Then it is over; someone has gone under the water, and remains there. The lyrical voice of the poet intrudes, to be summarily met with the calm indifference of nature, caring no more for a human dragged under water than for a fish dragged above it.

This is an unalterable sequence. The first haiku could stand alone and be fully intelligible—but it pulls us onward. We only come to fully understand the action of verse II and the depth of III in the light of the previous verses.

By 1974 *Haiku Magazine* devoted several pages to haiku sequences, many of them narratives. Today virtually all of the

English language haiku magazines publish sequences of haiku, most of which fall into one of three categories. Some, like the Japanese gunsaku or the *"Apuntes"* of Antonio Machado, portray various aspects of a particular subject or topic in relatively independent haiku. Others seem to fall between the rensaku Japanese poets were writing in the 1930s and 1940s and the sort of tightly structured narrative exemplified in Hayden's "Smelt Fishing". And, during the last decade or so, several haiku sequences have appeared that consist of poems which can stand separately, but which are linked to one another in much the same way as the stanzas in a renga.

The following sequence of one-line haiku was assembled from notes taken during a 1966 trip to Africa; the piece was worked up over a long period of time and finally published in a 1981 issue of *Frogpond*. Here is Elizabeth Searle Lamb's

A Sequence from Lagos, Nigeria

mosquitoes in airport's hot moist air hum

"dash me, dash me"   all the kids begging ha'pennies

a mammy-wagon named *Daddy Come Soon* rattling down the
                                                                         street

after drinking palm wine young men toss down empty gourds

the 16 Palm Nuts   thrown to fall 'according to the will of Ifa'

how cold the bronze   this ancient Benin warrior

way back in the market's chattering crush   monkey skull

a street vendor sleeping in a doorway   his candle burning the storyteller turns round to pee into the dusk

into the deepest of the nightdark   the talking drums

A variety of resonances holds all these images together. The swarming, humming mosquitoes become the swarming, shouting children. One characteristic expression leads to another, as children's cries give way to the noise of a rattletrap bus carrying its vivid name and ladies who sell their wares to market. The bus finds its echo in the rattling of gourds. Falling gourds immediately become palm nuts, thrown in careful ritual, as some look for their fortunes in divination while others drink theirs. The will of Ifa suggests the warrior's fate, and the clatter and crash of ancient warfare suggest the bustle of the marketplace itself, which yields another silent relic of noisier days. As the market grows quiet, a street vendor falls asleep, his life almost hard to detect in the lengthening shadows, dimly pierced by candlelight. Yet there is activity in the shadows, as a storyteller pauses in pouring out his tale to pour out another sign of life. And the drops spattering in the dust find their deeper echo in another form of communication as old as the story itself, the talking drums.

Part of the excitement of Lamb's sequence, for me at least, comes from the earthiness and exoticism of the images to one raised in a large modern city. But that excitement is greatly enhanced by the skillful shifting that takes place from one image to the next. While each seems perfectly natural to its time and place, and to the sequence of events from daylight to dark, the inner connections from verse to verse raise their own excitement. Whether I analyze them or not, these inner connections are psychologically "right", in effect discovering and capitalizing on the archetypal sensations embedded in each minute experience.

BEYOND HAIKU?

Since the kinds of writing discussed in this chapter developed after the era of Bashō, who the Japanese consider the father of haiku, I have called the chapter Beyond Haiku. But the independent hokku-become-haiku and the independent tsukeku-become-senryu share a common beginning in renga. And the haiku sequence, of whatever variety, derives from the impulse to group individual perceptions in ways that are aesthetically pleasing—the foundation of renga. In effect, this handbook should be called Beyond Renga, since all but a few of its topics derive from renga directly or indirectly.

If the single image, the elemental fibre of human perception, is like haiku or senryu, then human understanding and pleasure result from the bringing together of these fibres into the stronger cords of renga. The Japanese that initiated, nurtured, and enjoyed the renga for several centuries developed a powerful unity of spirit and aesthetic. This aesthetic spirit pervades many aspects of Japanese society, not just those associated with haiku, senryu, and so on. Perhaps by studying one or another of these branches of literature we can develop our own understanding of and participation in this spirit.

16

The Uses of Haiku

WHY THIS CHAPTER?

Chapter 10, Sharing Haiku, offers writers a number of suggestions for sharing their haiku. Readers will find other books of haiku listed in Resources, following this chapter. But beyond the sharing that is the heart of haiku, and all literature, there are several specific ways that the haiku has helped people with a wide variety of interests. In particular, the haiku has served as an introduction to other subjects, and as a means of learning and using several skills.

Since haiku involve two basic acts, reading and writing, the bulk of this chapter approaches the uses of haiku in one or the other of these two ways. This is something of an artificial distinction, for both reading and writing are parts of one larger process, language. I hope that readers will find ideas of interest to them in the section for writers, and vice-versa.

Teachers, whether of language, literature, history, or the social sciences, should find much here to take them beyond the simple introductions to the writing of haiku found in Part Three of this book. For literature exists because people write, and put life into their writings. And that life goes far beyond literature itself.

FOR THE READER

Reading haiku helps us to respect the experience of others. Through reading haiku we can come to know the sensations and events which have moved fellow human beings. We can begin to understand again how deeply human beings in all times and places identify with the environment in which they live, and the creatures that live there with them, as in this excellent haiku in Arabic by Abdelhadi Barchale, of Casablanca, Morocco:

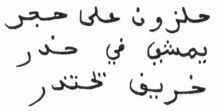

a snail on the stones
advances with care.
autumn draws to an end.

Robert Bly, in an essay called "Dropping the Reader", offers both a justification for the writing of a short poem, and some thoughts on the benefits of reading a short poem. Here is part of it:

> Most of the emotions we have are brief: they appear suddenly and vanish. They are part of the swift life of the intelligence. . . . A brief poem does without the scaffolding of secondary ideas. Because of this, it moves more swiftly than the longer poem and with more intellectual exhilaration. . . . In the brief poem . . . the poet takes the reader to the edge of a cliff, as a mother eagle takes its nestling, and then drops him. Readers with a strong imagination enjoy it, and discover they can fly. The others fall down to the rocks where they are killed instantly.

The writer of a short poem—and particularly a haiku—invites the reader to take off, to become dynamically involved in the poetic process. As with music, the poem only begins in the writing, and finds its completion in a process that includes the sounding of the poem in the reader or hearer's mind, and the echoes it awakens there.

While a haiku itself is brief and extremely limited in what it directly presents, the responses to a haiku are not. In the late 1960s I had the honor of the author's help in translating a Japanese newspaper article called "My Favorite Poems—From the Traveler's Heart". In it Takahashi Nobuyuki quotes a poem by Kawamoto Gafu, haiku master and editor of *Itadori* magazine, and offers his own response to Gafu's poem:

> *akashiya no*   by the acacia's
> *shiroku ōki na*   large, white blossoms
> *hana ni furare*   fallen on . . .

This poem calls to mind the figure of the poet, tall and at ease, and imparts to me the calm of having returned from a long journey. The poem, ending with the passive "fallen on", shows exactly the position and attitude of the relaxed writer. The combination of such a poet and the large, white blossoms causes me to remember Fugen Bodhisattva mounted on a white elephant or seated upon a white lotus bloom, giving me the feeling of having returned to the home of the spirit. Then, too, perhaps I may recall the roadside acacias of my childhood, passed in Dairen, China, and the lifetime of my father.

The haiku triggers our own thoughts and memories based on our own experiences. Here Professor Takahashi responds to Gafu's poem with a picture of the poet in "the calm of having returned from a long journey". Then the image of the poet in his mind shifts to that of Fugen Bodhisattva, who is associated with white through the elephant and the lotus. This image moves Professor Takahashi to the "home of the spirit". Now he remembers his childhood home, where acacias bloomed, and his father in those days. In each of these mental images the figure represents authority, and the flowers are associated with the calmness, the comfort of home in the poet's return, the spiritual home, the childhood home.

Haiku teach us not only to respect the experience of others, but to recall and treasure our own experience. In letting his mind contemplate Gafu's haiku, Professor Takahashi discovered connections among poetry, religion, and his own personal history. May we all learn to find such rich rewards in our own reading!

Aside from the deeply personal rewards of reading haiku, the study of the Japanese haiku in this or any book on the subject quickly leads to other, related subjects. Obviously, haiku is a good place to begin the study of Japanese poetry. Many other aspects of Japanese culture gradually reveal themselves to the student of haiku, as well. But haiku has been important in much of modern world literature, and studying it will help us understand not only the techniques of some modern writers, but some of the aspects of life and literature which they found important.

Despite its brevity, and the difficulty which that creates for many mature Westerners (it is not usually a difficulty for children), the haiku genre rewards a conscientious student more quickly than almost any other kind of Japanese poetry. Some Japanese haiku require a considerable understanding of other Chinese and Japanese literature before their meaning becomes clear. But many are fully understandable on first reading. The history and technique of haiku place it central among the other genres of Japanese poetry. From haiku, as this book suggests, one can branch out to explore the intricacies of the closely allied renga and senryu, and begin to look at the deep tradition of the tanka. Indeed, the earliest tanka remind one of haiku, with their directness and simplicity. Also, the haibun relates to a variety of Japanese prose writings, particularly the long tradition of poetic travel journals and diaries. Finally, the history of haiku since the beginning of the influx of Western literature into Japan gives a window on the upheavals in all of Japanese literature during the modern era. Thus haiku offers one of the best places to begin studying Japanese literature.

As the amount of haiku activity in Japan today suggests, haiku is also a major manifestation of Japanese culture generally. For example, those who wish to understand the underlying principles of traditional Japanese art would do well to begin with the study of haiku painting, called *haiga*. The haiku poet Buson was one of the finest painters of his day, a pillar of the *Nanga*, "Southern Style", or *Bunjinga*, "Literati Style" of painting, and a master of haiga.

Haiga involve a spare, sketch-like picture and a haiku in calligraphy in the same piece of art. Such scrolls and art objects frequently grace the focal center of the main room in a traditional Japanese house, and usually provide the only visual relief in the plain room reserved for the famous Japanese tea ceremony. An understanding of this poetry and art will put one in the correct frame of mind for participating in the ceremony, so some knowledge of Japanese poetry and painting becomes necessary for the full appreciation of the ritual.

Similarly, many of the Japanese traditional arts, but particularly the haiku, have a special connection with Zen Buddhism. Indeed, some authors, such as D. T. Suzuki and Alan Watts, seem unable to mention haiku without noting what they see as its characteristic Zen. This point of view also dominates the works of R. H. Blyth. While I have not emphasized the connection in this handbook, ignoring it would be like ignoring the connection of Christianity with the paintings of Michelangelo and the music of J. S. Bach. Christianity undoubtedly had much to do with many of the arts of Western Europe, not only providing artists with their subject matter in many cases, but helping to create the world view from which their artistry grew. To this extent one may study Japanese haiku as part of the milieu which flowered from the interaction of native Japanese culture and the culture and religion imported from Korea and China. This interaction resulted in many adaptations of continental government, philosophy, art, religion (including Zen), and literature to the needs of the Japanese sensibility.

Along with Buddhism, Zen or otherwise, we can find Confucianism in haiku. For example, there is Shiki's

jūnen no	ten years'
kugaku ke no naki	hard study threadbare
mōfu kana	this blanket

—the first four words of which (three in the original) Shiki quotes directly from the Confucian *Analects*. Thus Shiki pays homage to Confucius and notes the long devotion which he has given to the study of haiku, in spite of hardship. His wry humor adds a hint of Japanese spice to the otherwise Chinese flavor of this verse.

Beyond Japanese culture, haiku has been important for many Western poets, from Pound and Ginsberg to Eluard and Seferis, each of whom wrote haiku during their early decades in the art of poetry. Some critics have maintained that these Western poets have only poorly understood haiku, and that haiku was relatively unimportant in their development. As far as the poets' understanding of haiku goes, the following quotation should help set the record straight. The writer is John Gould Fletcher, a colleague of Ezra Pound and Amy Lowell during the days of Imagism in London; he is introducing the first book to contain both translations of Japanese haiku and an extensive selection of original haiku in English, Kenneth Yasuda's *A Pepper-Pod*, published in 1946. Fletcher tells, directly and simply, what modern Western poetry owes to haiku:

> The only difference between the Japanese *haiku* poet and the Western . . . poets is this: the Japanese is content to suggest an object, and leaves the resulting emotion for the reader to complete in his own mind. The Western poet states the emotion, along with the object or objects that provoked it; and frequently in stating his emotion, he overdoes it.

I cannot imagine a better critique of much eighteenth and nineteenth century Western poetry, or introduction to that of the twentieth. From the Imagists on, the better Western poets of our era have largely tried to present the causes of their emotions, clean of the emoting that clutters so much earlier work.

Not only poets, but novelists and essayists have been influenced by haiku. Among modern Japanese fiction writers, Natsume Sōseki (1867–1916), Akutagawa Ryūnosuke (1892–1927), and Kawabata Yasunari (1899–1972) have all been intimately connected with haiku throughout their careers. Sōseki and Akutagawa (as they are usually called in Western critical writing, using the pen name of one and the surname of the other) both wrote and published haiku regularly. The story-telling impulse can be seen in some of their haiku:

> *kao arau*   face-washing
> *tarai ni tatsu*   in the basin rises
> *aki no kage*   autumn's shadow
>
>   *Sōseki*

> *arijigoku*   ant lion's trap—
> *kage shite botan*   making shade, the peony
> *hana akaki*   blossom is red
>
> *Gaki (Akutagawa's haiku pen name)*

Although Kawabata was not widely known as a haiku poet, he occasionally wrote some, and his novels dwell on the minute details of everyday life with an aesthetic distance akin to that of the haiku.

Among Western novelists Jack Kerouac stands out as the one most interested in haiku. As noted in Chapter 5, The Haiku Movement in English, his *Dharma Bums* introduced haiku to many American readers; it also portrays his own introduction to the genre, which was to figure so strongly in the early portion of *Desolation Angels*. The irony and humor that pervade much of Kerouac's writing also came out in his "haikus", particularly his senryu:

> Missing a kick
>   at the icebox door
> It closed anyway.

Western essayists, too, have fallen under the spell of Japanese literature, and particularly the haiku. Lafcadio Hearn (1850–1904) was already a lover of the macabre before he arrived in Japan and collected a number of Japanese folk tales and weird stories. But the style of Japanese haiku may have influenced his prose, which seems more lucid and free of unnecessary decoration in the books he wrote in Japan. An extreme example, perhaps, is his diary of a climb up Mount Fuji, in *Exotics and Retrospectives;* here is a short, haibun-like excerpt:

> Open country with scattered clumps of trees,—larch and pine. Nothing in the horizon but scraggy tree-tops above what seems to be the rim of a vast down [i.e., hill]. No sign of Fuji. . . . For the first time I noticed that the road is black,—black sand and cinders apparently, volcanic cinders: the wheels of the kuruma [i.e., cart] and the feet of the runners sink into it with a crunching sound.

> The rain has stopped, and the sky becomes a clearer gray. . . . The trees decrease in size and number as we advance.

(Ellipses as in the original.) Pretty crisp language for a book published in 1898! The last part is like a concluding haiku.

Most recently, the French critic Roland Barthes (1915–1980) found in haiku an epitome of Japanese culture, and devoted a major portion of one of his last books, *Empire of Signs*, to a discussion of haiku that seems more relevant to Barthes' ideas about language than to haiku itself. In effect the haiku illuminates his thought, rather than the other way around. Perhaps that is as he wished it.

The haiku, with its apparent simplicity and directness, helped to generate—and points to—a vast body of literature written by people who intend to be understood. The whole of literature is like an endless net; pick it up at any knotting of the strands, and you find yourself connected to all the rest.

FOR THE WRITER

For the writer haiku brings direct and immediate rewards. Writing haiku claims and confirms one's experience of the world, and offers an opportunity to construct ideal experiences which enrich one's inner life. Haiku poets must clarify their language, due to the imposed brevity, and they must base their writing in images, the most powerful tool of all writing. Whether Japanese or Western, haiku poets enter directly into an experience of Japanese culture, art, and thought at a level that long-term visitors in Japan may never achieve. Deeply understood, the act of writing haiku affords an opportunity for meditation that may be a rewarding philosophical or religious experience.

Canadian haiku poet and physician George Swede, in an article entitled "The Role of Haiku in Poetry Therapy", says:

> Haiku is a poetic form which avoids the use of metaphor, simile, and other poetic devices, obtaining its effects primarily through the juxtaposition of sensory impressions. If done successfully, this juxtaposition creates a moment of acute awareness about the external world. The person wrapped up in himself is forced outward to a consideration of the unity of nature.

While there is certainly subjectivity in writing a haiku, the act usually involves trying hard to see, and to remember accurately what one has seen; to hear, and so on. While the pathologically self-involved may need this discipline, I suspect that we all could use some of it. They say Gautama Siddhartha was a very rich young man, and that only after he left the confines of his luxurious home and gazed on the commoners' world outside did he begin the long seeking that resulted in Buddhahood. I take this as a parable for the fact that only after we examine the minute particulars of our daily lives can we come to a knowledge of "life". Perhaps the many persons who find themselves bored with their lives could come to enjoy them through writing haiku.

Shiki suggested that haiku poets write mainly from their actual, direct experience. But even he allowed fiction into haiku, and the Buson he admired was a master at creating fantasy haiku. This does not mean that haiku should go beyond the realistic possibilities of this world, but that one may, on occasion, create a new experience in the process of making haiku. Here is how I wrote one such poem:

Walking home from the post office, I heard for some moments a metal wind chime tinkling in the wind. I recalled that it was the day of the winter solstice, so I started to construct a haiku with the words "solstice . . . wind in the / wind chimes".

Still hearing the wind chimes, I noticed the smell of wood smoke. Though it was earlier, I decided to place the experience at dusk, a time when wood smoke is more smelled than seen. When I got home I played around with a few versions, at one point writing:

> winter solstice
>
>   dusk
>
> smoke in the
> wind in the wind
>
>   chimes

As I was repeating my written versions aloud, I realized that the word "smoke" alone provided a visual image rather than the scent of wood smoke I had experienced. So I added "wood" to the formation. While writing and sounding a few different arrangements with "wood smoke" my own wooden wind chimes came to mind, providing a sound that I preferred to the brassier wind chimes I had actually heard.

Now I had moved time forward an hour or so from afternoon to dusk, and changed the wind chimes from metal to wood. Recalling that in the original experience the sound of wind chimes had preceded the smell of wood smoke, I reorganized the images in an order closer to the original experience. Since the words "winter solstice" weighed the poem down more than a haiku can stand, but I wanted the sense of the solstice in it, I decided to title the haiku, something not done very often. The final haiku:

Winter Solstice

wooden wind chimes
in the wind in the
wood smoke dusk

This haiku combines associations that I have not in fact encountered all together. Whenever I smell wood smoke I recall my grandmother's cottage in the trees and its wood stove. The words "dusk" and "smoke" set up a special resonance for me with their elemental sounds. Dusk on the day of the winter solstice comes early, accentuating our desire to be at home by the fire. Wind and wood smoke also suggest to me wind roaring through the trees high overhead, as I often experienced them at my grandmother's. And all this is suffused with the rare music of wooden wind chimes, bringing to mind the entrance of the Chinese block in Bartok's "Music for Strings, Percussion, and Celesta". These images reawaken in me the joys that I have had at such moments in my life, and combine to create a new moment in my imagination to join the rest.

Taking up the haiku will help us make our language more accurate, base our writing in images, and cut our words to the essentials. Gwendolyn Brooks, who began her own "Poets in the Prisons" program, visiting inmates who were trying to write long before it became fashionable or remunerative to do so, introduced

Etheridge Knight to haiku. Later, Knight said:

> my poems/were/too 'prosy'—too filled with 'abstractions'
> rather/than/images . . .

> I really got into haiku when I learned (read/or/"heard"
> somewhere) that the "original" haiku poets/were in to
> haiku *primarily* as/an/oral/being and the "written" poem
> as secondary—as simply an/ extension of the spoken
> word . . .

During his stay in prison Knight taught himself to write strik-
ing poems, and his haiku are no exception:

> Under moon shadows
> A tall boy flashes knife and
> Slices star bright ice.

The Penal Farm

> The wire fence is tall.
> The lights in the prison barracks
> Flick off, one by one.

Haiku poets who are open enough to let it happen can join
Selma Stefanile, for whom "Sometimes the haiku impulse works
as my 'touchstone' towards a [different kind of] poem." When we
set out to write a haiku we may have to give up that objective and
let the poem come as it must, as in this tanka-like piece of hers,
which probably began as an attempt at haiku:

Wabash

> the old rowboat
> will rest on the bank
> under the sycamore
> all winter
> the doll in the fishnet

The experience of writing haiku undoubtedly accounts for the sharpness of the images and language in Stefanile's other poems as well as in her haiku.

Those who write haiku—in Japanese or any other language— come to know a bit of Japanese art and thought from the inside. How deeply the practice of haiku permeates Japanese life may be seen from these comments by Fujiwara Noburo, made during an interview with Lucien Stryk a few years ago. Noburo, then fifty, is a member of the Tenrō School of haiku, and a practicing Zen Buddhist.

Like all children I learnt about [haiku] in school, was strongly drawn to them, especially Bashō's. We were encouraged from time to time to write our own, as a form of writing exercise leading to the cultivation of good style. The practical element was emphasized, the rules held all important—the spirit of the poems only occasionally looked into . . . .

What [the leaders of the Tenrō School of haiku] tell us is every place is full of poetry. All one has to do is go find the poems . . . . We select an interesting and beautiful place and, on the spot, compose *its* poetry.

. . . The main thing is we really open our eyes, whether or not good poems come—and so discover a spirit there. We're made aware through active seeking of the presence of poetry all around us, begin, slowly to be sure, to see our personal world in the same spirit. . . .

[Regarding the clarity and directness of Japanese art:]

I suspect it has much to do with our attempt to discover essences—about which Zen teaches us more than anything else. Take a sumie work [black-ink painting]: purely the essence of a scene, details absorbed, harmonized. In haiku it's the same—a weeding out of all that would clutter, muddy, confuse, leading to great incisiveness, clear purpose. What we are looking for, guided by Zen, is revelation . . . .

[To the question, "Why do you write haiku?"]

Because I love haiku, and because I am Japanese; it expresses the spirit of our people. It makes one feel part of something essential to the culture of our nation.

A glimmer of the depth of the tradition Noburo feels himself part of may be seen in the following haiku by Yamaguchi Seishi, founder of the Tenrō School:

hanano ni wa	in the flower-field
iwa ari kubo ari	are rocks, are hollows,
hana arite	and are flowers

Japanese, and those of Japanese descent living outside of Japan, have practiced haiku wherever they found themselves, thus retaining one of the deepest and most characteristic features of their culture despite the trials their ethnicity may have caused them. Earlier I mentioned Kenneth Yasuda's book, *A Pepper-Pod*, with his translations of Japanese haiku and original haiku in English. Yasuda, an American citizen born in California, was studying Japanese literature in Japan when he broke off his studies and came home shortly before the war between Japan and the United States erupted. Toward the end of the war he was forced from his home and imprisoned in "relocation centers" in Arkansas and Wyoming, losing all his possessions in the process. Despite the violence between nations, Yasuda continued to work at adapting his ancestral culture to the landscape and language of his homeland. The delicacy of his best work shows in these haiku, originally written in English, from *A Pepper-Pod*:

The Rain

Tenderly again
On the peony I hear
Whispers of the rain.

Irises

Irises in bloom,
Soon the white one too will fade
Into the gathering gloom.

The Mississippi River

Under the low grey
Winter skies water pushes
Water on its way.

Another Japanese-American, Soichi Furuta, has written both
as a translator and poet of haiku. Furuta, who lives in New York
City, writes in both Japanese and English—and translates both
ways—a wide variety of work, much of it published both here
and in Japan. He composes his haiku in Japanese; here are a pair
with his own translations, written originally to accompany the
photographs of Frank Dituri and appearing in their book, *a man
never becoming a line . . . . . .*, published in 1979:

koto kurete	a late day in Vienna
chōzō no ashi	I come upon statues' bare legs
torihada su	goose-fleshed

gūrū no	a guru leering
ichigei aki no	right out of a torn poster
yare posutā	in autumn light

In 1981 The Coach House Press in Toronto published *Paper
Doors*, one of the finest anthologies of poetry by those of Japanese
descent yet seen on this continent. From among poems in many
styles by Japanese-Canadian authors, here are three of the several
haiku included by editors Gerry Shikatani and David Aylward,
with Aylward's translations into English:

rokkiisan	Soundless
yogiri oto naku	Rocky Mountain
kayote naku	foggy night:

Coyote's cry.

Takeo Ujō Nakano

momo taburu	Peach
warabe ubu ge no	munching
maruki hoho	kiddies'
	downy
	round
	cheeks

Tomi Nishimura

asatsuyu ni	Soaked
shimeri chūsha no	in morning dew
ihanhyō	a parking ticket

Chūsaburō Koshū Itō

Whether one is a Westerner or a Japanese, the exercises of reading and writing haiku bring a wide range of personal benefits, some intellectual and aesthetic, some practical.

FOR THE EARTH

The arts have always transcended national boundaries, as this book demonstrates for the haiku. The haiku has also been a democratizing force; since before Bashō's day people of all levels of society have written what we call haiku. As people within a society, or in different societies, share with one another the objects and events that mean something in their lives they come to know one another better. Perhaps the haiku, in its small way, will help us toward a world with greater understanding among all people, of whatever class or nation.

Haiku reading and writing can lead to a deeper understanding and appreciation for life, and in particular for our environment. When Mori Sumio writes of the few geese migrating overhead he recalls that in former days geese were much more plentiful, as reflected in both his own memory and the whole span of Japanese literature. Perhaps through his poem we will come to reflect upon the loss of geese in the modern world, and this may motivate us to "live more lightly on the earth"—as some American Indians have expressed it.

According to Bashō, putting our eyes and our thoughts on nature is the highest refinement of civilization. Here is how he expressed it in *Oi no kobumi (Notes of a Pack-Basket)*, a travel diary written in 1687–1688, a year or two after the "old pond" haiku. Saigyō and Sōgi we have already met; Sesshū (1420–1506) was a great Zen painter; Sen no Rikyū (1522–1591) the greatest master of the tea ceremony. Bashō has told how the way of poetry came to dominate his life; now he allies himself with the tradition of all high art, and explains its source:

> Through the waka of Saigyō, the renga of Sōgi, the painting of Sesshū, and the tea of Rikyū, one thing flows. People of such refinement submit to nature and befriend the four seasons. Where they look is nothing but flowers, what they think is nothing but the moon. Perceiving shapes other than flowers amounts to being a barbarian. Holding thoughts other than the moon is akin to being a beast. Come out from barbarians, depart from beasts. Submit to nature, return to nature.

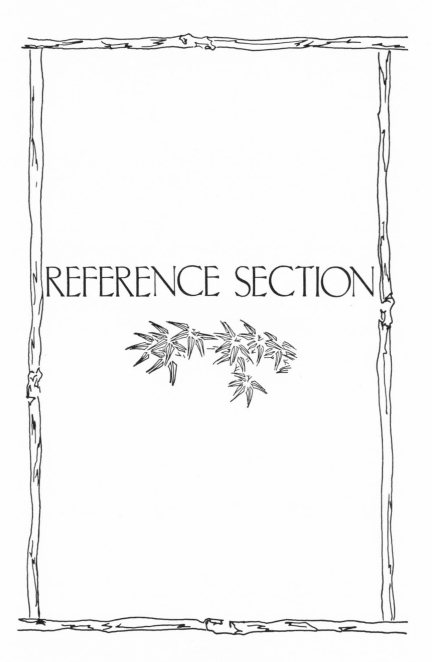

REFERENCE SECTION

Season–Word List
and Index

Chapter 7, Nature and Haiku, gives the rationale behind seasonal topics (kidai) in traditional Japanese poetry. A season-word list collects the "season words" (kigo) poets have used to incorporate kidai in their poems, and organizes these words for reference. The list below contains about 600 words and phrases, arranged in their traditional seasons and categories. By Japanese standards this is a very short list, but I have saved space by leaving out all kigo which name the season, except those in the poems translated in this handbook.

This list is also an index to the Japanese haiku and tanka in the handbook which have traditional season words; their page numbers follow the entry where appropriate. However, this index does not work for Japanese poems without season words, or for Western-language poems.

Each entry gives the Japanese kigo, followed by a relatively literal English translation (with an explanation in parentheses, if needed). Occasionally, where two Japanese terms have the same meaning I have placed them together with a slant between. A comma separates equally valid translations, with the first usually the more literal. If the word "or" separates two meanings, they are quite different, and only context will show which is intended. In a few instances I have saved space by judicious use of parentheses. Square brackets indicate a meaning not justified in the Japanese words, but which a Japanese reader will normally assume.

Traditional analysts organize kidai and kigo into one of six or seven categories within each season. I have chosen a relatively conservative breakdown, including:

jikō (season, climate)—the most basic seasonal phenomena relating to time and temperature;

tenmon (astronomy)—all sky phenomena, precipitation, winds;

chiri (geography)—surface phenomena, on land and water;

gyōji* (observances)—sacred and secular holidays;

seikatsu* (livelihood, life)—human work, play, and rest;

dōbutsu (animals)—from mammals and birds to bugs and worms;

shokubutsu (plants)—flowers and foliage from trees to seaweed.

A few moments spent perusing one season from beginning to end will familiarize you with the organization.

The New Year—a holiday period traditionally combining features of such Western celebrations as Bastille Day or the Fourth of July, Christmas or Hanukkah, Thanksgiving, and, in premodern times, the beginning of spring and everyone's personal birthday—has a section of its own at the end of the list, and is not divided into categories.

Please note that the Japanese feel the equinoxes and solstices as the peaks of the seasons, not the beginnings of them as we do

---

*Some authorities combine *gyōji* and *seikatsu* into *jinji* (human affairs).

in the West. Accordingly, their seasons start more than a month before ours. I have indicated the modern months of each season at its beginning.

Also note that there is no distinction between singular and plural for most nouns. In haiku, with a few exceptions, nouns should be interpreted as singular. A parenthetical *s* after an English translation indicates that this word should sometimes be taken as plural.

HARU	**SPRING** (February, March, April)
JIKŌ	SEASON, CLIMATE
saekaeru	clear and cold
atataka	warm
uraraka	bright
nodoka(sa)	tranquil(lity)
nagaki hi	long day
hi no nagai	day is long
osoki hi	slow day
shunchū	spring noon, 38, 231
haru no yume	spring dream
haru no kure	spring's end, 21, 28
natsu chikaki	summer near, 26
TENMON	ASTRONOMY
wasurejimo	forgotten frost
oborozuki	hazy moon
oboroyo	hazy [moonlit] night
tsuki no kasa	halo of the moon
kasumi/kasumu	mist/to mist, 24
usugasumi	thin mist
yūgasumi	evening mist
kagerō	heat shimmer, heat waves, 18
kaze hikaru	wind is bright
kochi	east wind
kunpū	fragrant breeze, balmy breeze

CHIRI	GEOGRAPHY
yukima	between snowfalls, or, in the snow
nokoru yuki	leftover snow, 23
yukidoke	melting snow
ukikōri	floating ice, ice floes
nadare	snow-slide, avalanche
mizu nurumu	water warms up
haru no mizu	waters of spring, 14
yama warau	mountains/hills smile (i.e., with flowers)

GYŌJI	OBSERVANCES
saohime	Saohime, goddess of spring (compare Flora)
ise mairi	Ise pilgrimage
kamiji yama	Mt. Kamiji (lit., "Gods' Path Mountain"; at Ise Shrine)
omizutori	getting holy water
higan	equinox week, Nirvana week
chūnichi	equinox, middle day [of *higan*]
nehan-e/nehanzō	Nirvana picture, Nirvana portrait [of Buddha]
efumi	[Christ-] picture-trampling (to demonstrate one was not Christian, during an Inquisition)
yabuiri	Servants' Day, Menials' Day
hina matsuri	Doll Festival
hina	doll
uri-hina	doll(s) for sale

SEIKATSU	LIVELIHOOD, LIFE
yake (no) no	burnt-over field(s), 183
tagayasu	to plow

hata (o) utsu	till the field, hoe the field
nawashiro	rice-seedling field
monotane	seeds
kaiko	silkworms
kogai	tending silkworms
shiohi	low tide
shiohigata	low-tide beach, 18, 117
kai hirou	gather shells
cha tsumi	tea [leaf] picking
rofusagi	closing the fireplace
tako	kite (the toy), 103
fūsen	balloon
furakoko	swing

DŌBUTSU   ANIMALS

neko no koi	cats in love, the love-making of cats
neko no ko	kitten(s)
momonga	flying squirrel(s)
nezumi no su	nest of mice, rats' nest
uguisu	nightingale, bush warbler, 98
hibari	skylark(s)
agehibari	soaring skylark, 103
kiji	pheasant
yamadori	copper pheasant
komadori	robin
tsubame	swallow(s)
kari/gan/kigan/ karigane	[wild] geese, [wild] goose
kaeru kari	returning [wild] geese
tsuru	crane, stork
suzume	sparrow(s), 29, 108, 187
momochidori	ten thousand birds, 142
saezuri	twittering [of birds]
washi no su	eagle's nest

270 Reference Section

shirauo	white fish, whitebait
awabi	abalone, 185
kato	tadpoles
kawazu/kaeru	frog(s), 9, 103, 122, 126, 224, 229
tokage	lizard
chō/kochō	butterfly, 129
abu	horse-fly
tanishi	paddy-snail(s), snail(s), mud-snail(s), 35

SHOKUBUTSU — PLANTS

ume (no hana)	plum (blossoms)*
yanagi	willow, 13
tsubaki	camellia [blossom(s)]
hatsuzakura	first cherry [blossoms]
sakura (no hana)	cherry (blossoms)
yamazakura	mountain cherry [blossoms]
itozakura	thread cherry, weeping cherry [blossoms]
yaezakura	double cherry [blossoms]
sakura saku	cherries bloom
sakura chiru	cherries [blossoms] fall
hana	[cherry] blossoms (anciently, plum)
hana no kumo	cloud(s) of [cherry] blossoms
hana chiru	[cherry] blossoms fall, 99
chiru hana	falling [cherry] blossoms

*Unless otherwise specified, the name of a flowering tree or shrub indicates the flowers of that tree or shrub; however, the words *no hana* ('s blossoms) are sometimes included.

rakka	fallen [cherry] blossoms
sakuragari	cherry [-blossom-] viewing
hanami	[cherry-] flower-viewing
hana no hagoshi	[moon] through [cherry-] blossom petals
oigi no hana	old [cherry] tree's flowers
matsu (no) hana	pine flowers
momo (no hana)	peach (blossoms)
nashi (no hana)	pear (blossoms), 22
anzu no hana	apricot blossoms
na no hana	mustard flowers (usually called "rape flowers" in English; the plants are similar)
nabatake	field(s) of mustard
fuji (no hana)	wisteria (blossoms)
chūrippu	tulip(s)
yamabuki	mountain rose(s), yellow rose(s)
bara no hana	bramble blossoms (not to be confused with its homonym, *bara*, rose, a summer season word)
azami (no hana)	thistle (blossom(s)), 127
tsutsuji	azaleas
tanpopo	dandelions
nazuna (hana)	shepherd's purse
itadori	giant knotweed (lit., "tiger cane")
asagao	morning glory
sumire (-gusa)	violets
seri	parsley
kusa moyuru	grass sprouts
ko no me	tree buds
meudo	asparagus sprouts
negi no hana	onion flowers
warabi	bracken
nori	[edible] seaweed, laver

NATSU

SUMMER (May, June, July)

JIKŌ

SEASON, CLIMATE

natsu-mekite	summer-appearing, 87
kachō	summer morn, 33
natsu no yo	summer night, 34
mijikayo	short night
satsuki yami	June darkness, 35
suzushi(sa)	cool(ness), 19
atsusa	heat

TENMON

ASTRONOMY

kumo no mine	cloud peaks, billowing clouds
samidare	June rains, 210
yūdachi	evening shower, sudden shower
niji	rainbow, 109
inazuma	lightning, 228, 229
enten	burning sky, burning sunshine
atsuki hi	hot sun
suzukaze	cool breeze
asakaze	morning breeze
kaze no kaori	wind scent, 125

CHIRI

GEOGRAPHY

aoi yama	green hills/mountains, 30
aota	green [rice] fields/paddies
shimizu	clear water, 3, 13
yamashimizu	clear mountain water
kiyotaki	clear waterfall
natsugawa	summer river, 24
yakezuna	scorching sand

GYŌJI	OBSERVANCES
kidachi	wooden sword
ryūtō	floating lantern, 36
nobori	[carp] banner
degawari	change of servants, or, departing servant
koromogae	change of clothes

SEIKATSU	LIVELIHOOD, LIFE
taue	[rice-] paddy-planting
taue-uta	paddy-planting song, rice-planting song
take ueru	to plant bamboo
amagoi	prayers for rain
mugi karu	cutting barley
aoume	green plums, or, a kind of pickled plum
ume tsukeru	to pickle plums
uchiwa/sen	fan, paper fan
ōgi	fan, folding fan
hirune	midday nap
suzumi	cooling [oneself], 195
yūsuzumi/yoisuzumi	cooling at evening
aisukuriimu	ice cream (Japanese word derived from English)
oyogi	swimming
kayari(bi)	mosquito smudge
kaya	mosquito net
yūgatō	bug-trap lamp
shimi	silverfish
u	cormorant
ubune	cormorant [fishing] boat
sushi	sushi (a food, often taken on picnics)

DŌBUTSU	ANIMALS
ka no ko	fawn
uma no ko	foal
(ō)neko	(huge) cat
hototogisu	cuckoo, 229
kankodori	cuckoo, (a different species from *hototogisu*)
kuina	water hen, moor hen
kawasemi	kingfisher
aosagi	blue heron, grey heron, 12
shirosagi	white heron
yoshikiri	oriole, reed warbler
ayu	trout, or sweetfish
hatsugatsuo	first bonito
medaka	killifish
kani	crab
aogaeru/amagaeru	green frog(s)/rain frog(s), tree frog(s)
hikigaeru/gama	toad
nomi	fleas
shirami	lice
hae	fly, flies, 17
ka	mosquito(es), 227
yabuka	bush mosquito(es)
kabashira	column of mosquitoes, pillar of gnats
natsu no chō	summer butterfly, 39
hotaru	firefly
ōbotaru	huge firefly, 127
ari	ants
yama-ari	mountain ants
ha-ari	winged ants, flying ants
semi	cicada, 11
matsu no semi	pine cicada
hebi	snake
kumo	spider

haramigumo	pregnant spider
katatsumuri	snail (different species from *tanishi*, spring)
namekuji(ri)	slug
ga	moth
hitorimushi	tiger moth (lit., "light-taking moth")
bōfura/bōfuri	mosquito larvae
maimai/mizusumashi	water beetle, whirligig
kemushi	caterpillar

SHOKUBUTSU   PLANTS

u no hana	*deutzia scabra* (perhaps resembles saxifrage?)
botan	peony, 35, 39, 116, 249
shakuyaku	peony (a different species)
kakitsubata	iris(es)
yuri (no hana)	lily (blossom(s))
kōhone	[yellow] water lily/lilies
kiri no hana	paulownia flower(s)
hō (no hana)	magnolia (blossom(s)), 35
bara	rose(s), 28
ibara	wild rose(s)
shirobara	white rose(s)
nebu (no hana)	mimosa (blossom(s))
akashiya (no hana)	acacia (blossom(s)), 245
ajisai	hydrangea
aoi	hollyhock
hirugao	bindweed, convolvulus (lit., "noon-face")
yūgao	moonflower, bottle gourd (sometimes also translated as convolvulus; lit., "evening-face")
uri (no hana)	melon (blossom(s))
himawari	sunflower

nindō	honeysuckle
hasu no hana/fuyō	lotus flower
keshi (no hana)	poppy (flower(s))
beni (no hana)	safflower
mo no hana	duckweed flower
sarusuberi	crepe myrtle
hyakunichisō	zinnia(s)
wakaba	young leaves, 103
banryoku	myriad green leaves
ki no shita	under the trees
hayanagi	leafy willow trees
shigeri	luxuriance (of foliage)
kuwa no ha	mulberry leaves
aoi kusa	green grass, 34
kusa ikire	sultry grass, rank grass
natsugusa	summer grass, 22, 120
ukikusa	floating grass
take (no ko)	bamboo (shoots)
takebayashi	bamboo grove, stand of bamboo
wasuregusa	day lily (lit., "forgetting plant")
mugi (no ho)	barley (ears)
mame	beans

AKI	**AUTUMN** (August, September, October)

JIKŌ	SEASON, CLIMATE
zansho	lingering [summer] heat
asasamu	morning chill, morning cold
aki (no) hi	autumn day, 37, 108
aki harete	autumn clear, 24
aki no kure	autumn dusk, autumn's close, 9, 132, 133, 186

aki no yo	autumn night, 17
nagaki yo	long night
yosamu	night chill, cold night, 14
hazuki	leaf month, month of leaves

TENMON   ASTRONOMY

ama-no-gawa	River of Heaven, Milky Way, 29
mikazuki	crescent moon (lit., "three-day moon"), 37
hoshizukiyo	starry night (lit., "stars & moon night")
matsuyoi	waiting [for the moon] evening
tsuki	moon, 30, 43, 61, 196
kyō no tsuki	today's moon (i.e., tonight's)
tsukiyo	moon [lit] night
yūzuki	evening moon
meigetsu	bright moon, harvest moon, 121
tsukimi	moon-viewing, 11
kiri	fog, mist (distinguish *kasumi*, in spring)
kawagiri	river fog
yogiri	night fog, 258
asagiri	morning fog
tsuyu	dew
asatsuyu	morning dew, 19, 258
shiratsuyu	white dew
aki (no) kaze	autumn wind, 128, 182
nowaki	[autumn] storm (lit., "field-divider")
taifū	typhoon, 44

CHIRI   GEOGRAPHY

| *irozuku* | take color, color up (of fruits, tree leaves) |

hanano	flower field(s), 256
karita	reaped field(s), harvested field(s)
otoshimizu	drawn water (from the fields)
shiranui	phosphorescent light (lit., "unknown light")

GYŌJI — OBSERVANCES

aki matsuri	autumn festival, 45
tama matsuri	feast of all souls
tamadana	spirit-shelf (an altar in the home)
tanabata	Tanabata, Festival of the Weaver
negai no ito	prayer threads
kaji no ha	mulberry leaf (used in ritual)
(bon) odori	(Bon [Festival]) dance
tōrō	lantern
haka mairi	grave-visit
hanabi	fireworks (lit., "flower-fire"), 25

SEIKATSU — LIVELIHOOD, LIFE

inekari	rice-cutting
hasa/inakake	rice rack, 45
kakashi	scarecrow
takegari	mushroom-gathering
kinuta	fulling block, 126
mushiko	insect cage
shūshi	autumn loneliness, 45

DŌBUTSU — ANIMALS

shika	deer
kari wataru	geese migrate, 124
tsuru kitaru	cranes/storks come
mozu	shrike, butcher bird
uzura	quail

hiyo(dori)	bulbul
kitsutsuki	woodpecker
wataridori	bird of passage, migratory bird
shigi	snipe, longbill, 186
hiwa	siskin
kotori	little birds
sake	salmon, 41
akiaji	autumn mackerel, 43
ayu ochiru	trout fall, 213
tonbo	dragonfly, 31
akatonbo	red dragonfly
tonbotsuri	catching dragonflies (with a pole), 25
tōrō	praying mantis, 38
higurashi	clear-toned cicada, day-darkener, 36, 109
kirigirisu	katydid, 19
inago	grasshopper, locust
kōrogi/itodo	cricket(s) (two different species)
kajika	black frog (lit., "river deer")
kagerō	shadflies
minomushi	bagworm (lit., "straw-coat insect")
jimushi	ground beetle, 36
mushi no naku	insects cry, 190
aki no koe	voice(s) of autumn (i.e., insect cries), 213

SHOKUBUTSU   PLANTS

mukuge	rose of sharon
hagi	bush clover, 98
asagao	morning glory/glories
ominaeshi	maiden flower
fuyō	rose mallow
ran	orchid

nogiku	wild aster (lit., "field chrysanthemum")
kiku	chrysanthemum(s), 43, 107
shiragiku	white chrysanthemum(s)
kigiku	yellow chrysanthemum(s)
nadeshiko	pink(s)
ashi-no-hana/roka	reed flower(s), reed tassel(s)
susuki (no ho)	pampas grass (plume(s))
susuki no hana	pampas grass flower(s)
tsuta	vine(s)
tōkibi	maize
awa no ho	millet ear(s)
soba	buckwheat
momo taburu	peach munching, 258
ringo	apple, 123
nashi	pear, 22
kaki	persimmon
zakuro	pomegranate
budō	grapes
kuri	chestnuts
shii no mi	pasania nuts, 45
e no mi	hackberry
ko no mi	nuts, berries (lit., "seeds of trees")
hechima	sponge gourd
take	mushrooms, 212
matsutake	pine mushrooms
bashō	banana plant
kusa no hana	flowers of grasses, flowers of weeds
kusa no me darake	lush sprouting grass, 31
momiji/kōyō	autumn leaves (lit., "red leaves")
yanagi chiru	willow [leaves] fall, 12
kiri no ha chiru	paulownia leaves fall
konoha chiru	tree leaves fall, 31, 127
ochiba	fallen leaves

FUYU	**WINTER** (November, December, January*)

JIKŌ	SEASON, CLIMATE
fuyu no hajime	beginning of winter
kannazuki	godless month, November
fuyu no yo	winter night, 183
kanya	cold night, midwinter night
samuki yo	cold night
samusa/tsumetasa	the cold
sokobie	deep cold, 44
kan no uchi	middle of the cold
yuku toshi	departing year
toshi kurete	the year ends, 121
toshiwasure	New Year's Eve party (lit., "year-forgetting")

TENMON	ASTRONOMY
kangetsu	cold moon [light], icy moon [light]
tsuki samushi	moon is cold, moon is chill
fuyu no hoshi	winter stars, 43
fuyu no kumo	winter clouds, 34
kanrai	mid-winter thunder, 38
hatsushigure	first [winter] rain/drizzle
shigure	[winter] rain/drizzle, 30
shigururu	it's raining/drizzling [in winter], 18
yoshigure	[winter] night rain/drizzle
shimo	frost, 197
hatsushimo	first frost
shimoyo	frosty night

*See following section for the New Year.

shimogare	frost-withered
hatsuyuki	first snow
ōyuki	heavy snow
yuki	snow, 32
yuki maroge	snow ball
miyuki	deep snow
yukimi	snow-viewing, 11
fubuki	snow storm, driving snow, or, snow drift
mizore	sleet
arare	hail
tsurara	icicles
kogarashi	withering wind (lit., "tree-witherer") 18

CHIRI   GEOGRAPHY

kareno	withered field(s), withered moor
kōru	to freeze
hatsugōri	first ice
kōri	ice
tōdo	frozen ground
taki kareru	waterfall dries up
kan no mizu	icy water, mid-winter water

SEIKATSU   LIVELIHOOD, LIFE

susuharai	cleaning [the family altar] (literally, "soot-brushing"; objects from the altar are placed outdoors during the process)
sumi no hi	charcoal fire
umorebi	banked fire
hibachi/hioke	brazier
kotatsu	*kotatsu* (no Western equivalent; it is a

	central fire pit with a frame and quilt over it; one can sit with the lower body under the quilt, and make a table or desk of the top)
sumi	charcoal
fuyugomori	winter's bonds, winter seclusion, 98
mōfu	blanket, 248
kamiko	top coat (thin; made of treated paper)
nunoko	quilted cotton clothes
setta	snow sandals, 197
daikonhiki	radish-pulling
mugimaki	sowing barley
ajiro	wicker-work [fish trap]
takagari	falconry
furugoyomi	old calendar
takuan	pickled radish

DŌBUTSU   ANIMALS

kuma	bear, 41
washi	eagle
chidori	plover(s), 183
oshidori	mandarin duck
kamome	gull
kamo	wild duck(s)
kogamo/takabe	small duck, or, duckling
kaitsuburi	grebe
misosazai	wren, jenny wren
mizutori	water fowl
ukinedori	birds floating asleep
kujira	whale
kaki	oyster
namako	sea slugs
kogane mushi	gold bug

SHOKUBUTSU	PLANTS
kusu no ki	camphor tree
kangiku	winter chrysanthemum
karegiku	withered chrysanthemum
daikon	[Japanese long, white] radish
akakabura	red turnip
negi	onion, 26
uragare	desolate, withered (lit., "withered twigs")
karesusuki	withered pampas grass
chiru susuki	falling pampas grass fluffs
kare ashi	withered reeds
matsu	pine [tree]
suisen	daffodils, narcissus

SHINNEN	**THE NEW YEAR***
shinnen	the New Year
ganjitsu	New Year's Day
ganchō	New Year's morning
ōashita	great morning
hatsuhi	New Year's [Day] sun [rise]
shōgatsu	original, perfect month
... *no toshi*	Year of the . . . (*ne*, Rat; *ushi*, Ox; *tora*, Tiger; *u*, Hare; *tatsu*, Dragon; *mi*, Serpent; *uma*, Horse; *hitsuji*, Sheep; *saru*, Monkey; *tori*, Rooster; *inu*, Dog; (*w*)*i*, Boar—one of the twelve signs of the Chinese zodiac)

*Formerly same as the "Chinese New Year", early February, and associated with the coming of spring. Now celebrated during the first week of January. All of the objects named are associated with family or public celebrations.

kozo/kyonen	last year
kotoshi	this year
tarōtsuki	Tarō Month (January; old custom had all persons become one year older on New Year's Day; Tarō is the most common male given name)
hatsuashita	first morning
hatsu hi no de	first sunrise
hatsuzora	first sky
hōrai	Islands of Eternal Youth (equivalent of the Elysian Fields; a model used as decoration)
shimadai	island stand (for above)
wakaebisu	Young Ebisu (god of wealth and commerce)
kadomatsu	gate-pines (decorations)
matsukazari	pine decorations
matsutatte	putting up the pines, decorating with pines
mochi	rice cakes (offered on *shimadai*, as are the other foods, below)
shida	fern (used to decorate *mochi*)
wakana	young greens, young herbs
kushigaki	dried persimmon
kashiguri	dried chestnut
kaya no tane	pine seeds
kuromame	black beans
iwashi	sardine
kazu no ko	herring roe
mochibana	rice-cake flowers
koji	orange
oibane/hanetsuki	battledore and shuttlecock (traditional New Year's game for girls; forerunner of badminton)

tako	kite (traditional toy for boys at New Year)
temari	hand ball (used in New Year's games), 39
wakamizu	young water
fude no hajime	beginning with the brush, first writing
kakizome	first calligraphy
zōni	soup with rice cakes (for New Year's breakfast)
hatsu shibai	first theater [-going]
hatsuni	first freight, first load (boats and draft animals decorated for the occasion)
hatsuyume	first dream
manzai	comic [street] dancers
hatsu kasumi	first mist [of New Year, of spring]
jinjitsu	people day (seventh of January; last day of the week-long celebration)
dondo	bonfire (made by children to burn New Year's decorations, the morning of the fifteenth)

Glossary

This glossary contains the Japanese technical terms used in this handbook and a few more which the reader may encounter in other books on haiku and related subjects. For some of these words the index will lead to further information. A relatively literal translation of each Japanese word follows it in parentheses. All definitions supply the meaning of the word as used in Japanese; only in a few cases has a specifically Western sense been indicated. These Japanese words are all their own plurals, and where they name a poetic genre or form the same word is used for the generic (for example, "The *sonnet* came to England from Italy.") and the specific ("This *sonnet* by Shakespeare mocks the tradition."). All words defined in the glossary have been italicized throughout the glossary, though they appear in italics in the text of the handbook only on first occurrence.

ageku (completing verse)   Of *renga*, the final stanza.

aware (touchingness)   Moving, stirring; the kind of thing that evokes an emotional response; often in the phrase *mono no aware*, "the touchingness of things".

chiri (geography)   In the season-word list, a category including natural phenomena on land and water (hills, streams, etc.)

chōka, or *nagauta* (long poem)   Traditional verse form, usually spoken of as having alternating verse-lines of five and seven *onji*, plus one of seven *onji* at the end. An alternate interpretation suggests verse-lines of twelve *onji*, with a caesura dividing each line into five and seven, plus a concluding line of seven *onji*. The genre flourished in the era of the *Manyōshū*, and has had an occasional revival. See *ji-amari*.

dai (topic)   Originally, the circumstances under which a poem was written, given in a short preface; later, a set topic upon which a poem was composed.

daisan (the third)   Of *renga*, the third stanza.

dōbutsu (animals)   In the season-word list, a category including animals, especially birds and insects.

dodoitsu (city leisure / quickly city-to-city)   One traditional form for popular and folk songs, in seven-seven-seven-five *onji*. The name appears to derive from the speed with which songs in this form became popular. See *ji-amari*.

gunsaku (group work)   Of haiku and tanka, a group of poems on a single subject which illuminate the subject from various points of view, but can be read independently. See *rensaku*.

gyōji (observances)   In the season-word list, a category including festivals, holidays, and associated objects.

haibun (*haikai* prose)   Prose in terse style by a *haikai* or *haiku* poet, usually including *hokku* or *haiku*.

haiga (*haikai* painting)   A painting in a slightly abstract, rough style, including a *haiku* or *hokku* in calligraphy.

haigon (*haikai* word)   Words normally excluded from "serious" poems (for example, words from foreign languages, words too vulgar in meaning or diction, etc.), but which became a distinguishing feature of *haikai*, *haiku*, *senryū*, etc.

haijin (*haikai* or *haiku* person)   *Haikai* or *haiku* poet.

haikai (humor, joke)   Originally, a classification of humorous poems; later, an abbreviation for *haikai-no-renga*, and thus a generic term for all compositions relating to it, such as *haiku, maekuzuke, haibun,* etc. Occasionally in Japanese, and especially in French and Spanish, a synonym for *haiku.*

haikai-no-renga (humorous *renga*)   Originally, vulgar, earthy renga, also called *mushin renga;* by Bashō's day the dominant kind of renga.

haiku (verse of *haikai*)   Originally (and rarely used), any stanza of a *haikai-no-renga;* since Shiki, the *hokku* of *haikai-no-renga* considered as an independent genre. Traditionally, a *haiku* meets the criteria for *hokku*—containing a *kigo* (season word) and *kireji* (cutting word), and being in more or less five-seven-five *onji.* Bashō emphasized the depth of content and the sincerity of the poet as perceived in the poem, and was not overly concerned with *kigo* and *kireji,* though he used both and did promote *kisetsu* (seasonal aspect) in poetry; several of his poems have *ji-amari.* Some modern *haiku* poets have abandoned traditional form, *kigo,* and *kireji,* holding that *haiku* has a deeper essence based on our response to the objects and events of our lives. *Haiku* is now the most common word for writing of this genre in the West, whether referring to poems in Japanese or any of the Western adaptations.

hibiki (echo)   In *haikai-no-renga,* a relationship between two stanzas whose images seem strong in the same way.

hiraku (ordinary verse)   In *renga,* any stanza other than the *hokku, wakiku, daisan,* or *ageku.*

hokku (starting verse)   Originally, in *renga,* the first stanza, which later became an independent poem, now usually called *haiku* in Japan, with *hokku* reverting to its original meaning. For a time *hokku* was the most common word in English for what we now call *haiku*. See *haiku*.

hosomi (slenderness)   In *haikai-no-renga* and *haiku*, empathy, sometimes bordering on the pathetic fallacy.

hyakuin (hundred verses)   A *renga* of one hundred stanzas, the most popular length before Bashō's day.

ichigyoshi (one-column poem)   Equivalent to "one-line poem" in English; a pejorative term used by traditional haiku poets when referring to modern haiku in irregular form. (Note: quite different from traditional form with *ji-amari*.)

ji (ground)   In *renga*, term for a relatively unimpressive stanza that serves as a background to those more impressive *(mon)*.

ji-amari (character excess)   In traditional verse forms, the use of one or a few more *onji* than typical of the form; a fairly common practice.

jikō (season, climate)   In the season-word list, a category including climatic and certain seasonal phenomena, such as "spring day", "lingering heat" (in autumn), etc.

jinji (human affairs)   In the season-word list, an alternate category used in some modern references, which includes both *gyōji* and *seikatsu*.

kaishi (pocket paper)   Paper sheets used for writing poems, especially *renga*.

kanshi (Chinese poem)   Poem in classical Chinese by a Japanese.

kaori (scent, fragrance)   In *haikai-no-renga*, a relationship between two stanzas in which they both evoke the same emotion using different images.

karumi (lightness)   In *haikai* and *haiku*, the beauty of ordinary things.

kasen (poetic genius)   Originally, one of the thirty-six great poets of antiquity; hence, a *renga* of thirty-six stanzas, the length preferred by Bashō.

katauta (side poem)   A traditional verse form of the *Manyōshū* era, typically in five-seven-seven *onji*. See *sedōka*.

kidai (seasonal topic)   In *tanka* and *haiku*, a topic upon which a verse is to be composed. It can be a specific *kigo* or some seasonal event, or a combination. See *kisetsu*.

kisetsu (season, seasonal aspect)   The seasons. The seasonal aspect of the vocabulary *(kigo)* and subject matter *(kidai)* of traditional *tanka, renga,* and *haiku;* a deep feeling for the passage of time, as known through the objects and events of the seasonal cycle. (See *aware*.)

kigo (season word)   The name of a plant, animal, climatic condition, or other object or activity traditionally connected with a particular season in Japanese poetry.

kireji (cutting word)   In *hokku* and *haiku*, a word or suffix that indicates a pause and usually comes at one of the formal divisions or at the end. A *kireji* may be used within the second rhythmical unit, breaking the poem into a five-three-four-five rhythm, for example. The two types are verb and adjective suffixes that can end a clause, and short words that mark emphasis, a sort of spoken punctuation. Some common *kireji:*

> *ka*—emphasis; at the end of a phrase, makes a question.
>
> *kana*—emphasis; usually at the end of a poem, indicates an author's wonder at the object, scene, or event.
>
> *-keri*—verb suffix, (past) perfect tense, exclamatory.
>
> *-ramu* or *-ran*—verb suffix indicating probability, such as "it may be that . . . "
>
> *-shi*—adjective suffix; used to end a clause, it corre-

sponds to an English predicate adjective, as in *mine takashi*, "the peak is high".

-*tsu*—verb suffix, (present) perfect tense.

ya—emphasis; has the grammatical effect of a semicolon, separating two independent clauses (not necessarily grammatically complete); gives a sense of suspension, like an ellipsis.

kouta (little song)   Popular songs, often in *dodoitsu* form.

kyōka (mad poem)   Comic poem in *tanka* form, often bawdy.

maeku (previous verse)   In *renga*, *tsukeai*, and *maekuzuke*, the preceding stanza, to which another must be added; the first of a pair of stanzas.

maekuzuke (joining to a previous verse)   A game based on *renga*, in which one party gives a stanza *(maeku)* to which another adds a linking stanza *(tsukeku)*; a linked pair resulting from the game, a forerunner of *senryū*.

mankuawase (collection of myriad verses)   An anthology of *tsukeku* selected and published as the result of a *maekuzuke* contest.

mon (pattern)   In *renga*, a relatively impressive stanza that stands out against the "ground" stanzas. See *ji*.

mono no aware (the touchingness of things)   See *aware*.

mushin (without heart)   Of *renga*, frivolous, that is, unconcerned with the classical ideal of beauty in appropriate subject matter and diction, but featuring humor and unconventional language. (Other meanings in other contexts.) See *ushin*.

nagauta (long poem)   See *chōka*.

nioi (scent, smell)   See *kaori*.

on (sound)   In poetry, the smallest metrical unit, represented by a single written phonetic character. Abbreviation for *onji*.

onji (sound symbol)   A character in the Japanese phonetic

GLOSSARY 293

syllabary; hence, a technical term for the smallest metrical unit in Japanese poetry—equivalent to *mora* in Latin prosody (*not* simply "a syllable", as it is usually translated).

renga (linked poem) A poem of alternating stanzas of nominally five-seven-five and seven-seven *onji*, usually composed by two or more poets, and developing texture by shifting among several traditional topics without narrative progression. Typical renga run to 36, 50, 100, 1000 or more stanzas.

rensaku (linked work) Of *haiku* and *tanka* sequences, a longer work composed of individual *haiku* or *tanka* which function as stanzas of the whole, and are not independent. See *gunsaku*.

rensō (linked ideas) In *renga* and *haiku*, the association of images from one stanza to another, or within a verse.

renku (linked verse) Originally, linked verse in Chinese; now a modern term for renga, especially the *haikai-no-renga* of Bashō and later poets.

sabi (patina/loneliness) Beauty with a sense of loneliness in time, akin to, but deeper than, nostalgia.

sedōka (repeat head poem) A traditional verse form with metrically identical stanzas, usually *katauta*, found mainly in the *Manyōshū*. Sometimes composed as question and answer by two parties, and so a forerunner of *renga*.

seikatsu (livelihood, life) In the season-word list, a category including human activity, such as farming, working, playing.

senryū (river willow) A humorous or satiric poem dealing with human affairs, usually written in the same form as *haiku*. Derived from the name of a popular selector of *maekuzuke*.

shibumi (astringency) The beauty of subdued, rather than vibrant, images; Classical, rather than Romantic, in taste.

shikishi (square paper)   A square sheet of heavy paper for writing and painting, often used for a short poem.

shinku (close verse)   In renga, a close relationship between two succeeding stanzas. See *soku.*

shiori (bending, withering)   In *haikai* and *haiku,* sympathy mixed with ambiguity; used of verses with delicate, almost pathetic images.

shōfū (abbreviation for "Bashō style")   In *haikai* and *haiku,* in the refined style of Bashō, rather than the coarser, earlier styles.

shokubutsu (plants)   In the season-word list, a category including plants, flowers, trees, fruits, etc.

soku (distant verse)   In renga, a distant relationship between two succeeding stanzas. See *shinku.*

sono mama (as it is)   In *haikai* and *haiku,* presenting a thing or event just as it is, without flourishes or emotionalism.

tanka (short poem)   A lyric poem with the typical form five-seven-five-seven-seven *onji* (see *ji-amari*). In many ways equivalent to the sonnet in the West, the *tanka* was the primary genre of Japanese poetry from *Manyōshū* times through about the fourteenth century, and still flourishes. Now also called *waka* or *uta.*

tanrenga (short linked poem)   A modern term for ancient *tanka* composed by two authors, formerly called *renga,* to distinguish them from the longer *renga* of later times.

tanzaku (*tanka* sheet)   A narrow strip of paper on which a *tanka* or *haiku* may be written.

tenmon (astronomy)   In the season-word list, a category including sky phenomena, precipitation, etc.

tsukeai (joining together)   In *renga,* the linking of one stanza to another; hence, a pair of linked stanzas.

tsukeku (joined verse)   In *renga, tsukeai,* and *maekuzuke,* the second of a pair of linked stanzas.

ukiyo (floating world)   Originally, a Buddhist term indicating the ephemeral nature of life; later, a name for the entertainment quarters of large cities.

ushin (with heart)   Of *renga,* sincere, that is, concerned with the classical ideal of beauty, employing only classical diction, etc. See *mushin.*

uta, or *-ka* or *-ga* in compounds (song, poem)   Generic term for traditional poetry in Japanese, excluding all forms of foreign verse; now *uta* is practically synonymous with *tanka.*

uta-awase (poem competition)   In the tradition of the old Japanese court, the pretext for a party, at which participants composed *tanka* on assigned *dai.* Results were judged, and usually prizes given. *Mushin renga* began as a sort of game for the participants, once the serious business of composing and judging *tanka* was done.

utsuri (reflection)   In *renga,* a relationship between stanzas in which there is a sense of movement or transference between them; there may also be some visual harmony between the images.

wabi (loneliness, poverty)   Beauty with a sense of asceticism; austere beauty.

waka (Japanese poem)   Traditional poetry in Japanese language and style, particularly those varieties found in the *Manyōshū.* Today, virtually synonymous with *tanka.*

wakiku (side verse)   In *renga,* the second stanza.

yūgen (mystery)   Elegance, mystery, depth. (Several whole volumes in Japanese are devoted to this word, particularly in relation to the *nō* drama.)

Resources

This section does not list every work consulted in writing the handbook, but includes books and other resources which will help anyone wishing to look more deeply into the haiku and other genres, and Japanese culture generally. I have not mentioned works in Japanese; those interested should consult the catalogue of a good East Asian library. Anyone wishing to offer or request further information may write to me, William J. Higginson, c/o From Here Press, Box 219, Fanwood, NJ 07023 USA. (Please include a self-addressed, stamped envelope.)

This listing follows, roughly, the plan of the book. After General Works on Japanese Literature and Culture, works dealing specifically with haiku—Japanese or international—appear under logical subheadings in Resources for Parts One and Two, Haiku, ending with "Directories, Bibliographies, and Organizations".

Next come Resources for Part Three, Teaching Haiku. I have listed Resources for Part Four, Before and Beyond Haiku, genre-by-genre. The final chapter has a section for itself, Resources for Chapter 16, The Uses of Haiku, which presents a few works that have helped me to understand the relationship between haiku and various aspects of Japanese and Western culture.

GENERAL WORKS ON JAPANESE LITERATURE AND CULTURE

Bownas, Geoffrey, and Anthony Thwaite, editors and translators. *The Penguin Book of Japanese Verse*. Baltimore: Penguin, 1964. A valuable collection, recently surpassed in size, scope, and depth by Sato and Watson, below.

Keene, Donald, editor. *Anthology of Japanese Literature from the Earliest Era to the Mid-Nineteenth Century*. New York: Grove Press, 1955. All of Professor Keene's books on Japanese literature have fine material on haiku and related genres.

Keene, Donald, editor. *Modern Japanese Literature: An Anthology*. New York: Grove Press, 1956.

Keene, Donald. *World Within Walls: Japanese Literature of the Pre-Modern Era, 1600–1867*. New York: Holt, Rinehart & Winston, 1976.

Kwock, C. H., and Vincent McHugh, translators. *Old Friend From Far Away: 150 Chinese Poems from the Great Dynasties*. San Francisco: North Point Press, 1980. Classical Chinese poetry has been very important to Japanese poets. These are the *only* translations I know of in English that read as concisely and clearly as the originals.

Nippon Gakujutsu Shinkōkai, translators. *The Manyōshū: One Thousand Poems*. New York: Columbia Univ. Press, 1965.

Sansom, G. B. *Japan: A Short Cultural History*, Revised Edition. New York: Appleton-Century-Crofts, 1962.

Sato, Hiroaki, and Burton Watson, editors and translators. *From the Country of Eight Islands: An Anthology of Japanese Poetry*. Garden City, NY: Anchor/Doubleday, 1981. Excellent end matter provided by Thomas Rimer increases the value of this well-done collection. A nicely bound edition on good paper is available from the University of Washington Press, Seattle, and worth the expense.

Shiffert, Edith Marcombe, and Yūki Sawa, editors and translators. *Anthology of Modern Japanese Poetry*. Tokyo: Charles E. Tuttle, 1972. Small sections on modern tanka and haiku.

Tsunoda, Ryusaku, Wm. Theodore de Bary, and Donald Keene, editors. *Sources of Japanese Tradition*. New York: Columbia Univ. Press, 1958. Among other delights, contains Keene's essay "The Haiku and the Democracy of Poetry in Japan".

Ueda, Makoto. *Literary and Art Theories in Japan.* Cleveland: Press of
    Western Reserve Univ., 1967. Especially valuable essays on Tsura-
    yuki (tanka poet), Yoshimoto (early renga poet), and Bashō (haikai
    and haiku).

RESOURCES FOR PARTS ONE AND TWO, HAIKU

Japanese Haiku: Anthologies and Critical Works in English

Blyth, R. H. *Haiku.* Four volumes. Tokyo: Hokuseido Press, 1949–1952.
    Several hundred traditional haiku with Blyth's Zen-biased commen-
    tary. First volume has considerable background; others organized
    seasonally.

Blyth, R. H. *A History of Haiku.* Two volumes. Tokyo: Hokuseido Press,
    1963–1964. Includes many modern haiku, despite Blyth's evident
    lack of sympathy for them.

Henderson, Harold G. *An Introduction to Haiku: An Anthology of Poems
    and Poets from Bashō to Shiki.* Garden City, NY: Doubleday/Anchor,
    1958. A modest selection, most decently translated, with superfluous
    titles and a little background.

Higginson, William J., translator. *thistle brilliant morning.* Paterson, NJ:
    From Here Press, 1975. Twenty-eight modern haiku.

Miyamori, Asatarō, translator. *An Anthology of Haiku, Ancient and Mod-
    ern.* Westport, CT: Greenwood Press, 1970. First published in Tokyo,
    1932. Almost 1000 haiku; the latter 350 are by Shiki and later poets.
    All with superfluous, made-up titles and explanatory comments
    where needed, plus a 100-page introduction. Includes Western-lan-
    guage translations by others up to that time.

Nippon Gakujutsu Shinkōkai, translators. *Haikai and Haiku.* Tokyo:
    N.G.S., 1958. A selection of haiku by Bashō, Buson, Issa, Shiki, and
    a few other poets (no moderns after Shiki), plus examples of a haikai-
    no-renga, haibun, and one of Buson's mixed works, with notes and
    season-word index.

Shikitani, Gerry, editor, and David Aylward, editor and translator. *Paper
    Doors: An Anthology of Japanese-Canadian Poetry.* Toronto: Coach

House Press, 1981. Haiku and tanka in Japanese, with translations, plus original modern poems in English, by thirteen very fine poets.

Ueda, Makoto, editor and translator. *Modern Japanese Haiku: An Anthology*. Toronto: Univ. of Toronto Press, 1976. A good selection of work by twenty important poets, beginning with Shiki and ending with a few of today's major figures.

Yasuda, Kenneth. *The Japanese Haiku: Its Essential Nature, History, and Possibilities in English*. Tokyo: Charles E. Tuttle, 1957. Valuable for the many excerpts from classical and modern critical writing on haiku in Japanese. Also has some of Yasuda's own haiku in English, from *A Pepper Pod* (see below).

Japanese Haiku: Individual Authors in English Translation

Beichman, Janine. *Masaoka Shiki*. Boston: Twayne, 1982. A good brief biography, stressing the breadth of Shiki's work, especially in tanka and prose. Translation quality varies.

Furuta, Soichi, translator. *Cape Jasmine and Pomegranates: The Free-Meter Haiku of Ippekiro*. A Mushinsha Book. New York: Grossman, 1974. Over three hundred poems with translations.

Furuta, Soichi, author and translator. *a man never becoming a line....* Yonkers, NY: Edition Heliodor, 1979. Twelve haiku by Furuta, in his own English translations, written to photographs by Frank Dituri. A limited edition has the original Japanese.

Isaacson, Harold J., editor and translator. *Peonies Kana: Haiku by the Upasaka Shiki*. New York: Theater Arts Books, 1972. Over 300 of Shiki's haiku in semi-English.

Mackenzie, Lewis, translator. *The Autumn Wind: A Selection from the Poems of Issa*. London: John Murray, 1957. Over 300 haiku, with transliterated Japanese.

Sawa, Yuki, and Edith Marcombe Shiffert, translators. *Haiku Master Buson*. South San Francisco: Heian International, 1978. A wide range of materials; book poorly produced.

Stevens, John, translator. *Mountain Tasting: Zen Haiku by Santōka Taneda*. New York: Weatherhill, 1980. A short introduction followed by over 350 poems.

Ueda, Makoto. *Matsuo Bashō*. New York: Twayne, 1970. An overview of
    Bashō's life, hokku, haibun, renga, and critical writings. Now avail-
    able in paperback from Kodansha.

English-Language Haiku: Anthologies and Critical Works

Amann, Eric W. *The Wordless Poem: A Study of Zen in Haiku*, revised edi-
    tion. Toronto: Haiku Society of Canada, 1978. Examples by Japanese
    and English-language poets.

Duhaime, André, and Dorothy Howard, editors and translators. *Haiku:
    anthologie canadienne / Canadian Anthology*. Hull, Québec: Editions
    Asticou, in press. A large anthology of work by Canadian poets writ-
    ing in English, French, and Japanese, all bilingual English and
    French.

Higginson, William J. *Itadakimasu: Essays on Haiku and Senryu in English*.
    Kanona, NY: J & C Transcripts, 1971.

Horovitz, Michael, editor. *Children of Albion: Poetry of the Underground
    in Britain*. Baltimore: Penguin Books, 1969. A few haiku each by
    Chris Torrance and William Wyatt, as well as many other fine poems.

Lamb, Elizabeth Searle. *Haiku in English, 1910–1983: A History*, with a
    Checklist of Publications by Lamb and William J. Higginson. Glen Bur-
    nie, MD: Wind Chimes, in preparation.

Swede, George, editor. *Canadian Haiku Anthology*. Toronto: Three Trees
    Press, 1979.

van den Heuvel, Cor, editor. *The Haiku Anthology: English Language
    Haiku by Contemporary American and Canadian Poets*. Garden City,
    NY: Anchor/Doubleday, 1974. Outstanding.

English-Language Haiku: Individual Authors

Every poet writing haiku in English who is represented in this
handbook and has at least one book of haiku that I know of is
listed here. These books are not necessarily the sources of the
poems quoted in the text. This section supplements the roll call
of the haiku magazines in Chapter 5, The Haiku Movement in
English, for most of these collections came from the so-called

"small presses" that, with the "little magazines", keep all literature alive. An asterisk (*) after a title indicates that it is not primarily a book of haiku, though it contains some.

Amann, Eric. *Cicada Voices: Selected Haiku of Eric Amann 1966–1979*. George Swede, Editor. Battle Ground, IN: High/Coo, 1983.

Bostok, Janice. *On Sparse Brush.** Brisbane, Australia: Makar Press, 1978.

Brooks, Randy. *Barbwire Holds Its Ground.* Battle Ground, IN: High/Coo, 1981.

Davidson, L. A. *The Shape of the Tree.* Glen Burnie, MD: Wind Chimes, 1982.

[Drevniok, Betty, writing as] Makato. *Inland: Three Rivers From An Ocean.* Ottawa: Commoners' Publishing Society, 1977.

Dudley, Michael. *through the green fuse.* Battle Ground, IN: High/Coo, 1983.

Faiers, Chris. *Sleeping in Ruins: Haiku and Senryu 1968–1980.* Toronto: Unfinished Monument Press, 1981.

Ginsberg, Allen. *Mostly Sitting Haiku.* Paterson, NJ: From Here Press, 1978.

Gorman, LeRoy. *Heart's Garden.* Montréal: Guernica Editions, 1983.

Harr, Lorraine Ellis. *A Flight of Herons, Seascapes & Seasons In Haiku.* Portland, OR: Dragonfly, 1977.

Harter, Penny. *In the Broken Curve.* Sherbrooke, Québec: Burnt Lake Press, 1984.

Hayden, Robert. *Angle of Ascent: New and Selected Poems.** New York: Liveright, 1975.

Higginson, William J. *Paterson Pieces: Poems 1969–1979.** Fanwood, NJ: Old Plate Press, 1981.

Hotham, Gary. *Without the Mountains: Haiku & Senryu.* [Laurel, MD]: Yiqralo Press, 1976.

Hoyt, Clement. *Storm of Stars: The Collected Poems and Essays.** Baton Rouge, LA: The Green World, 1976.

Jewell, Foster. *Sand Waves.* El Rito, NM: Sangre de Cristo Press, 1969.

Kenny, Adele. *Notes from the Nursing Home.* Fanwood, NJ: From Here Press, 1982.

Kerouac, Jack. *Scattered Poems.** San Francisco: City Lights, 1971.

Knight, Etheridge. *Born of a Woman: New and Selected Poems.* * Boston: Houghton Mifflin, 1980.

Lamb, Elizabeth Searle. *in this blaze of sun.* Paterson, NJ: From Here Press, 1975.

Lester, Julius. *Who I Am: Poems.* * New York: Dial Press, 1974.

Lloyd, David. *The Circle: A Haiku Sequence with Illustrations.* Tokyo: Charles E. Tuttle, 1974.

Lowell, Amy. *Pictures of the Floating World.* * New York: Macmillan, 1919.

Lyles, Peggy Willis. *Still at the Edge.* Oneonta, NY: Swamp Press, 1980.

McClintock, Michael. *Maya: Poems 1968–1975.* * Los Angeles: Seer Ox, 1975.

Mosolino, William R. *Fifty Haiku.* [Self-published], 1977.

Pauly, Bill. *Wind the Clock by Bittersweet.* W. Lafayette, IN: High/Coo, 1977.

Pizzarelli, Alan. *Zenryu and other works 1974.* Paterson, NJ: From Here Press, 1975.

Pound, Ezra. *Personae: Collected Shorter Poems.* * New York: New Directions, 1926.

Pratt, Claire. *Haiku.* [Self-published], 1965.

Reznikoff, Charles. *Poems 1918–1936: Volume I of the Complete Poems.* * Edited by Seamus Cooney. Santa Barbara, CA: Black Sparrow Press, 1976.

Richardson, Marion Jane. *Kicking the Dust.* [Self-published], 1981.

Roseliep, Raymond. *Listen to Light: Haiku.* Ithaca, NY: Alembic Press, 1980.

Rotella, Alexis Kaye. *Clouds in My Teacup.* Glen Burnie, MD: Wind Chimes, 1982.

Saunders, Margaret. *Snapdragons! Haiku & Senryu.* London, Ontario: South Western Ontario Poetry, 1982.

Shea, Martin. *across the loud stream.* Los Angeles: Seer Ox, 1974.

Snyder, Gary. *Earth House Hold: Technical Notes & Queries To Fellow Dharma Revolutionaries.* * New York: New Directions, 1979.

Southard, O [also known as "Mabelsson Norway"]. *Marsh-grasses and other verses.* Platteville, WI: American Haiku, 1967.

Spiess, Robert. *The Shape of Water.* Madison, WI: Modern Haiku, 1982.

Stefanile, Selma. *The Poem Beyond My Reach.* West Lafayette, IN: Sparrow Press, 1982.

Stevens, Wallace. *The Collected Poems.** New York: Alfred A. Knopf, 1954.

Swede, George. *All of Her Shadows.* Battle Ground, IN: High/Coo, 1982.

Tipton, James. *Bittersweet.* Austin, TX: Cold Mountain Press, 1975.

van den Heuvel, Cor. *dark.* New York: Chant Press, 1982.

Virgil, Anita. *A 2nd Flake.* Montclair, NJ: self-published, 1974.

Virgilio, Nicholas A. *Selected Haiku.* Sherbrooke, Quebec: Burnt Lake Press, 1985.

Webb, Joyce W. *Return to Lincolnville.** Madison, WI: Wells Printing Co., 1968.

White, Beverly. *days of sun nights of moon.* No place or date.

Williams, Paul O. *The Edge of the Woods: 55 Haiku.* Elsah, IL: self-published, 1968.

Williams, William Carlos. *The Collected Earlier Poems.** New York: New Directions, 1951.

Willmot, Rodney Wilson. *Haiku.* Québec: Editions Particulières, 1969.

Wills, John. *River.* Statesboro, GA: self-published, 1970.

Wills, Marlene Morelock. *the old tin roof.* No place, 1976.

Wright, Ellen, and Michel Fabre, editors. *Richard Wright Reader.** New York: Harper & Row, 1978.

Wyatt, William E. *Songs of the Four Seasons.* Sutton, Surrey, UK: Origins-Diversions Publications, 1965.

Yarrow, Ruth. *no one sees the stems.* Battle Ground, IN: High/Coo, 1981.

Yasuda, Kenneth. *A Pepper-Pod: Classic Japanese Poems Together with Original Haiku.* New York: Alfred A. Knopf, 1947. Reprinted as *A Pepper-Pod: A Haiku Sampler.* Tokyo and Rutland, Vermont: Charles E. Tuttle Co., 1976.

Young, Virginia Brady. *Shedding the Water.* No place, 1978.

Haiku in Languages Other Than Japanese and English

My source for the early French haikai is William Leonard Schwartz's *The Imaginative Interpretation of the Far East in Modern*

French Literature 1800–1925, published at Paris, by Librarie Ancienne Honoré Champion, 1927. Works not found in the magazines mentioned in Chapter 6, Haiku Around the World, came mainly from the following books. I have listed a bilingual edition where known to me. An asterisk (*) indicates not primarily a book of haiku.

Bodmershof, Imma. *Löwenzahn: Die auf 17 Silben verkürzten Haiku.* Matsuyama, Ehime, Japan: Itadori Hakkosho, 1979.

Domenchina, Juan José. *Poesías Completas (1915–1934).** Madrid: Signo, 1936.

Duhaime, André. *haïkus d'ici.* Hull, Québec: Editions Asticou, 1981.

Eluard, Paul. *Premiers Poèmes 1913–1921.** Lausanne, Switzerland: Mermod, 1948.

Hammarskjöld, Dag. *Vägmärken.** Stockholm, Sweden: Albert Bonniers Förlag, 1963. (Translated by Leif Sjöberg and W. H. Auden as *Markings*, New York: Alfred A. Knopf, 1964.)

Hellemans, Karel. *De Heuvels Rondom: Haikoes en Senrioes.* No place, 1981.

Jappe, Hajo. *Haiku.* 5. Folge. No place or date.

Machado, Antonio. *Poesías Completas.** Séptima Edición. Madrid: Espasa-Calpe, 1956. *The Dream Below the Sun: Selected Poems,** translated by Willis Barnstone, contains some of the haiku-influenced work, and is bilingual. Trumansburg, NY: The Crossing Press, 1981.

Muñoz, María Luisa. *Miniaturas.* Wilton, CT: self-published, 1982.

Núñez, Ana Rosa. *Escamas del Caribe (Haikus de Cuba).* Miami: Ediciones Universal, 1971.

Paz, Octavio. *Early Poems 1935–1955.** Translated by Muriel Rukeyser, et al. New York: New Directions, 1973 [bilingual].

Reumer, Wanda, and Piet Zandboer. *Samen Oud Worden.* No place or date.

Rilke, Rainer Maria. *Sämtliche Werke.** Zweiter Band. Wiesbaden: Insel-Verlag, 1975.

Seferis, George. *Collected Poems 1924–1955.** Translated by Edmund Keeley and Philip Sherrard. Princeton, NJ: Princeton Univ. Press, 1967 [bilingual].

Tablada, José Juan. *Obras: I—Poesía.** México: Univ. Nacional Autónoma de México, 1971.

Uchida, Sono. *Haïku: le poème le plus court du monde.* Rabat, Morocco: Éditions Techniques Nord-Africaines, 1983. This essay on the haiku follows a preface by Léopold Sédar Senghor. Briefly introduces the haiku; a few poems each by Bashō, Buson, Issa, and Chiyo, followed by a couple of poems from each of twenty-five modern Japanese haiku poets, with comments. Talks of world-wide haiku, and concludes with examples from Senegal and Morocco, where Uchida has served as Ambassador from Japan, and instituted haiku contests.

Directories, Bibliographies, Organizations

Brooks, Randy, and Shirley Brooks, editors. *Haiku Review '80, Haiku Review '82,* and *Haiku Review '84.* Published by High/Coo, Route 1, Battle Ground, IN 47920. A series of biennial pamphlets detailing the publishing activities in English-language haiku during the previous two years.

Brower, Gary L., with David William Foster. *Haiku in Western Languages: An Annotated Bibliography (With Some Reference to Senryu).* Metuchen, NJ: Scarecrow Press, 1972. The index is somewhat helpful; otherwise, confusing and inaccurate.

Fulton, Len, and Ellen Ferber, editors. *The International Directory of Little Magazines and Small Presses.* Revised annually. Published by Dustbooks, P.O. Box 100, Paradise, CA 95969 USA. Best source for current English-language literary magazine and book publishers. See "haiku" in index.

Fulton, Len, and Ellen Ferber, editors. *Small Press Record of Books in Print.* Revised annually. Published by Dustbooks, address above. Best source for authors and titles of books published by small presses; includes ordering information. See "haiku" in subject index.

Japan P. E. N. Club. *Japanese Literature in European Languages.* No place, Japan P. E. N. Club, 1961. Much has happened since, but still valuable for thoroughness; titles presented in characters as well as transliteration, etc. Lists books and articles in literary, academic, and popular journals.

Rimer, J. Thomas, and Robert E. Morrel, editors. *Guide to Japanese Poetry.* Bonnie R. Crown, general editor, Asian Literature Bibliography Series. Boston: G. K. Hall, in press. Annotated bibliography of translations from Japanese into English and critical works.

The following organizations exist to help haiku poets and those interested in haiku. The Museum of Haiku Literature, in Japan, has recently been established to serve as a national archive, and is interested in overseas materials as well. Each of the other groups is a nationwide organization (international, in the case of the HSA) of poets, readers, and teachers of haiku. Each offers helpful information to newcomers to haiku study and composition, and can help in obtaining poets for readings, instruction, or contest judging. Some maintain libraries or keep up bibliographies. These organizations do not usually have paid staff, so be patient if you enter into correspondence with them.

In Japan: International Division, Museum of Haiku Literature. 3-28-10, Hyakunin-Cho, Shinjuku-Ku, Tokyo 160.

In The United States: Haiku Society of America, Inc. c/o Japan Society, 333 East 47th St., New York, NY 10017.

In Canada: Haiku Society of Canada. c/o Sandra Fuhringer, 70 Taymall St., Hamilton, Ontario L8W 2A1.

In Belgium: Haikoe Centrum Vlaanderen. Drogenberg 100, 1900 Overijse.

In Holland: Haiku Kring Nederland. Buiskendael 11, 3743 EA Baarn.

RESOURCES FOR PART THREE, TEACHING HAIKU

Includes the sources for the examples cited at the beginning of Chapter 11, Haiku for Kids, plus a few other useful books. See also such books as *The Haiku Anthology,* edited by Cor van den Heuvel, and others mentioned in Resources for Parts One and Two.

Henderson, Harold G. *Haiku in English*. Tokyo: Charles E. Tuttle, 1967. First published as a Japan Society (NY) pamphlet in 1965, previously this was the only work on the teaching of haiku in English. A bit off the mark in places, but Henderson's review of Japanese haiku characteristics at the beginning is still helpful.

Kusano Shimpei. *frogs &. others*. Cid Corman and Kamaike Susumu, translators. A Mushinsha Book. New York: Grossman, 1969. Modern Japanese free-verse in excellent translations.

Lewis, Richard, editor; Haruna Kimura, translator. *There Are Two Lives: Poems by Children of Japan*. New York: Simon & Schuster, 1970. Free-verse poems by children ages 6 to 11, so good I use them in professional adult writing workshops.

Philippi, Donald, translator. *This Wine of Peace, This Wine of Laughter: A Complete Anthology of Japan's Earliest Songs*. A Mushinsha Book. New York: Grossman, 1968. Poems, mainly chōka and tanka, that the *Manyōshū* missed. Excellent.

Sackheim, Eric, editor and translator. *The Silent Firefly: Japanese Songs of Love and Other Things*. Tokyo: Kodansha International, 1963. Folk songs, mostly in dodoitsu form, collected in the early twentieth century. Excellent.

Zavatsky, Bill, and Ron Padgett, editors. *The Whole Word Catalogue 2*. New York: Teachers & Writers/McGraw-Hill, 1977. Writing ideas, plus in-depth articles on everything from keeping journals in first grade to following up on high school graduates, writing genre fiction, making media of all sorts, etc. Parts of Chapter 11 of this handbook first appeared there. Good idea: Send for the T&W catalogue of books on all aspects of teaching writing. Teachers & Writers, 5 Union Square West, New York, NY 10003.

RESOURCES FOR PART FOUR, BEFORE AND BEYOND HAIKU

Tanka and Kyōka: Translations from Japanese

Brower, Robert H., and Earl Miner. *Japanese Court Poetry*. Stanford, CA: Stanford Univ. Press, 1961. The standard work on the courtly tanka, down to the fourteenth century. Dull.

Fujiwara Teika, editor. *Superior Poems of Our Time: A Thirteenth-Century Poetic Treatise and Sequence*. Robert H. Brower and Earl Miner, translators. Stanford, CA: Stanford Univ. Press, 1967. A major contribution to understanding how an editor built up a sequence of tanka in an anthology, foreshadowing several important characteristics of renga composition. Translations so-so.

[Ishikawa] Takuboku. *Poems to Eat*. Carl Sesar, translator. Tokyo: Kodansha International, 1966. Selected tanka, in clear, accurate translations that work as poems in English. Includes Japanese originals. Watch for a reprint.

Ishikawa Takuboku. *Sad Toys*. Sanford Goldstein and Seishi Shinoda, translators. West Lafayette, IN: Purdue Univ. Press, 1977. Complete text in Japanese, transliteration, and good translation of Takuboku's last book of tanka.

[Kitagawa] Utamaro. *A Chorus of Birds*. James T. Kenny, translator. New York: Metropolitan Museum of Art/Viking Press, 1981. Fifteen wood-block prints of birds by the eighteenth century master; each print depicts two birds, and contains two pseudonymous kyōka. An appendix identifies the birds, and gives transliterations and translations.

Miner, Earl. *An Introduction to Japanese Court Poetry*. With translations by the author and Robert H. Brower. Stanford, CA: Stanford Univ. Press, 1968. Based on the first item in this section; much shorter, with a slightly different emphasis—on the purposes for which the poems were written.

Morris, Ivan. *The World of the Shining Prince: Court Life in Ancient Japan*. New York: Alfred A. Knopf, 1964. Masterful presentation of the society in which the tanka flourished.

Murasaki Shikibu. *The Tale of Genji*. Edward G. Seidensticker, translator. New York: Alfred A. Knopf, 1976. A novel containing some 800 tanka, intimately necessary to the action, as they were to the style of life portrayed.

Saigyō. *Mirror for the Moon: A Selection of Poems*. William R. LaFleur, editor and translator. New York: New Directions, 1978. A good selection; translations so-so.

Waley, Arthur, editor and translator. *Japanese Poetry: The 'Uta'*. Oxford: Clarendon Press, 1919, and later editions. Mostly tanka, from the *Manyōshū* through the fourteenth century, in transliteration and translations especially helpful to the student of Japanese language.

Yosano, Akiko. *Tangled Hair: Selected Tanka from Midaregami.* Sanford Goldstein and Seishi Tsunoda, editors and translators. West Lafayette, IN: Purdue Univ. Studies, 1971. Slightly fewer than one-half of the poems from the most important book by the major Romantic poet and feminist, in Japanese, transliteration, and good translation.

Tanka: Originals in Western Languages

Borges, Jorge Luis. *The Gold of the Tigers: Selected Later Poems.* Alastair Reid, translator. New York: E. P. Dutton, 1977. A bilingual edition, including six interesting tanka.

Goldstein, Sanford. *Gaijin Aesthetics.* LaCrosse, WI: Juniper Press, 1974. Goldstein's personal gains from the study of Takuboku and Akiko.

McClintock, Michael. *Man With No Face.* No place: Shelters Press, 1974. Best tanka I have seen in the West.

Renga: Translations from Japanese

Matsuo Bashō. *Monkey's Raincoat.* Maeda Cana, translator. A Mushinsha Book. New York: Grossman, 1973. Translations, with notes and transliteration, of four kasen from *Sarumino*, the best-known anthology of the Bashō school. Although Bashō was instrumental in the book, it was actually edited by two of his disciples, and contains work by several poets. Translation is sometimes a bit awkward, but repays study.

Miner, Earl. *Japanese Linked Poetry: An Account with Translations of Renga and Haikai Sequences.* Princeton, NJ: Princeton Univ. Press, 1979. Highly technical history and criticism, with several awkwardly presented translations and transliterated text.

Miner, Earl, and Hiroko Odagiri, translators. *The Monkey's Straw Raincoat and Other Poetry of the Bashō School.* Princeton, NJ: Princeton Univ. Press, 1981. As in *Japanese Linked Poetry*, the renga are presented as a succession of tsukeai, making it impossible to get a sense of the movement over a series of verses—perhaps the most important single characteristic of a whole renga. Technical discussion and transliteration.

Sato, Hiroaki. *One Hundred Frogs: From Renga to Haiku to English.* New York: Weatherhill, 1983. A clear, concise, and enjoyable introduction to the essentials of renga composition. Also presents over a hundred translations and adaptations in English of Bashō's famous frog poem, in chronological order, and Sato's thoughts on translating renga and haiku. Finally, *100 Frogs* ends with an anthology of haiku, tsukeai, and renga composed in English by several fine poets.

Renga: Originals in Western Languages

Kondo, Tadashi, Kris Young, Robert Reed, Philip Meredith, and others. *Twelve Tokyo Renga 1980–1982*. Fanwood, NJ: From Here Press, in press.

McClintock, Michael, S. L. Poulter, and Virginia Brady Young. *Jesus Leaving Vegas*. Milwaukee, WI: Pentagram Press, 1976. Seems more like a collaborative haiku sequence, each verse independent.

Paz, Octavio, Jacques Roubaud, Edoardo Sanguineti, and Charles Tomlinson. *Renga: A Chain of Poems*. Charles Tomlinson, translator. New York: George Braziller, 1971. A collaborative sonnet sequence in Spanish, French, Italian, and English, with facing English translation. Inspired by Japanese renga, to which it bears little resemblance.

Sato, Hiroaki. *One Hundred Frogs*. See last entry in previous section.

Haibun: Translations from Japanese

Keene, Dennis, translator. *The Modern Japanese Prose Poem: An Anthology of Six Poets*. Princeton, NJ: Princeton Univ. Press, 1980. A broad range of work, showing a mixture of influences from French Surrealist prose poems and traditional Japanese haibun.

[Kobayashi] Issa. *The Year of My Life: A Translation of Issa's Oraga Haru*. Nobuyuki Yuasa, translator. Berkeley, CA: Univ. of California Press, 1960. Issa's journal for one full year in a wordy translation.

[Matsuo] Bashō. *Back Roads to Far Towns: Bashō's Oku-no-hosomichi*. Cid Corman and Kamaike Susumu, translators. A Mushinsha Book. New York: Grossman, 1968. The *only* complete translation of this work into English that gives a sense of Bashō's masterful prose style. Includes Japanese text and notes.

[Matsuo] Bashō. *The Narrow Road to the Deep North and Other Travel Sketches*. Nobuyuki Yuasa, translator. Baltimore, MD: Penguin Books, 1966. Includes *Oku no hosomichi* and four other important journals; translations mediocre.

Miner, Earl, editor and translator. *Japanese Poetic Diaries*. Berkeley, CA: Univ. of California Press, 1969. Places Bashō's *Oku no hosomichi* and a short journal by Shiki in the long tradition of the Japanese poetic diary. The two other pieces have many tanka.

Haibun: Originals in Western Languages

Kerouac, Jack. *Desolation Angels.* New York: Coward-McCann, 1965. The first part of this novel is in haibun style.

Little, Geraldine Clinton. *Separation: Seasons in Space: A Western Haibun.* West Lafayette, IN: Sparrow Press, 1979.

Roth, Hal. *Behind the Fireflies.* Glen Burnie, MD: Wind Chimes, 1982.

Spiess, Robert. *Five Caribbean Haibun.* Madison, WI: Wells Printing Co., 1972.

Tulloss, Rod. *December 1975.* Paterson, NJ: From Here Press, 1978.

Senryu: Translations from Japanese

Blyth, R. H. *Edo Satirical Verse Anthologies.* Tokyo: Hokuseido Press, 1961. A chronological survey of the main eighteenth century anthologies, with Japanese, transliteration, translations, and commentary.

Blyth, R. H. *Japanese Life and Character in Senryu.* Tokyo: Hokuseido Press, 1960. A history and selection of senryu from its beginnings in the late seventeenth century through the mid-twentieth century. Plus over three hundred pages of poems catalogued under various topics, and a large number of poems categorized by season.

Blyth, R. H. *Senryu: Japanese Satirical Verses.* Tokyo: Hokuseido Press, 1949. Some fifty pages devoted to a useful comparison of haiku and senryu; a large number of senryu classified by topic. One of the better books for the student of haiku who wishes to expand horizons.

Isaacson, Harold J., translator and editor. *The Throat of the Peacock: A book of modern senryu on parents and children, with a sutra by the Buddha about filial devotion.* New York: Theater Arts Books, 1974. An oddity in distressed English.

Levy, Howard S., and Junko Ohsawa, translators. *One Hundred Senryu.* South Pasadena, CA: Langstaff Publications, 1979. Short-but-good introduction; original Japanese and good translations. Best short book on the subject.

NOTE: Several of the works listed in Resources for Parts One and Two, under "English-Language Haiku", contain senryu as well as haiku, but there are few collections exclusively of senryu in Western languages.

Haiku Sequences

I know of no works in Western languages which include a substantial number of haiku sequences translated from Japanese. Many of the haiku books listed in Resources for Parts One and Two contain original sequences in Western languages.

RESOURCES FOR CHAPTER 16, THE USES OF HAIKU

French, Calvin L. *The Poet-Painters: Buson and His Followers.* Ann Arbor, MI: Univ. of Michigan Museum of Art, 1974. This catalogue for an art exhibit contains an excellent chapter on Buson, and translations of the inscriptions on the paintings. One can see in Buson's painting his extraordinary capacity for detail harmonized with his powerful sense of abstraction, both qualities of his haiku as well. Matsumura Goshun (1752–1811) and Ki Batei (1734–1810), two of his disciples in painting, also incorporate Chinese poems and haiku (frequently Buson's) into their works, as do the other painters represented. Several of these works are haiga. (Reproductions in black and white.)

Herrigel, Eugene. *Zen.* R. F. C. Hull, translator. New York: McGraw-Hill, 1964. Includes his famous essay, "Zen in the Art of Archery"; anyone wanting to take up any art should read this description of studying under a master.

Miner, Earl. *The Japanese Tradition in British and American Literature.* Princeton, NJ: Princeton Univ. Press, 1966. Originally completed before the rise of the "Beat" poets, this work does not deal with anyone past the generation of Pound, Williams, and Amy Lowell. It makes clear how these, and Yeats in his plays, appropriated techniques and concerns from Japanese literature.

Okakura Kakuzo. *The Book of Tea.* Many editions since the first, American, in 1906. Illustrates the Romantic notion of Japan's traditional culture held by many, Japanese and Westerners, as the old ways gave way to modernization.

Philippi, Donald, L., translator. *Kojiki.* Tokyo: Univ. of Tokyo Press, 1968. The major repository of Japan's earliest mythology; essentially Shinto scripture. Its songs and poems abound in joy akin to the *Song of Solomon.* Very helpful introduction and back matter.

Ross, Nancy Wilson, editor. *The World of Zen: An East-West Anthology.* New York: Vintage, 1960. Along with a number of excellent essays on Zen itself are several on Zen and the arts, including painting, gardens, haiku, tea ceremony, architecture, drama, and humor. Leads to a host of other books on its subject.

Tanizaki, Junichirō. *In Praise of Shadows.* Thomas J. Harper and Edward G. Seidensticker, translators. New Haven: Leete's Island Books, 1977. Wonderful essay on the modern world and traditional Japanese culture by a major novelist.

Zolbrod, Leon M. *Haiku Painting.* Tokyo: Kodansha, 1982. Many color plates. Follows the development of haiga from the seventeenth century through Bashō, Buson, and later painters. The *joie de vivre* of the paintings matches the often playful inscriptions, translated in the text.

Credits and Acknowledgments

Every effort has been made to contact copyright holders. The author would be pleased to hear from any copyright holders not acknowledged below.

The majority of Chapter 11, Haiku for Kids, is adapted from the essay "Japanese Poems for American School Kids? or Why and How to Not Teach Haiku", by William J. Higginson, from *The Whole Word Catalogue 2*, edited by Bill Zavatsky and Ron Padgett, published by McGraw-Hill Paperbacks, New York, copyright © 1977 by Teachers & Writers Collaborative.

An additional portion of Chapter 11 is by Ron Padgett, consisting of excerpts from his essay "Haiku", from *The Whole Word Catalogue 2*, edited by Bill Zavatsky and Ron Padgett, published by McGraw-Hill Paperbacks, New York, copyright © 1977 by Teachers & Writers Collaborative, and specially revised for *The Haiku Handbook*; copyright © 1985 by Ron Padgett; used by permission of the author.

Chapter 12, A Lesson Plan that Works, was written specially for *The Haiku Handbook* by Penny Harter; copyright © 1985 by Penny Harter; used by permission of the author.

Clarence Matsuo-Allard: "somewhere", from *Cicada*; copyright © 1980 by Eric W. Amann; by permission of the publisher. • Eric W. Amann: "September rains", from *Haiku* (1967), and "Snow falling" and "Billboards", from *The Haiku Anthology*, copyright © 1974 by Cor van den Heuvel; by permission of the author. • Nick Avis: "whale spray!", from *Tickle Ace*, copyright 1982 by Nick Avis; by permission of the author.

Abdelhadi Barchale: "a snail on the stones", copyright © 1985 by Abdelhadi Barchale; all rights reserved. • Manya Bean: translations from the Greek of George Seferis specially made for this book, copyright © 1985 by Manya Bean and Willim J. Higginson; by permission of Manya Bean. • Robert Bly: excerpt from "Dropping the Reader", in *The Sea and the Honeycomb*, The Sixties Press, 1966; by permission of the author. • R. H. Blyth, translator: "'What's this for?'", from *Senryu: Japanese Satirical Verses*, published by Hokuseido Press, Tokyo, 1949, all rights reserved; by permission of the publisher. • Imma von Bodmershof: "Im grünen Wasser", "Der große Fluß schweigt", and "Rückkehr aus Sonne und Schnee" (first version), from *Haiku*, published by Albert Langen Georg Müller Verlag, München, copyright © 1962 by Albert Langen Georg Müller Verlag, and "Gräber im Nebel" and "Rückkehr aus Sonne und Schnee" (second version), from *Löwenzahn*, published by Itadori-Hakkosho, Matsuyama, Japan, copyright 1979 by Imma von Bodmershof; by permission of Ehrenfels-Abeille. • Jorge Luis Borges and Alastair Reid: "Alto en la cumbre" and the translation, "High on the summit", from *El Oro de los Tigres*, published by Emecé Editores, Buenos Aires, and *The Gold of the Tigers: Selected Later Poems*, published by E. P. Dutton, New York, Spanish copyright © 1972, 1975 by Emecé Editores, translation copyright © 1976, 1977 by Alastair Reid; by permission of the publishers. • Janice M. Bostok: "Pregnant again" and "wind" from *Walking into the Sun*, copyright © 1974 by Janice M. Bostok; by permission of the author. • Chuck Brickley: "the ledger blurs", from *Modern Haiku*, copyright © 1982 by Chuck Brickley; by permission of the author. • Randy Brooks: "late afternoon", from *Barbwire Holds its Ground*, copyright © 1981 by Randy Brooks; by permission of the author.

314

Jack Cain: "fog moves through", "an empty elevator", and "someone's newspaper", from *Haiku* copyright © 1969 by Eric W. Amann; by permission of the publisher.   •   Mark Cramer: translation of "El Saúz" by José Juan Tablada, previously published in *Haiku Magazine*, copyright © 1972 by William J. Higginson; by permission of the translator.

L. A. Davidson: "On the gray church wall", from *Haiku West*, copyright © 1975 by Leroy Kanterman, "beyond", from *Haiku Magazine*, copyright © 1972 by William J. Higginson, and "after all these lighthouses", from *Wind Chimes*, copyright © 1982 by L. A. Davidson; by permission of the author.   •   Vladimir Devidé: "Pod kopitima", from *Haiku*, copyright 1979 by Vladimir Devidé; by permission of the author.   •   Juan José Domenchina: "Pájaro muerto", from *Poesias Completas (1915-1934)*, published by Signo, Madrid, copyright © 1935 by Juan José Domenchina; all rights reserved.   •   Betty Drevniok: "Wading out", from *Cicada*, copyright © 1978 by Betty Drevniok; by permission of the author.   •   Michael Dudley: "empty shopping mall", from *through the green fuse*, copyright © 1983 by Michael Dudley; by permission of the author.   •   André Duhaime: "une dent en or", from *Cicada*, copyright 1981 by André Duhaime; by permission of the author. André Duhaime and Dorothy Howard, editors and translators, for selections and translations from *Haïku: anthologie canadienne/Canadian Anthology*, published by Les éditions Asticou enrg., copyright © 1985 by André Duhaime and Dorothy Howard; by permission of the editors.

Paul Eluard: "La petite" and "Une plume donne au chapeau", from *Premiers Poèmes, 1913-1921*, published by Mermod; © by Editions Gallimard; reprinted by permission.   •   Dee Evetts: "a small ceremony", from *Haiku Byways*, all rights reserved, copyright © 1985 by Dee Evetts; by permission of the author.

Christopher Faiers: "Vine Leaves", from *Sleeping in Ruins* (1981); by permission of the author.   •   John Gould Fletcher: an excerpt from the introduction to Kenneth Yasuda's *A Pepper-Pod: Classic Japanese Poems together with Original Haiku*, published by Alfred A. Knopf, New York, copyright 1946 by Alfred A. Knopf; reprinted as *A Pepper-Pod: A Haiku Sampler*, by Charles E. Tuttle Co., Tokyo and Rutland, Vermont, copyright 1976 by Kenneth Yasuda; by permission of Charles E. Tuttle Co.   •   Soichi Furuta: "a late day in Vienna" and "a guru leering", from *a man never becoming a line. . . .* , copyright © 1979 Edition Heliodor; by permission of the author.

Larry Gates: "Test Pattern", from *Haiku*, copyright © 1971 by Eric W. Amann; by permission of the author.   •   Anton Gerits: "een duivepaar", from *Alleen wanneer ik kijk*, published by De Oude Degel, Eemnes, Netherlands, copyright © 1984 by Anton Gerits; by permission of the author.   •   Allen Ginsberg: "Looking over my shoulder", "Lying on my side", "Winter Haiku", and "Haiku = objective images . . . ", all from *Journals: Early Fifties Early Sixties*, copyright © 1977 by Allen Ginsberg; by permission of the author.   •   Sanford Goldstein: "this summer night", from *This Tanka World*, copyright © 1977 by Sanford Goldstein; by permission of the author.   •   LeRoy Gorman: "a diver brings up the body", from *High/Coo*, copyright © 1978 by LeRoy Gorman, and "she dresses", from the *Canadian Haiku Anthology*, copyright © 1979 by LeRoy Gorman; by permission of the author.

Dag Hammarskjöld: "Snö i april", "Cikadorna skrek", and "Ännu långt från stranden", from *Vägmärken*, published by Albert Bonniers Förlag, Stockholm, copyright © 1963 by Albert Bonniers Förlag; by permission of the publisher. • Lorraine Ellis Harr: "Spring moon", from *Modern Haiku*, copyright © 1974 by Kay T. Mormino; by permission of the author. • Penny Harter: "the old doll", from *The Orange Balloon*, copyright © 1980 by Penny Harter; "spring rain", from *Cicada*, copyright © 1981 by Penny Harter; and "snowflakes", copyright © 1985 by Penny Harter; by permission of the author. • Hashimoto Takako: *kiri no naka*, copyright 1941 by Hashimoto Takako; *hi o keseba*, copyright 1948 by Hashimoto Takako; *araigami*, copyright 1962 by Hashimoto Takako; and *ryūtō ni*, copyright 1959 by Hashimoto Takako; by permission of Hashimoto Miyoko. • Robert Hayden: "Smelt Fishing", from *The Night-Blooming Cereus*, from *Angle of Ascent: New and Selected Poems*, by Robert Hayden, published by Liveright, New York, copyright © 1975, 1972, 1970, 1966 by Robert Hayden; reprinted by permission of Liveright Publishing Corporation. • Karel Hellemans: "de asters bloeian", from *De Heuvels Rondom*, copyright © 1981 by Karel Hellemans; by permission of the author • Ilse Hensel: "auf kahlem acker", from *apropos*, number 1/82; copyright © 1985 by Ilse Hensel; by permission of the author. • William J. Higginson: "Pause after", from *Haiku*, copyright © 1970 by Eric W. Amann, "drove past", from "Riverdale Walk", which appeared in the *Third Coast Haiku Anthology*, copyright © 1978 by William J. Higginson, "Holding the water", from *Haiku West*, copyright © 1970 by Leroy Kanterman, and excerpts from "Traditional Haiku Techniques", which first appeared in *The Windless Orchard*, copyright © 1971 by William J. Higginson; by permission of the author. William J. Higginson, translator: "the nail box" by Ozaki Hōsai, from *thistle brilliant morning*, copyright © 1975 by William J. Higginson, by permission of the translator; "Mid-Mountain Dialogue" by Li Po, from *Sun*, copyright © 1977 by Bill Zavatsky, by permission of the publisher; for excerpts from "From the Traveller's Heart", published in *Haiku*, copyright © 1969 by Eric W. Amann, by permission of the publisher; for excerpts from "Poems from Itadori", published in *Haiku*, copyright © 1968 by Eric W. Amann, by permission of the publisher. William J. Higginson and Tadashi Kondo, translators: Bashō's "Record of Rakushusha", from *Haiku Magazine*, copyright © 1976 by William J. Higginson; by permission of the translators. • Gary Hotham: "to hear them", from *Without the Mountains*, copyright © 1976 by Gary Hotham, and "Sunset dying", from *Haiku Magazine*, copyright © 1969 by Eric W. Amann; by permission of the author. • Clement Hoyt: "A Hallowe'en mask", from *Storm of Stars*, published by The Green World, Baton Rouge, copyright © 1976 by Violet Hoyt, and "While the guests order", from *American Haiku*, copyright © 1963 by James Bull; by permission of Esther Jean Hoyt, Isabel H. Browning, Vera G. Heath, and Constance L. Heath.

Ishikawa Takuboku: "came to", translated by Carl Sesar, from *Takuboku: Poems to Eat*, published by Kodansha International Ltd., copyright © 1966 by Carl Sesar; by permission of the translator. • Itadori Hakkosho: "Autumn Loneliness Selections": by Ueda Isemi, Takahashi Kazuo, Fujimoto Kanseki, Matsuura Takuya, Sakai Yamahiko, Kinoshita Michiteru, Oka Sueno, Takeda Chie, Ebisuya

Kiyoko, and Izumi Sumie, from *Itadori*, copyright 1967; by permission of Kawamoto Yōgo. • Chūsaburō Koshū Itō: *asatsuyu ni*, from *Paper Doors: An Anthology of Japanese-Canadian Poetry*, published by The Coach House Press, Toronto, copyright © 1981 by Chūsaburō Koshū Itō; by permission of the author.

The Japan Society for the Promotion of Science (The Nippon Gakujutsu Shinkōkai): excerpts from *Haikai and Haiku*, published in 1958 by The Nippon Gakujutsu Shinkōkai, Tokyo; all rights reserved; by permission of the publisher. • Hajo Jappe: "Fern nun die Berge", from *Haiku*, Folge 2, copyright © 1970 by Hajo Jappe; by permission of the author. • Foster Jewell: "Only scattered stars", from *American Haiku*, copyright © 1968 by James Bull, and "Under ledges", from *Sand Waves*, copyright 1969 by Foster Jewell; by permission of Rhoda de Long Jewell. • Brian Joyce: "straightening up", from *Tweed*, copyright © 1974 by Janice M. Bostok; by permission of the publisher.

Kamiko Yoshiko: "Daddy", and Haruna Kimura for the English translation, from *There Are Two Lives: Poems by Children of Japan*, edited by Richard Lewis, published by Simon & Schuster, New York, copyright © 1970 by Richard Lewis and Haruna Kimura; reprinted by permission of Simon & Schuster, Inc. • Kaneko Tōta: *kawa no ha yuku*, copyright 1971 by Kaneko Tōta; two poems beginning *aoi kuma*, and three beginning *hone no sake*, copyright 1972 by Kaneko Tōta; by permission of the author. • Katō Shūson: *kanrai ya*, copyright 1948 by Katō Shūson; *tōrō no* and *hi no oku ni*, copyright 1948 by Katō Shūson; *ganka tsugaru* and *uma arau*, copyright 1955 by Katō Shūson; *kajikamitsutsu* and *hiete takumashi*, copyright 1967 by Katō Shūson; all rights reserved. • Kawahigashi Hekigodō: *tō hanabi*, copyright 1896 by Kawahigashi Hekigodō; *konogoro tsuma naki*, copyright 1926 by Kawahigashi Hekigodō; *tonbo tsuru*, copyright 1929 by Kawahigashi Hekigodō; and *tōku tataki ki*, copyright 1914 by Kawahigashi Hekigodō; all rights reserved. • Kawamoto Gafu, Takahashi Nobuyuki, and William J. Higginson: an excerpt from "My Favorite Poems—From the Traveler's Heart", originally published in the *Ehime Shimbun*, copyright © 1969, translation from *Haiku*, copyright © 1969; by permission of Kawamoto Yōgo, Takahashi Nobuyuki, and William J. Higginson. • Adele Kenny: "turning in bed", from *High/Coo*, copyright © 1980 by Adele Kenny; by permission of the author. • Jack Kerouac: "Birds singing", "Useless, useless", and "Missing a kick", from *Scattered Poems*, published by City Lights Books, San Francisco, copyright © 1971 by the estate of Jack Kerouac; by permission of the publisher. Jack Kerouac: excerpt from *Desolation Angels*, published by Coward-McCann, Inc., New York, copyright © 1960, 1963, 1965 by Jack Kerouac; reprinted by permission of Coward-McCann, Inc. and The Sterling Lord Agency, Inc. • Gustave Keyser: "Steady fall of rain", from *Haiku West*, copyright © 1972 by Leroy Kanterman; by permission of the publisher. • Etheridge Knight: excerpts from "A Statement from Etheridge Knight", from *Frogpond*, copyright © 1982 by Etheridge Knight; and for "Under moon shadows" and "The Penal Farm", from *Born of a Woman: New and Selected Poems*, published by Houghton Mifflin Co., Boston, copyright © 1980 by Etheridge Knight; by permission of the author. • Tadashi Kondo: excerpts from a letter on renga, copyright © 1985 by Tadashi Kondo; by permission of the author. • Kusano Shimpei: excerpt from "hachijo rhapsody", from *frogs &. others.*, translated by Cid Corman and Kamaike Susumu, a Mushinsha Limited Book, published in 1969 by Grossman Publishers, New York, all rights reserved; by permission of Mushinsha Limited.

Elizabeth Searle Lamb: "pausing", "in the hot sun", "Deep into this world", and "Broken kite, sprawled", from *in this blaze of sun*, copyright © 1975 by Elizabeth Searle Lamb; "a plastic rose", from *Brussels Sprout*, copyright © 1982 by Elizabeth Searle Lamb; and "Sequence from Lagos, Nigeria", from *Frogpond*, copyright 1981 by Elizabeth Searle Lamb; by permission of the author. • Julius Lester: "Spring dawn", from *Kaleidoscope: Poems by American Negro Poets*, copyright © 1967 by Julius Lester; by permission of the author. • Geraldine C. Little: "The white spider", from *Dragonfly*, copyright © 1973 by J & C Transcripts; "a warm wind", from *Frogpond*, copyright 1982 by Geraldine C. Little; and "Fallen horse", from *Haiku Magazine*, copyright © 1971 by William J. Higginson; by permission of the author. • David Lloyd: "The silence", from *Dragonfly*, copyright © 1973 by J & C Transcripts; and "Moonlit sleet", from *Haiku*, copyright © 1971 by Eric W. Amann; by permission of the author. • Gerry Loose: "each", from *Tweed*, copyright © 1972 by Janice M. Bostok; by permission of the publisher. • Amy Lowell: "Autumn Haze", from *Pictures of the Floating World*, from *The Complete Poetical Works of Amy Lowell*, copyright © 1955 by Houghton Mifflin Company, copyright renewed by Houghton Mifflin Company, Brinton P. Roberts, Esq., G. D'Andelot Belin, Esq.; reprinted by permission of Houghton Mifflin Company. • Peggy Willis Lyles: "Still damp", from *Wind Chimes*, copyright © 1982 by Peggy Willis Lyles, and "Before we knew", from *Brussels Sprout*, copyright 1981 by Peggy Willis Lyles; by permission of the author.

Antonio Machado: "Canta, canta, canta", and excerpts from "Apuntes", from *Poesias Completas*, seventh edition, published by Espasa-Calpe, S. A., Madrid, copyright 1956 by Espasa-Calpe, S. A.; all rights reserved. • Michael McClintock: "as far toward the trees", and "the old pond", from *Maya*, copyright © 1975 by Michael McClintock; "rowing downstream" (first version), from *Haiku Byways*, copyright 1971 by Michael McClintock; "rowing downstream" (second version), and "dead cat", from *Light Run*, copyright © 1971 by Michael McClintock; "hungry", from *Man With No Face*, copyright © 1974 by Michael McClintock; by permission of the author. • Philip Meredith, Tadashi Kondo, Robert Reed, Kris Young, and Timothy Knowles: "Eleven Hours, or Morning Wind", copyright © 1985 by Tadashi Kondo and Kris Young; by permission of the authors. • Miyamori Asatarō: an excerpt from *An Anthology of Haiku Ancient and Modern*, published by Maruzen Company, Ltd., Tokyo, copyright © 1932 by Miyamori Asatarō; and reprinted by Taiseido Shobu Co., Tokyo; all rights reserved. • Mizuhara Shūōshi: *tsubo ni shite*, copyright 1935 by Mizuhara Shūōshi; *ōki inu*, copyright 1952 by Mizuhara Shūōshi; *numa mo ta mo*, copyright 1973 by Mizuhara Shūōshi; and *moya nokoru*, copyright 1973 by Mizuhara Shūōshi; by permission of Mizuhara Shizu. • Mori Sumio: *kari no kazu*, copyright 1972 by Mori Sumio; by permission of the author. • Ivan Morris: an excerpt from *The World of the Shining Prince: Court Life in Ancient Japan*, published by Alfred A. Knopf, Inc., New York, copyright © 1964 by Ivan Morris; by per-

Haiku Anthology, copyright © 1979 by Claire Pratt; by permission of the author.
• Marjory Bates Pratt: "Not a breath of air", from *American Haiku,* copyright ©
1965 by James Bull; by permission of the publisher. • Katarina Pśak: "Drndaju
kola", from *Haiku,* copyright 1977 by Katarina Pśak; by permission of the author.
Charles Reznikoff: "The twigs tinge the winter sky", from *Poems 1918–1936
Volume I of The Complete Poems of Charles Reznikoff,* edited by Seamus Cooney,
published by Black Sparrow Press, Santa Barbara, copyright © 1976 by Charles
Reznikoff, and for "Horsefly", from *Poems 1937–1975 Volume II of The Complete
Poems of Charles Reznikoff,* edited by Seamus Cooney, published by Black Sparrow
Press, Santa Barbara, copyright © 1977 by Marie Syrkin Reznikoff; by permission
of the publisher. • Marion J. Richardson: "Twilight", from *Wind Chimes,* copy-
right © 1982 by Marion Richardson; by permission of the author. • Rainer
Maria Rilke for *"Kleine Motten taumeln schauernd quer aus dem Buchs",* and *"Entre
ses vingt fards",* from *Sämtliche Werke,* published by Insel-Verlag, Wiesbaden,
copyright © 1957 by Insel-Verlag; by permission of the publisher. • Frank K.
Robinson: "the elevator", from *Bonsai,* copyright © 1976 by Jan and Mary Streif;
by permission of the author. • Raymond Roseliep: "after Beethoven", from
Cicada, copyright © 1981 by Raymond Roseliep, and "factory whistle", from
Firefly in My Eyecup, published by High/Coo, copyright © 1979 by Raymond
Roseliep; by permission of the Estate of Raymond Roseliep. • Sydell Rosenberg:
"In the laundermat", from *Modern Haiku,* copyright © 1972 by Kay T. Mormino,
"Library closing", from *Haiku,* copyright © 1968 by Eric W. Amann, and "As the
sun sets", from *American Haiku,* copyright © 1967 by James Bull; by permission
of the author. • Alexis Rotella: "Shiva", from *Clouds in My Teacup,* copyright
© 1982 by Alexis Rotella; by permission of the author. • Hal Roth: "lightning
flash", from *Frogpond,* copyright © 1982 by Hal Roth, and excerpts from *Behind
the Fireflies,* copyright © 1982 by Hal Roth; by permission of the author.
Eric Sackheim, translator: "Fog Clings", from *The Silent Firefly: Japanese Songs
of Love and Other Things,* published by Kodansha International Ltd., Tokyo, copy-
right © 1963 by Eric Sackheim; by permission of the translator. • Saitō Moki-
chi: poems included here by permission of Saitō Shigeta. • Emiko Sakurai: who
collaborated with me in producing seven of the translations from the work of Issa
in this book (identified in the text); copyright © 1985 by Emiko Sakurai and Wil-
liam J. Higginson; by permission of the translators. • Margaret Saunders:
"After", from *Cicada,* copyright © 1978 by Margaret Saunders; by permission of
the author. • William Leonard Schwartz: reprinting the following authors and
works indicated in *The Imaginative Interpretation of The Far East in Modern French
Literature, 1800–1925,* published at Paris by Librairie Ancienne Honoré Champion,
1927: Julien Vocance, excerpts from «Cent Visions de Guerre», from *Grande
Revue,* May 1916; Maurice Betz, "Un trou d'obus", from *Scaferlati pour troupes,*
1921; René Maublanc, "Démontés après la fête", from *Poèmes,* 1922, and "Le ciel
noir", from *Cent Haïkaï,* published in Maupré, 1924; Albert Poncin, "Le banc de
bois est humide", from *Le Pampre,* October 1923; Jean Beaucomont, "Le train arri-
vait", from *Gouttelettes, Haïkaï et Outa,* published in Maupré, 1924; reprinted by

permission of Slatkine Reprints. • George Seferis: "Drip in the lake", "In the Museum Garden", "Night, the wind", and "You write", from *Tetradio Gymnasmaton*, published by Icaros, Athens, copyright © 1940, and "1 January [1931]", from *Meres*, Volume I, 16 February 1925—17 August 1931, published by Icaros, Athens, copyright © 1975 by Ikaros; by permission of the publisher. • Martin Shea: "the long night", from *Modern Haiku*, copyright © 1973 by Kay T. Mormino; by permission of the author • Gerry Shikatani and David Aylward, editors: Aylward's translations from *Paper Doors: An Anthology of Japanese-Canadian Poetry*, published by The Coach House Press, Toronto, copyright © 1981 by Gerry Shikitani and David Aylward; by permission of the authors and translator. • Gary Snyder: "This morning" and "leaning in the doorway whistling", from *Earth House Hold*, published by New Directions, copyright © 1969 by Gary Snyder; reprinted by permission of New Directions Publishing Corporation. • Sabine Sommerkamp: "Mein Gärtchen verkauft—", copyright © 1985 by Sabine Sommerkamp; by permission of the author. • Mabelsson O Southard: "The water deepens", from *American Haiku*, copyright © 1965 by James Bull; by permission of the author. • Robert Spiess: "Snowing", from *The Shape of Water*, copyright © 1982 by Robert Spiess; "An evening cricket", from *American Haiku*, copyright © 1968 by James Bull, "Muttering thunder", from *The Turtle's Ears*, copyright © 1971 by Robert Spiess; by permission of the author. • Ruby Spriggs: "moment of birth", from *Haiku: anthologie canadienne/ Canadian Anthology*, published by Les éditions Asticou enrg., copyright © 1985 by André Duhaime and Dorothy Howard; by permission of the author. • Selma Stefanile: "a yellow leaf", from *I Know a Wise Bird*, copyright © 1980 by Selma Stefanile, and "Wabash", from *The Poem Beyond My Reach*, copyright © 1982 by Selma Stefanile; by permission of the author. • Wallace Stevens: an excerpt from "Thirteen Ways of Looking at a Blackbird", from *The Collected Poems of Wallace Stevens*, published by Alfred A. Knopf, Inc., New York, copyright 1954 by Wallace Stevens; by permission of the publisher. • Lucien Stryk: excerpts from "Noboru Fujiwara, Haiku Poet", in *Encounter with Zen: Writings on Poetry and Zen* by Lucien Stryk, published 1982 by Swallow Press, copyright 1979 by *The Georgia Review*; reprinted with the permission of Ohio University Press. • George Swede: "Passport check", from *Cicada*, copyright © 1978 by George Swede, and for an excerpt from "The Role of Haiku in Poetry Therapy", from *Cicada*, copyright © 1978 by George Swede; by permission of the author.

José Juan Tablada: "El Saúz", "Oiseau", and "Looping the Loop", from *Obras, I—Poesía*, edited by Héctor Valdés, published by Universidad Nacional Autónoma de México, Ciudad Universitaria, copyright © 1971 by Universidad Nacional Autónoma de México; by permission of the publisher. • Takahama Kyoshi: poems included here by permission of Takahama Kimiko, owner, Hototogisu Publishing Company. • Takayanagi Shigenobu: *mi o sorasu*, copyright 1950 by Takayanagi Shigenobu, and *sanmyaku no*, copyright 1951 by Takayanagi Shigenobu; by permission of Nakamura Sonoko. • Taneda Santoka: poems included here by permission of Oyama Sumita. • Tanizaki Junichirō: excerpt from *In Praise of*

Shadows, translated by Thomas J. Harper and Edward G. Seidensticker, published by Leete's Island Books, Box 1131, New Haven, CT 06505, copyright © 1977 by Thomas J. Harper and Edward G. Seidensticker; by permission of the publisher. • James Tipton: "A boy wading", from *Haiku Highlights,* copyright © 1970 by J & C Transcripts, and "the old barber", from *Haiku Magazine,* copyright © 1972 by William J. Higginson; by permission of the author. • Tomiyasu Fūsei: *hana kuzu ni,* copyright 1920, by permission of Tomiyasu Toshiko. • Tomizawa Kakio: *tōten ni,* copyright 1940 by Tomizawa Kakio, and *Junko!,* copyright 1941 by Tomizawa Kakio; by permission of Miyoshi Junko. • Chris Torrance: "white butterfly, blue cabbage", from *Haiku Byways,* copyright 1971 by Chris Torrance, by permission of the author.

Cor van den Heuvel: "in the toy pail", "snow!", and "a black model-T ford", from *sun in skull,* copyright 1961 by Cor van den Heuvel; "an empty wheelchair" and "in the hotel lobby", from *the window-washer's pail,* copyright 1963 by Cor van den Heuvel; "a milkweed seed", from *dark,* copyright 1982 by Cor van den Heuvel; and "the little girl", from a personal note, copyright © 1985 by Cor van den Heuvel; by permission of the author. • Jocelyne Villeneuve: "Pique-nique", from *Haiku: anthologie canadienne/ Canadian Anthology,* published by Les éditions Asticou enrg., copyright © 1985 by André Duhaime and Dorothy Howard; by permission of the author. • Anita Virgil: "not seeing", "red flipped out", and "walking the snow-crust", from *A 2nd Flake,* copyright © 1974 by Anita Virgil; by permission of Anita Virgil Garner. • Nicholas Virgilio: "Bass", from *American Haiku,* copyright © 1963 by James Bull; "Into the blinding sun", from *American Haiku,* copyright © 1964 by James Bull; and "Autumn twilight", from *Haiku West,* copyright © 1967 by Leroy Kanterman; by permission of the author.

Joyce Webb: "rain . . . washing away", from *Haiku Highlights,* copyright © 1970 by J & C Transcripts; by permission of the publisher. • Beverly White: "where peonies bloom", from *days of sun nights of moon;* by permission of the author. • Larry Wiggin: "cleaning whelks", from *Haiku,* copyright © 1970 by Eric W. Amann; by permission of the publisher. • Paul O. Williams: "the flick of high beams", from *Frogpond,* copyright © 1982 by Paul O. Williams; by permission of the author. • William Carlos Williams: "Lines", from *The Collected Earlier Poems of William Carlos Williams,* published by New Directions Publishing Corporation, New York, copyright 1938 by New Directions Publishing Corporation, and an excerpt from the "Author's Introduction" to *The Wedge,* from *The Collected Later Poems of William Carlos Williams,* published by New Directions Publishing Corporation, New York, copyright © 1944 by William Carlos Williams; reprinted by permission of New Directions Publishing Corporation. • Rod Willmot: "Listening", from *Haiku,* published by Les Éditions Particulières, Québec, copyright © 1969 by Les Éditions Particulières; by permission of the author. • John Wills: "New Year's Day", from *Haiku,* copyright 1969 by Eric W. Amann; "the moon at dawn", and "a mayfly" from *river,* copyright 1970 by John Wills; and "keep out sign", printed on notepaper; by permission of the author. • Richard Wright: "Coming from the woods", "Just enough of rain", and "In the falling snow", fron *Richard Wright Reader,* edited by Ellen Wright and Michel Fabre,

Index

（新装版）英文版 俳句ハンドブック
The Haiku Handbook

2009 年 11 月 25 日　第 1 刷発行

著　者	ウィリアム・ヒギンスン、ペニー・ハーター
発行者	廣田浩二
発行所	講談社インターナショナル株式会社
	〒112-8652 東京都文京区音羽 1-17-14
	電話　03-3944-6493 (編集部)
	03-3944-6492 (マーケティング部・業務部)
	ホームページ　www.kodansha-intl.com

印刷・製本所　大日本印刷株式会社